Wilton C. Eddis

Manual for Accountants, Canada

Volume I.

Wilton C. Eddis

Manual for Accountants, Canada
Volume I.

ISBN/EAN: 9783337188658

Printed in Europe, USA, Canada, Australia, Japan

Cover: Foto ©ninafisch / pixelio.de

More available books at **www.hansebooks.com**

MANUAL FOR ACCOUNTANTS.

CANADA.

VOLUME I.

BEING THE QUESTIONS SET BY THE INSTITUTE OF CHARTERED ACCOUNTANTS, AND THE ANSWERS THERETO, FORMING A TEXT BOOK FOR ACCOUNTANTS, BOOK-KEEPERS, AND BUSINESS MEN.

THE ANSWERS TO THE INTERMEDIATE QUESTIONS BY
MR. DAVID HOSKINS, C.A.,
TORONTO.

EDITED AND PUBLISHED BY
WILTON C. EDDIS, F.C.A.,
TORONTO.

1899.
PRESS OF DOUGLAS FORD, LOMBARD STREET, TORONTO.

Entered according to Act of Parliament of Canada, by WILTON C. EDDIS, F.C.A., at the Department of Agriculture, Ottawa, March, 1899.

PREFACE.

THE Institute of Chartered Accountants has for many years endeavored to raise the standard of Accountancy work in Canada, and with this object in view, has held periodically examinations, as a means of testing the knowledge and experience of those students who have wished to obtain its diplomas and honors. The standing of the Chartered Accountant is at the present time fully recognized and appreciated by the business community, and as this title can now only be obtained by passing the Institute's examinations, subject to other qualifications as laid down in its by-laws, it has necessarily created a demand for publications bearing on the subjects on which such candidates are examined. The Institute of Chartered Accountants of Ontario is conducted on similar lines to the English Institute, and its diplomas conferred on those, who have passed its examinations, are highly prized and duly recognized all over this continent.

The object of this work is primarily to supply candidates with a text book, which will assist them in preparing for their examinations, and while it has been produced in the form of questions and answers, yet it must not be taken as showing specimens of the answers required by the examiners, but rather as a guide and help for future students. To have simply answered the questions as they would be in the time allotted at the examinations referred to, would, no doubt, have been useful, but the object as aforesaid has been also to give to the public a text book, which deals with the subjects from a practical standpoint as well as the theoretical.

The forms of accounts shown in this book are for actual use, and the Mercantile House and the Office have been looked to for illustrations in preference to books.

The Editor, in publishing this book, desires to express his acknowledgements for the work done by Mr. David Hoskin, C.A., of Toronto, in writing the answers to the Intermediate questions. It may be mentioned that Mr. Hoskins has been very successful in preparing candidates for the Institute Examinations.

PREFACE.

He also desires to thank Mr. H. T. Canniff, Barrister-at-Law, for his valuable assistance in supervising the answers as far as they touched on legal matters.

And further he wishes to acknowledge the many useful hints and information received from Mr. W. B. Tindall, C.A., as he feels that to the ability of the above gentlemen many of the merits of this publication are due.

No pains have been spared to make the Manual useful, up to-date, and as complete as possible; and it is hoped that it will be received with a kind criticism that will look for the good points and not for its defects.

WILTON C. EDDIS, F.C.A.

CONTENTS.

Chapter.					Page.
I.	BOOK-KEEPING—Intermediate Exminaation, 1897				1
II.	"	"	"	1898	11
III.	"	Final	"	1897	22
IV.	"	"	"	1898	41
V.	SHAREHOLDERS AND PARTNERS' ACCOUNTS—				
		Intermediate Examination, 1897			56
VI.		"	"	1898	65
VII.	PARTNERSHIP AND EXECUTORSHIP ACCOUNTS—				
		Final	Examination, 1897		78
VIII.		"	"	1898.	94
IX.	JOINT STOCK COMPANIES—				
		Final	Examination, 1897		108
X.	"	"	"	1898	122
XI.	AUDITING—	Intermediate Examination, 1897			136
XII.	"	"	"	1898	145
XIII.	"	Final	"	1897	151
XIV.	"	"	"	1898	166
XV.	INSOLVENCY—	Intermediate Examination, 1897			175
XVI.	"	"	"	1898	184
XVII.	"	Final	"	1897	189
XVIII.	"	"	"	1898	196
XIX.	NEGOTIABLE INSTRUMENTS—				
		Intermediate Examination, 1897			206
XX.	"	"	"	1898	216
XXI.	MERCANTILE LAW—Final	Examination, 1897			221
XXII.	"	"	"	1898	229
XXIII.	MERCANTILE ARITHMETIC—				
		Intermediate Examination, 1897			236
XXIV.	"	"	"	1898	244

(v.)

ERRATA.

Heading to Chapter I. should be only "Book-Keeping."

For dates of Examinations see page 5.

In answer to Question No. 6, page 47, it is implied that the Bank allows a standing overdraft, whereas it discounts the firm's own paper. There is practically little difference. The Bank would hold the proceeds of the notes, held as collateral security, to retire firm's notes as they matured.

DEBENTURES.

In answer to question under this heading the following may be included: (See page 212.)

By chapter 119 of R. S. O., 1897, sec. 38: The bonds or debentures of corporations, made payable to bearer, or to any person named therein or bearer, may be transferred by delivery, and if payable to any person or order shall (after general endorsation thereof by such person) be transferable by delivery from the time of the indorsation. Any such transfer shall vest the property of such bonds or debentures in the holder thereof to enable him to maintain an action thereon in his own name.

INDEX.

	Pages.
Accommodation Note, Points in	219
" " When Dishonored	227
Accountant, The, Extracts from Paper	212
Accounts, Personal and Impersonal	1
" Accrued Due, etc.	5, 144
" Executors	170
Accrued Interest on Investment	161
Active Partner—Definition	56
Adjusting Balances in Business with Branches	48
Adjustment of Losses, Example of	34
" Partners' Accounts—Examples	
65, 66, 67, 69, 76, 78, 80, 91, 97, 99, 104, 230	
Administrator, Provisions Statute of Frauds	222
Advances by Bank on Collateral Bills	48
Advantages of Cost Accounts	152
" of Double Entry	23
Agencies, Accounts of	141
Agent, Minor Acting as Such	230
Agreement Between Two or More Persons	221
Alligation, Rules as to	242
Allotment of Shares	125
Amalgamation of Two Businesses	71
" of Joint Stock Companies	120
Annual Return, Joint Stock Companies	134
Annuities and Sinking Funds, Principles Explained	254
Answering Examination Questions—Advice	53
Application of Payments (see Appropriation of Payments)	
Appropriation of Payments	80, 224
" " Barred Debts	225
" " Example of	30
" " Procedure by the Court	231
" " Provisions Statute of Limitations	225
" " Rights of the Creditor	231
" " Rights of the Debtor	231
" " When only One Debt	231

INDEX.

	Pages.
Arbitration—Award, Details as to	234
" Essentials of Proper	228
Arbitrator, Conduct and Duty of	234
Articles of Partnership, Definition	94
" " Essential Features	94
" " Importance of, Practical Illustration	104
Assets of Manufacturer, Audit	147
Assignee, Rights of with Regard to Hypothecated Securities	196
" Statement	176, 178
Assignments and Preferences Act—	
" Assignee Carrying on Business—Legal Position	203
" Assignment of Security at Advance of Ten Per Cent	196, 203
" Changing Assignee	202
" Claim Based upon Negotiable Instruments	196
" Encumbered Assets	179
" Fraudulent Preference	186
" How Claims may be Legally Barred	194
" Inspector's Duties	184
" Main Provisions of	175
" Preference Claims	187, 202
" Re Deed of Assignment	185
" Rights of Creditors	204
" Security Given Under Pressure	198
" Votes of Creditors	177, 187, 195
" What Vested in Assignee	185
Audit, Assets of Manufacturing Company	147
" Bank Account	139, 171
" Bills Receivable	147
" Books and Information Required	136
" Branch Accounts	173
" Capital Account	149
" Cash, Checking Same	147
" Experience a Guide	136
" First of Joint Stock Company	136
" Good Will	151
" Inventories	142, 156, 160
" Interest on Investments	143
" Joint Stock Company	136
" Joint Stock Company and Firm	145
" Machinery	157
" Manufacturing Business	137
" Minimum Royalties	162
" Municipal Accounts	168
" New Trading Co	146

INDEX.

	Pages
Audit, Object and Scope of	145
" Office and Shop Furniture and Fittings	157
" Outstanding Liabilities	144
" Partnership Accounts	148
" Patent Rights	151
" Preliminary Expenses	162
" Savings and Loan Co.	167
" Statutory Books	166
" Stock Ledger, etc.	166
" Stock-taking	142, 156, 160
" Trustees' Accounts	171
" Vouchers	146
" Wages	138, 150
Auditor, Why he Counts Cash, etc.	171
Auditors, Duties of and Responsibility	145
" Fees Not a Preferred Claim	203
Available Assets—and Good Will	158
Award in Arbitration, Must be according to Terms	228
" Must be Clear	228
" Must be Legal	228
" Must be in Writing	228
" Must Cover all Points	228
Bad Debts—Provision for	147
Balance Sheet—Business with Branches	48, 142
" Form of Account 10, 12, 19, 20, 33, 40, 55, 65, 98, 160
" How to Prepare	4, 18
" Information Required	18
" In Skeleton	12
" Insolvent Company	201
" Outstanding Liabilities	143
" Showing Partners " Capital Accounts " 33, 40, 101
Balancing Separate Ledgers	26
Ballot, Voting by, at Meetings	128
Bank Account, Audit of	139, 171
" Compared with Cash Book	4, 139
" Kept in Separate Book	28
" Various Ways of Keeping	26
Bank Bill or Note, Negotiable Instrument	212
" Statute of Limitations	211, 224
Bank Collateral Account	48
Bank Reconciliation Account, Form of	4
Bank Draft—Definition	207
Bankrupt Refusing to Assign	197
Bankruptcy Act—Advantages of	198

INDEX.

	Pages.
Barred Debts	223, 225, 231
Beneficiaries—Example	88, 103
Bills Lodged as Collateral Security	48
Bills of Exchange—See Promissory Notes.	
" Definition	232
" Object or Force of an Endorsement	208
Bill of Lading, Commonly Supposed to be Negotiable	215
" Definition of	232
Bills Receivable, Audit of	147
" Rules re	148, 211
Book Debts, Valuation of	147
Book-keeping, High Class	152
Books of Savings & Loan Company, Duties of Auditor	167
" Required by Statute, J. S. Company	75, 166
" Required for First Audit	136
Borrowing on Debentures	122
Bought and Sold Returns	1
Branches, Account of	141
" Audit of	173
British North America Act, Bankruptcy	198
Buildings, Deprecistion of	140
Business, Carried on by Assignee	203
" Conversion of Into Company	79, 89
" Converting same into J. S. Co	20
Call Register, Form of	60
Calls on Shares, Provisions as to	117
Capital Account Partner's	8, 9
" " What it Represents	149
Capital Authorized, Provisions	109
" Impaired Joint Stock Co	159
" Paid In, Provisions	109
" Subscribed, Provisions	109
Cash, Audit of	147
Cash Book, Form of	3, 14, 25, 29
" Used as Journal	26
Cash Receipts, Audit of	137
Certificate Bank Balance, Should be Obtained by Auditors	139
Changing Name of Joint Stock Company	120
Charter of Company, How to Surrender	123
Chartered Accountants' Student Society of London, Extract from Paper	212
Cheque, Definition of	207
" "Generally" Crossed	220
" "Specially" Crossed	220
" Negotiable	216
" Object of Endorsement	208

INDEX. XIII.

	Pages.
Cheque, Statute of Limitations	211
" Where Payee, Fictitious Person	207
Claims, How They may be Legally Barred	194
Closing Books for Financial Year	17
Coffee, How to make Mixtures to sell at Given Prices	212
Colliery Audit, Minimum Royalties	162
Commission Business, Examples re Consignments	41
" on Issue of Debenture Stock	161
Common Stock, Definition of	130
Companies' Act, Books Required by Statute	75, 166
" Compared	109, 129
" Incorporation under	112, 129
Companies, Amalgamation of	120
Company's Books, Journal Entries to Open	21
Consideration, Definition	222
" Standard Definition	222
Consignment Ledger	41
Consignor's Accounts, Example of	41
Contents of Bin, to Find	241
Contract, a Void	221, 223
" Definition of	221
" Made by a Minor	230
" Marriage	223
" Sale of Lands	223
" Statute of Frauds	223
" Verbal, Amount Limited	223
" " How Limited	222
" Voidable, a	233
" What must be in Writing	222
" What Necessary to make it Enforceable at Law	221
Contracts under Seal	221
Contributories, Different Classes of	182, 193
" Legal Effect, Settlement Name	193
" Liability of	181, 182
" Procedure in Dealing with	181
" Settling Accounts Amongst	183
Contingent Fund, How to Treat	165
Corpus of Estate, Illustration	83
Cost Accounts, Applied to Wages	139
" Article on and Forms	152, 153, 154, 155, 159
" Object of	152
Cost Ledger, Accounts	17
" Forms	155
Creditors, As Against Partner	66
" Bankrupt Refusing to Assign	197

INDEX.

	Pages
Creditors, Changing Assignee	202
" Claim Based Upon Negotiable Instruments	196
" Effect of Pressure	198
" Failing to Value Security	196
" How Claims Rank	185, 202
" Insolvent, Partner in Another Business	180
" Must Value Security	196, 203
" Remedy When Undue Delay	203
" Rights of Execution Creditor	187
" Rights With Assignee	204
" Secured, How They Rank	177, 179, 203
" Statement of Debtor's Affairs	181
" " for Meeting	176
" Status Where Claim Not Formally Proved	195
" " " " is Disputed	195
" " " " is for Amount not Matured	195
" Voting Power at Meetings	177, 187, 195
" When Debts Not Due	197
" Who Have Not Proved Debts	205
Creditors of Joint Stock Companies, Powers of	117
Creditors' Relief Act, Application of	197
Crossed Cheques, When in Common Use	220
Crossing Cheque, Meaning of and Examples	220
Currency, to Purchase Bill of Exchange on London, Eng	238
Debenture, Lost by Owner	212
Debentures, Are They Negotiable Investments	212
" Coommission on	161
" How secured	122
" How to Calculate Amounts Payable Yearly	236
" Rights of Lender	122
Debtor, Managing Assigned Business	203
" On Eve of Insolvency, Effect of Pressure	198
" (see Insolvency).	
Debtor's Rights, Secret Preference	229
Debts, Ordinary, Statute of Limitations	223
" Provisions, Appropriation of Payments	224, 225, 231
" " Statute of Limitations	223
Deed of Composition, Creditor's Position	229
Deferred Stock, Definition of	130
Definition of Active Partner	56
" Bank Draft	207
" Bill of Exchange	232
" Cheque	207
" Common Stock	130

		Pages.
Definition of Condition Insolvency "Limited Company"		199
" " " " Sole Trader		199
" Consideration		221
" Contract		221
" Deferred Stock		130
" Deposit Receipt		207
" Depreciation		140
" Discharge in Bankruptcy		188
" Dormant Partner		56
" Double Ranking		186
" Endorsement		218
" Expenditure		150
" Extraordinary Resolution		189
" Foreign Bill		207
" Fraud		229
" Fraudulent Preference		186
" General Partner		56
" Good Will		151
" Guarantee		229
" Income and Expenditure Account		149
" Law Merchant		215
" Legal Consideration		222
" Limited Partner		56
" Moral Consideration		222
" Negotiable Instruments		216
" " Promissory Note		206
" " Security		233
" Not Negotiable Promissory Note		206
" Order		207
" Over-issued Stock		131
" Patent Right Bill		210
" Preferred Stock		131
" Promissory Note		207
" Receipts and Payments		150
" Reserve Fund		162
" Silent Partner		56
" Sinking Fund		162
" Special Partner		56
" Special Resolution		189
" Stoppage in Transit		227
" Submission to Arbitration		234
" Treasury Stock		131
" Void Contract		233
" Voidable Contract		233

INDEX

	Pages
Definition of Voucher	146
" Warehouse Receipt	232
" Watered Stock	131
Departments, Three Semi-dependent	156
Deposit Receipt, Auditing	167
" Definition of	207
Depreciation, Balance Sheet	4
" Buildings	140
" Definition of	140
" Good Will	158
" Horses	158
" Leases	140, 158
" Loose Machinery, Utensils, Tools, etc.	158
" Office and Shop Furniture and Fittings	158
" Plant and Machinery	141, 157
" Stocks and Shares	141
Difference between a Negotiable Security and a Security Passing only by Assignment	233
" Condition Insolvency, Sole Trader and Limited Company	199
" Income and Expenditure Accounts and Receipts and Payments	149
" Legal and Moral Consideration	221
" Patent Right Bill and an Ordinary Bill	210
" Single and Double Entry Book-keeping	22
" Void and Voidable Contracts	233
Directors, Liabilities of	122, 132
" Improperly Elected	128
" Not less than Three nor more than Fifteen	108
" Qualifications of	108
" re Forfeiting Shares	64
" re Payment of Calls	117
" Voting at Meetings	128
Discharge in Bankruptcy, What is Meant	188
Discount on Book Debts and Liabilities	5
" Shares, How to Treat	44, 49
Discounted Note, When Proceeds and Rate Known to Find Face Value	239
Dishonored Bills, How to Treat	148
Dishonored Note, Journal Entries for	211
" Protest, Full Details	226
" Treatment of	231
Dispute in Arbitration	228
Dividend, How to Determine Propriety of	148
Dividends, Due Shareholders, Provisions Statute of L.	224
" Shareholders Entitled to	148

INDEX. xvii.

	Pages.
Dividends, Entries for	49
Dominion Bankruptcy Act	198
" Bills, Negotiable Instruments	216
" Companies Act (see Companies Act)	
" Winding Up Act, Conditions Insolvency	194, 200
Dormant Partner, Definition of	56
Double Entry Book-keeping, Advantages of	23
" " How to Start from Single Entry System, with Example Worked Out	35
" " Remarks on	22
Doubtful Debts, How to Provide for	147
Endorsement, Definition	218
" Object or Force of	208, 218
" Various Ways of Endorsing Bills	209
Endorser, How Discharged of Liability	226
" How to Hold Liable	231
" Notice, Entitled to	219
" Waiving Notice	218
Errors in Book-keeping, Correction of	14
Essentials of a Proper Award	228
Excess of Capital, Interest on	9
Exchange, Old Par of	238
Execution Creditor, Rights of	187
Executor, Accounts of	170
" Improper Investments	86, 102
" Power as to Investments	102
" Provisions, Statute of Frauds	222
" Responsibilities of	86
" Statement of Accounts	83, 84, 87
Extraordinary Resolution, Winding Up	189
Factory Expenses, Cost Accounts	152
Federal Bankruptcy Act, Advantages of	198
" Winding Up Act, Nature of	194
Financial Companies, Audit of	167
" " Interest as an Asset	143
" " Reserve Fund	163
" Statement for Business with Three Offices	48
Fire Insurance, Unused Premium	165
First Audit of a Company, General Instructions	146
" " " Special Points	136
Foreign Bill, Definition of	208
" Protest Compulsory	226
Forfeited Shares, Disposal of	64

INDEX.

	Pages.
Forfeited Shares, Entries for	49
" How Dealt with	63, 116
" Rights of Shareholder	51
Form of Accounts for Social Club	46
" " Shewing Accrued Items	6, 7
" Adjustment of Losses	34
" Allotting Shares	125
" Application for Shares	125
" Balance Sheet	8, 10, 12, 19, 40, 55, 65, 98, 160
" Bank Account	28
" Bank Reconciliation Account	4
" Call Register	60
" Cash Book	3, 15, 25, 29
" Columnar Ledger Account	13
" Cost Ledger Accounts	155
" Executor's Accounts	84, 87
" Instalment Scrip	126
" Investment Account	84, 87
" Journal Entry	18, 21
" Ledger Account for Gas Company or Water Undertaking	31
" Memorandum of Agreement, Shareholders	59
" Negotiable Promissory Note	206
" Not Negotiable Promissory Note	206
" Profit and Loss Account	8, 10, 11, 19, 33, 55, 70
" Partner's Balance Sheet, Shewing Their Capital Accounts	33, 40
" Partner's Capital Account	8, 9, 69, 70, 76, 98, 101
" Realization Account	84, 69
" Register of Transfers	59
" Revenue Account	19, 39
" Sales Book for Consignments	41
" " " Manufacturer	16
" Stock Book, J. S. Company	59
" Stock Certificate	127
" Stock Ledger	60, 61
" Statement for Meeting of Creditors	176
" " " Shareholders	192
" " Shewing Result Realization of Assets	178
" " " Position of Contributories	182
" Trading Account	10, 12, 19, 54, 79
" Trial Balance	18, 54, 69
" Venture Accounts	95
Fraud, What it is	229
Fraudulent Preference, Defined	186
Freight Account	16

INDEX.

xix

	Pages.
Full Endorsement, Example	209
Furniture Business, Three Departments	156
Gas Account, Customers' Ledger	31
Gas Company, With Three Departments Semi-Dependent	156
General Partners, Definition	56
Gold Coin, Compared with Bank Note or Bill	216
Goods and Chattels, Company Question on	123
" Finished But Not Sold, How Valued	156
" in Course of Manufacture, "	156
" Manufactured, "	156
" on Sale or Consignment	41
" Sold on Credit, Stoppage in Transitu	227
" Sold "to Arrive" " "	228
Good Will, As an Asset	151
" Depreciation of	158
Grocery Business, Specimen Prospectus	123
Guaranty, Definition of	229
" What Necessary to Make Enforceable at Law	229
Higher Powers of Numbers, Notes on	238
Holder in Due Course, Rights of	208, 217
Holder of a Promissory Note, Defined	210
" " Effects of Giving Time	226
Horses, Depreciation of	158
Hypothecated Securities, Rights of Assignee	196
Impairment and Deficiency Account	159
Impersonal Accounts, Meaning of	22
Imprest System of Cash, Illustration	174
Income and Expenditure Account Compared	149
Incorporation Under "Companies Act"	110
" "Ontario Companies Act"	111
" "Quebec Companies Act"	114
" "Manitoba Companies Act"	112
Indenture of Mortgage, Actions upon any Covenant	224
Inland Bill, Definition of	208
Insolvency, Classes of Contributories	182, 193
" Discharge in Bankruptcy, How Obtained	188
" Distribution of Assets Available for Dividend	188
" Duties and Powers of Inspectors	184
" How Claims may be Legally Barred	194
" Partner in Another Business	180
" Preference Claims	187, 202
" Ranking of Creditors	177, 188
" Rights of Execution Creditor	187

INDEX

	Pages.
" Security to be Valued	194
" Sole Trader and Limited Company	199
" Statement for Meeting of Creditors, Form of	176
" " of Debtor's Affairs	181
" " Realization of Assets	178
" Voluntary Liquidation of Company	189
" Votes of Creditors	177, 188
" Winding up Estate	177
Inspectors of an Insolvent Estate, Appointment, etc	185
" " Duties of	184
Instalment Scrip, Form of	126
Insurance, Unearned	5
Interest, on Excess Capital	9
" on Ledger Balances, to Calculate	249
" on Partners' Withdrawals	9
" on Promissory Note	219
" When an Asset	143
Intestate Estates, Table of Distribution	92
Inventories, Auditors' Duties	142, 147, 156
Inventory, of Merchandise	4
Investing Money, Most Profitable Way, Example	238
Investments, by Trustees, Powers as to	102
" in Stocks and Shares	141
" to Calculate Rate %	256
Invoice Goods, to Find List Prices	240
Joint Adventure in Wheat, Example	95
Joint Stock Companies, Acquiring Business of Another Company	120
" " Acts Compared	129
" " Advances on Goods and Chattels	123
" " Allotment of Shares	63
" " Amalgamation of	120
" " Annual Returns	134
" " Books and Information Required by Auditor	136
" " Call Register	60
" " Capital Authorized	109
" " " Paid in	109
" " " Subscribed	109
" " Changing Partnership into	79
" " Charter, How to Surrender	123
" " Common Stock	130
" " Condition of Insolvency	199
" " Contributories, re	117
" " Converting Business into	20
" " Dealing in its Own Shares	116

INDEX. xxi.

			Pages.
Joint Stock Companies,		Debentures	122
"	"	Deferred Stock	130
"	"	Discount upon Shares Issued	49
"	"	Dividend	148
"	"	Dividends upon Paid up Capital	49
"	"	Five Shareholders Necessary	68, 118
"	"	Forfeited Shares	49, 116
"	"	Form of Statement for Creditors	181
"	"	Hypothecated Shares	63
"	"	Incorporation in the Various Provinces 111, 110, 112,	113
"	"	Instalment Scrip	126
"	"	Liquidator's Statement	192
"	"	Memo. of Agreement	59
"	"	Number of Directors	108
"	"	Over-Issued Stock	131
"	"	Payments upon Forfeited Shares	49
"	"	Pledges, Shares	128, 135
"	"	Powers of Creditors	117
"	"	Preference Stock	80, 116
"	"	Preferred Stock	131
"	"	Procedure in Dealing with Contributories	181, 183
"	"	Procedure to Place a Company in Voluntary Liquidation	189
"	"	Profit and Loss	81
"	"	Qualification Directors	108
"	"	Real Estate, to Hold	132
"	"	Reduction, Capital Stock	74
"	"	" of Paid up Capital	49
"	"	Register of Transfers	59
"	"	Rules re Wages	132
"	"	Shareholders Entitled to Vote	128, 173
"	"	Shares Sold at a Discount	62
"	"	Statistical Books	166
"	"	Statutory Books to be Kept	75, 166
"	"	Stock Book, Form of	59
"	"	" Certificate	127
"	"	" Register	60, 61
"	"	To Reduce Capital	159
"	"	To Stay Liquidation Proceedings	191
"	"	Transfers of Shares	118, 132, 133
"	"	Treasury Stock	131
"	"	Voting Power of Shareholder	63, 128
"	"	Watered Stock	131

	Pages.
Joint Stock Companies, What Authorities Govern	116
" " What Act to be Wound Up Under	193
Journal, Entries, Examples 13, 17, 42, 43, 49	211
" Uses of	26
Judgment Creditor, Rights of	199
Law Merchant, What it is	215
Leasehold Property, Depreciation..................................140,	158
Leases, Depreciation 140,	158
Ledger Accounts With Branches	142
" " Mining Co 43,	44
" " Classification of	45
" How to Open Double Entry	35
" Sketch on Cost	155
Legal Consideration, Defined	221
Legatee, When Entitled to Interest	101
Lex Mercatoria, Is it Capable of Expansion	214
" Views of Different Authorities	214
Liability of Accountant, *re* Prospectus	119
Liens on Machinery	47
Limited Partners, Definition	56
Liquidator, Powers and Duties of	190
Loan Company, Audit of	167
" Debentures	122
" Notes *re* Charter	123
" Stock Subscribed	109
Lord Tenterden's Act	223
Losses on Partner's Capital, How Borne	97
Lumber Account...12,	13
Machinery, Audit of	147
" Depreciation	141
Manage of Business, Assignment	204
Manitoba R. S., ch. 25, Incorporation Under	112
Manufacturing Accounts, Cost Accounts	152
" " Exchange of	32
" " Form of Balance Sheet	160
" " Goods and Stores, to Value	156
" " Profits, When Earned	156
" " Registration Partnerships	56
" " Three Departments, Semi-Dependent on the Other	156
Marked Cheques, How Treated	173
Meeting of Creditors, Statement for	176

INDEX.

		Pages.
Mercantile Arithmetic,	Alligation Method	242
" "	Annuities and Sinking Fund	254
" "	Apportioning Freight	247
" "	Coupons	236
" "	Current Rate 10%, Meaning of	238
" "	Debentures	236
" "	Flour Trading Account	238
" "	Interest on Ledger Balances	248
" "	Investment Calculations	251, 253, 256
" "	Investments Compared	238
" "	Invoice Goods, to Find List Prices	240
" "	Mortgage Investments	237
" "	Multiplication by Contracted Method	250
" "	Old Par of Exchange	238
" "	Percentages, Profit and Loss	255
" "	Proceeds, Note Discounted	238
" "	Shipping Example	244
" "	Sum in English, French and German Money Converted Into Currency	249
" "	to Find Contents of Bin	241
" "	to Make Mixture, Coffee	243
" "	" " of Given Fineness Gold	252
Merchandise, Account		1, 5
"	(see Trading Account)	
"	Cost Accounts	152
"	"In Transitu"	49
Mining Company, Shares Sold at Discount		63, 132
"	Showing Sales of Treasury Stock and Entries	42
Mining Partnerships, Registration		58
Minor, Validity of Contracts		230
Minute Book, Auditors' Duties		166
Money in Sheriff's Hands, Assignment		199
Moral Consideration, Defined		221
Mortgage, Costs Attending a		160
"	Investments, How to Calculate	237, 251, 253
Mortgages, Audit of		167
"	in Assigned Estates	179
Multiplication by Contracted Method		250
Municipal Debentures, to Calculate Annual Payments		236
Municipal Accounts, Audit of		168
Negotiable Instruments, as Contracts		221
" "	Debentures	213
" "	Definition	216
" "	Examples	212, 216

INDEX.

	Pages.
Negotiable Instruments, Law Merchant	215
" " List of, Not Finally Closed	215
" " Their Advantages	216
Negotiable Promissory Note, Definition	206
" " Examples of	206
" Security Defined	232
Not Negotiable Promissory Note, Definition	206
" " Examples of	206
" " How Transferred	217
Nominal Partner, **Definition**	57
Notice of Dishonor, Rules *re*	212
" When Dispensed with	218
Old Par of Exchange Explained	238
One Man Companies	89
Ontario Companies Act Compared	109, 129
" " Incorporation Under	112, 129
Open Endorsement, Example	209
Opening Books of Company, Journal Entries	21
Order, Definition of	207
Order Book	17
" Cost Accounts	153
Ordinary Debts, Provisions Statute of Limitations	223
Outstanding Liabilities, Auditor's Duty	143
Over-Issued Stock, Definition of	130
Overdue Bills, How to Treat	148, 212
Partially Manufactured Goods, **How to Value**	156
Partnership, Adjusting Accounts....65, 66, 67, 69, 76, 78, 80, 91, 97, 99, 104
" Agreements, Definition	94
" Amalgamation Two Firms	71
" Assignment by Partners for Benefit of Creditors	185
" Balance Sheet, Form of	33, 40
" Capital **Account**	165
" Different Kinds of Partners	56
" Division of Profits, Example	78
" Forming Into **Joint** Stock Company	79, 89
" **Liability as to** Creditors	66
" Limited, Laws as to	56
" Mutual Obligations	57
" Partner Assigning Share	94
" Personal Drawings	57
" Steps **on** Retiring	58
" Taking New Partner	65
" When Registration Necessary	56

INDEX.

	Pages.
Part Payments, Applied to Barred Debts	225
Patent Rights, as an Asset	151
Patent Right Bills, What They Are	210
" Important Feature	211
Payments, How Appropriated	224
Percentages, Guide to Auditor	160
" How to Calculate in Trading Account	239
" Profit and Loss Account	255
Personal and Impersonal Accounts	1
Plant and Machinery, Depreciation	141
Possession, "Actual" and "Constructive"	228
Preferred Claims, What Are, and to What Extent	187, 202
Preferred Stock, Advantages	62
" Definition of	130
" Example of	80
" How Created	62, 116
" Provisions for	109
Preliminary Expenses, as an Asset	162
Premium Given for Lease, How Valued	160
Presentation for Payment, Proper	217
Pressure by a Creditor, Effect of	198
Private Joint Stock Company, Remarks	89
Profit and Loss Account, Dividends	82
" " Form of	7, 10, 11, 19, 33, 55, 70
" " How to Prepare	4
" " In Skeleton	11
" " Under Different Systems, Compared	22, 81
" " Under Single Entry System	100
Profit, Not Available for Dividend	148
Profits, Apportioning to Partners	7, 92
Promissory Note, Acquired After Maturity	210
" " Computing Claim	219
" " Definition of	232
" " Effect of Alterations	227
" " Holder of, Defined	210
" " Holder in Due Course	208, 210
" " Interest Thereon	219
" " Journal Entries	211
" " Law Merchant	214
" " Must They be Protested	225
" " Negotiable, Defined	206, 207
" " Not Dated, Valid	218
" " Object or Force of Endorsement	208
" " Presentation for Payment	217
" " Protesting Same	218, 225

INDEX.

	Pages.
Promisory Note, **Provisions**, Statute of Limitations	211, 224
" " To Hold Endorser Liable	231
" " Various Ways of Endorsing	209
Proper Award, Essentials of a	228
Prospectus, for Grocery Business	123
Protesting Bill of Exchange, Advantages **of**	226
" " Compulsory in Quebec	226
" " Essential Points	218
" " Full Details	225
" " Meaning of	218, 225
" " Should All Bills be Protested	225
" " What Required to Make Legal	225
" " Who Can Protest	218, 225
Provincial Bankruptcy Laws, Provisions British North America Act	198
Provisions for Bad and Doubtful Debts	164
Purchases Account	1
" Precautions to Adopt	138
Qualification of **a** Director, How Varied	108
Qualified Endorsement, Example	209, 218
Quebec, Protesting Bills	227
" Revised Statutes, 1888, Incorporation Under	114
Raw Material, **a Factor in Costing**	152
Realization **Account, Example of**	69, 76
" Form of	34
Reasonable Award	228
Receipts and Payments, Compared	149
Receipts, Vouching of	137, 160
Reduction Capital Stock, Procedure	74
" Paid Up Capital, Journal Entries	49
Register of Shareholders, Audit	166
" " Form of	59
" Wages	153
" Stores	153
Rent, Accrued Due, How to Treat	6
" As a Preference Claim	187, 202
" Actions for	224
Repairs, to **be** Charged to Revenue **Account**	140
Report, by Liquidator, Example	192
Reserve Fund, What it is	162
" Compared with Sinking **Fund**	162
" Should it be Specially Invested?	163
Residuary Legatee, Example	85
Restrictive Endorsement, Example	209

INDEX.   xxvii

	Pages.
Retiring Partner, Steps to Take	58
Return Sales	172
Revenue Account, Examples of	39, 162
" to Prepare	18
Rights as to Appropriation of Payments	224
" of Assignee	196
" of Creditors	117, 204
Sales Account	1
" Book, Form of	16, 41
Sans Recours, Effect of When Endorsing	218
Savings and Loan Company, Points in Audit	167
Scope of Audit	145
Security Given by Debtor Under Pressure	198
Shareholders, Dividends	148
" Hypothecated Shares	63, 181
" Liability of, When Less Than Five	68, 119
" Voting, Powers of	63, 128
" What " Double Ranking " is	186
Share in Profits to Employee	58
Share Ledger, Audit of	166
Shares, Form of Allotting	125
" " Application	125
" How Forfeited	63
" Issued at a Discount	132
" Sold " "	62, 132
" Under Pledge	128, 135
Shingles Account	12
Silent Partner, Definition of	56
Single Entry Book-keeping, Remarks on	22
" " To Change	35
Single Ship Company, Example	51
Sinking Fund, Explained	162
Social Club, Method of Keeping Accounts	46
Sole Trader, Condition of Insolvency	199
Special Endorsement, Examples of	209
Special Partner, Definition of	56
Statistical Books, List of	166
Statute of Frauds, Detailed as Regards Contracts	222
" Important Bearings on Commercial Transactions	222
" What it is	222
Statute of Limitations, Actions for Damages, Etc	223
" " " Rent	223
" " " On Accounts	223
" " " Upon Bonds	223

		Pages.
Statute of Limitations, Actions Upon Covenant		228
" " Applied to Cheque		211
" " Appropriation of Payments		224
" " Bank Note or Bill		211
" " Effect on Debts		223
" " Promissory Notes, Etc		211, 228
Stock Certificate, Form of		127
" Ledger, Audit of		166
" " Form of		60, 61
" Register, "		59
Stocktaking, Audit		142, 147, 156
" How to Value Stock		156
Stoppage in Transitu, How Can Seller's Rights be Annulled?		227
" " Meaning of		227
" " When Goods Sold "to arrive"		228
Stores (see Cost Accounts)		152
Submission in Arbitration		228
" " Definition of		234
Subrogation, Doctrine of, Example		53
Table of Distribution, Intestate Estate		92
Taxes, in Assigned Estate		208
" Municipal, How to Trace		168
Time Register		17
Trade Discount, Form of Account		7
Trade Discounts, Calculations in		240
Trading Account		1
" in Skeleton		12
" Example		10, 12, 19, 39, 54, 70
Trading Company, Incorporated Under Dominion Act, to Wind Up		194
Trading Partnership, Paying Same Debt Twice		217
" Registration		56
" Withdrawal from		58
Transfer of Shares, Made by Sale under Execution		118
" Position of Parties		118
" to be Valid		133
Treasury Stock, Definition of		130
Trial Balance, Manufacturer's Account		32
" Form of		18, 69
" What it Proves		23
Trustee, Interest to Legatee		101
Used Capital, Rights of Creditors		117
Usage, Origin of *Lex Mercatoria* a to Negotiable Instruments		215

INDEX.

	Pages.
Validity of Contracts	230
Valuation of Assets	147
" Book Debts	147
" Bills Receivable	147
" Goodwill	151
" Interest as an Asset	143
" Manufactured Stock	158
" Partly Manufactured Stock	156
" Goods Sold but Not Delivered	156
" Patent Right	151
Verbal Contract, How Limited	222
Void Contract, Defined	233
Voidable Contract, Defined	230, 233
Voluntary Liquidation of Company, Procedure	189
Voucher, Definition of	146
Voting at Creditors' Meetings	117, 187, 195
" Power of Shareholder	63
" Rules, as to	128, 173
Wages, Adequate System for	138, 150, 152
" Book	17
" Cost Accounts	152
" Liability of Directors	131, 187
" Preference Claim	187, 202
" Voucher for	150
Warehouse Receipt, Defined	232
Water Account, Ledger	31
Watered Stock, Definition of	130
Wheat, Joint Adventure	95
Wilson, B.A., W.R., Barrister, Extract from Paper	212
Winding Up Amendment Act, 1889	202
Winding Up Companies' Act, Company's Choice as to	194
" " Extraordinary Resolution	189
" " Powers of Inspectors	184
" " Rights of Creditors	201
" " Special Resolution	190
" " Voluntary Liquidation	189
Winding Up Partners' Accounts, Example	34
Without Recourse, Effect of, When Endorsing	218

MANUAL FOR ACCOUNTANTS.

CHAPTER I.

INTERMEDIATE EXAMINATION, 1897.

BOOK-KEEPING.

Question 1.—What is the reason of the division of Accounts into Personal and Impersonal, and what are the two widely different characteristics of the latter?

A.—To enable the complete records of any business to be kept, this being one of the principles of Double Entry Book-keeping.

The different characteristics are that personal accounts can only represent liabilities and assets, but that impersonal accounts may also represent, besides liabilities and assets, the profit and loss accounts.

Question 2.—In the course of trading you make and receive certain charges or allowances for Bought and Sold Returns. How would you deal with these?

A.—The best method of dealing with the Trading or Merchandise account is to open two separate accounts termed Purchases and Sales Accounts respectively. To these accounts all charges or allowances should be debited or credited, as follows:—

Purchased goods returned, or allowances, would be credited to "Purchases Account."

Goods **sold** and returned, or allowances thereon, **would be** debited to " Sales Account."

When the books are balanced, the charges **or** allowances would **be** deducted as a total from their respective accounts.

Question 3.—Plan a simple but effective Cash Book (with Bank Columns) and evidence working by twelve entries each debit and credit and draw balance.

Dr. CASH.   CONTRA. Cr.

Date.	Particulars	Fol.	Totals	Sundries	Cash Sales	Bills Rec'ble	Bank	Date.	Particulars	Fol.	Totals	Sundries	Expense	Interest	Bank
1868 July 31	To Cash on hand		$ 36 00	$ 36 00				1868 July 31	By Bank Balance		$ 184 26				$184 26
Aug. 1	" Balance in Bank		184 26	184 26				Aug. 1	" Deposit		300 00				300 00
"	" Cash Sales		76 00		76 00			"	" Bell Telephone		22 50		22 50		
"	" Cheque 123		22 50				22 50	"	" Gas Co.		6 18		6 18		
"	" " 184		6 18				6 18	"	" Purchases %, J. J. B. & Co.	100	176 00	176 00			
"	" " 185		176 00				176 00	"	" Bills payable, No. 68	150	225 12	225 12			
"	" " 196		225 12				225 12	Aug. 2	" Bill Disc'd, No. 74		100 00				
"	" B.R. No. 74		100 00		100 00			"	" Freight on goods	6	8 17	8 17			
"	" " 75		300 00		300 00			"	" Duty J. J. Co.	10	17 00	17 00			
Aug. 2	" J. Smith	316	16 34	16 34				"	" Wages		37 00		37 00		
"	" H. Brown	353	84 00	84 00				"	" Jones & Co.	340	96 00	96 00			
"	" Cash Sales		68 18		68 18			"	" Postage		3 00		3 00		
									" Balance in Bank		1176 55	523 29	68 68	1 30	583 06
	" Balance in Bank		1195 68	320 70	144 18	300 00	430 80		" Cash on hand		152 26		Fo.	Fo.	152 26
			152 26		Fo.	Fo.	152 26				19 35				
			$1347 94				$583 06				$1347 94				
Aug. 2	" Cash Balance		19 35					Aug. 2	" Balance in Bank		152 26				152 26
"	" Balance in Bank		152 26				152 26								

Memo.—The columns can be arranged to suit any business, and columns for Trade Discounts can often be added with great advantage.

The Bank Account can be posted direct to the Ledger, or a Bank Reconciliation Account opened at foot of Cash Book, for form of which see answer to Question 4.

Question 4.—Draft a Bank Reconciliation Account, bringing the Cash Book and Bank Pass Book in harmony at the close of a determined period

BANK RECONCILIATION ACCOUNT,

As taken from the Cash Book in previous answer.

1898 July 31	Bank Balance	$184 36		
Aug. 2	Deposits	398 70		
		583 06		
Aug. 2	Cheques, etc.	430 80		
	Balance as per firm's books	152 26		
Aug. 2	Balance as per Bank Pass Book		$554 38	
	Outstanding Cheques:			
	No. 135 .... $176 00			
	" 136 .... 226 12			
			402 12	
				$152 26

Question 5.—How would you set to work to prepare a Profit and Loss Account for a period, and a Balance Sheet at the close of it?

A.—First get inventories, of Merchandise, Stock, etc., on hand at date of closing, also ascertain what, if any, liabilities are outstanding. Also see what provision has to be made for such items as wages accrued, interest accrued, etc. See that provisions for depreciation are made as required on Machinery, Leasehold, etc. Then see that a Trial Balance has been properly taken from the ledger and duly balances. The next step would be to close all the Profit and Loss Accounts in the ledger, transferring the balances through the journal to an account called Profit and Loss Account. The balance at this account would show the profit or loss made. (From this account in the ledger a proper Profit and Loss statement, giving fuller details where required, may be made.)

Before closing Merchandise or similar accounts, to arrive at the profit made thereon, the amount of merchandise on hand taken from the inventory at the date of closing accounts, must be credited, or deducted from the debits and carried forward as a debit balance. If the total credits are in excess of the total debits, the difference is the gross profit and is transferred to Profit and Loss Account.

The remaining accounts must then be properly classified under suitable headings, showing the Liabilities and Assets.

A form of balance sheet is shown on page 12.

Question 6.—When making up final accounts there will be certain items Accrued Due to be brought in or vice versa Rebates to be dealt with: For instance, Discount being ⌀ on Book Debts and Liabilities, Rent, Insurance, Wages, Travellers' Commissions, Auditors' Fees.

How would you deal with these?

Give illustrative entries.

A.—At the end of the year or when closing the books, all amounts of expenditure, such as rent prepaid or unexpired, or insurance, should be credited to the accounts to which they have been charged and shown in the Balance Sheets as Assets, the principle being to only charge to the current period the expenses properly belonging thereto. Similarly, income earned but not received should be duly credited. In all such cases a Suspense Account or other suitable accounts may be opened to which to charge Asset items of this sort and to credit Liability items. For instance, Auditor's fees would be charged to Expense and credited to said Suspense Account, unless an account was opened in the Auditor's name.

This may be termed the orthodox way of dealing with such items, but in general work the following simple and effective method is preferred and adopted by many practical accountants:

Enter all accounts accrued due to or by the firm in **the Inventory book** or other suitable book; then charge or credit these items directly to **proper** Profit and Loss Accounts and carry them forward as balances in the same way as **the** Stock on hand is treated in a Trading or Merchandise account. These balances must of course be treated as Liabilities or Assets in the Balance Sheet. The **following illustrations will clearly show the method to be adopted:**

RENT.

1898				1898			
Apr.	1	Cash..................	$200 00	Dec. 31	Profit and Loss Acct..	$800 00	
July	1	"	200 00				
Oct.	1	"	200 00				
Dec.	31	Rent accrued due....	200 00				
			$800 00			$800 00	
				Jan.	1	Balance due........	200 00

Dr. **GENERAL EXPENSES.** *Cr.*

1898				1898			
		Brought forward.	$680 00				
Dec. 31		Wages 3 days due....	18 00	Dec. 31	Unexpired Insurance.	$ 13 00	
Dec. 31		Commission.........	9 00	Dec. 31	Profit and Loss......	684 00	
Dec. 31		Auditor's fees due....	40 00				
			$697 00			$697 00	
1898				1898			
Jan.	1	Unexpired Insurance.	13 00	Jan.	1	Wages 3 days due....	18 00
						Commission due.....	9 00
						Auditor's fees due ...	40 00

TRADE DISCOUNT.

1898 Dec. 31	Brought forward. Estimated discounts on book debts Profit and Loss Acct..	$150 00 30 00 60 00 $240 00	1898 Dec. 31	Brought forward. Estimated discounts on liabilities	$220 00 20 00 $240 00
1898 Jan. 1	Balance forward (being provision for discounts due on on liabilities).	20 00	1898 Jan. 1	Balance forward, (being provision for discounts on book debts)	30 00

Question 7.—Brown & Robinson's business for the half year ending 30th June, 1897, shows a gross profit of $4,000. The rent was $300.00, taxes $75.00, salaries $500.00, sundry expenses $250.00. Brown's capital was $3,500 and Robinson's $2,000.00 They were to be credited with 5% interest on capital. Draw a Profit and Loss account showing Net Profits, and apportion 7-11 to Brown and 4-11 to Robinson.

PROFIT AND LOSS ACCOUNT.

June 30	To Rent " Taxes " Salaries " Sundry exp.. " Int. on Capital. Net profit: Brown's share, 7-11 Robinson's " 4-11	$ 300 00 75 00 500 00 250 00 137 50 1,742 05 995 45	$1,262 50 2,737 50 $4,000 00	June 30	By Gross Profit	$4,000 00 $4,000 00

Question 8.—Draw Brown & Robinson's Balance Sheet as on 30th June, 1897, the amount of their debts receivable being $7,000 and of their debts payable $5,525, the balance at their bank $1,000; cash in hand $150; stock on hand $1,500; furniture and fixtures valued at $500. Brown has drawn $2,500 and Robinson $1,250.

BALANCE SHEET, June 30th, 1897.

Liabilities.			Assets.		
Debts payable		$5,525 00	Debts receivable		$7,000 00
Brown's Capital %:			Balance in bank	$1,000 00	
Investment	$3,500 00		Cash on hand	150 00	
Withdrawls.	2,500 00				1,150 00
	$1,000 00		Stock on hand		1,500 00
Add ½ year's int. on			Furniture and Fixtures		500 00
Capital	87 50				
Add 7-11 profits	1,742 05				
		2,829 55			
Robinson's Capital %:					
Investment	2,000 00				
Withdrawals	1,250 00				
	750 00				
Add ½ year's int. on					
Capital	50 00				
Add 4-11 profits	995 45	1,795 45			
		$10,150 00			$10,150 00

Question 9.—Smith and Jones are trading as partners. Their Capital Accounts are respectively $8,000 and $5,000. Their respective drawings are $1,000 and $800. You have prepared the Profit and Loss Account for the year and have to credit them respectively $700 and $500. Excess of Capital is to be charged at the rate of 5% per annum.

Complete the Capital Accounts of Smith and Jones.

SMITH "CAPITAL ACCOUNT."

To Drawings	$1,000 00	By Balance		$8,000 00
" Balance	7,762 50	" Share profit		700 00
		" Jones, int. on excess		
		Capital		62 50
	$8,762 50			$8,762 50
		" Balance		7,762 50

BOOK-KEEPING.

JONES' "CAPITAL ACCOUNT."

To Drawings	$ 800 00	By Balance	$5,000 00	
" Smith int. on excess Capital	62 50	" Share profit	500 00	
" Balance	4,637 50			
	$5,500 00		$5,000 00	
		" Balance	4,637 50	

Excess of Capital is $3,000,—interest thereon at 5% = $150.

Smith and Jones share profits at 7-12 and 5-12 respectively. Smith pays of this interest 7-12 or $87.50; he is credited $150—$87.50=$62.50; and Jones is debited the same amount.

No mention is made as to charging interest on their respective drawings, so these are not considered in calculating same.

Question 10.—John Staunton starts in business with a Cash Capital of $9,080 on January 1st, 1896, and the following is a summary of his accounts in his books for twelve months trading:

Purchases	$100,000
Sales	121,600
Trade discount allowed	2,130
" " received	1,920
Cash in hand, 31/12/96	50
Bank account overdrawn, 31/12/96	625
Creditors on open account	23,100
Debtors	35,795
Stock, 31/12/96	10,600
Reserve for bad and doubtful debts	1,250
" " rent, taxes, etc.	580
Trade expenses paid	6,100
Loan to P. Trew as 1st April to bear 5% interest	15,000
Bills payable	7,250

Private drawings $375 per month.
Draw up the usual accounts for the proprietor.

TRADING ACCOUNT.

1896 Dec. 31	To purchases .... " Less trade discount .	$100,000 00 1,920 00		1896 Dec. 31	By Sales .... " Less trade discount .	$121,600 00 2,130 00
	" Deduct stock on hand	98,080 00 10,600 00				
	" Balance gross profit.	87,480 00 31,990 00				
		$119,470 00				$119,470 00

PROFIT AND LOSS ACCOUNT.

1896 Dec. 31	To Trade expenses...... " Reserve for bad and doubtful debts.... " Provisions for rent, taxes, etc.	$ 6,100 00 1,250 00 580 00		1896 Dec. 31	By Balance, gross profit " Interest accrued, R. Trew.............	$31,990 00 562 50
	" Profit	7,930 00 24,622 50				
		$32,552 50				$32,552 50

BALANCE SHEET.

Liabilities.				*Assets.*		
Bank % overdrawn. Crediors' open %... Bills payable ..	 $23,100 00 7,250 00	$ 625 00 30,350 00		Cash on hand .... Debtors' open %...... Less reserve for bad and doubtful debts..	 $35,795 00 1,250 00	$ 50 00 34,545 00
Reserve for rents, etc. J. Staunton, Capital % Balance.. .... Drawings .	 9,080 00 4,500 00	580 00		Stock on hand........ P. Trew, loan %...... Interest accrued..	 15,000 00 562 50	10,600 00 15,562 50
Profit	4,580 00 24,622 50	 29,202 50				
		$60,757 50				$60,757 50

CHAPTER II.

BOOK-KEEPING.

Question 1.—From the following list of accounts draw Profit and Loss account in skeleton, and also Balance Sheet, placing the accounts in the division to which they properly belong, and on the proper side of each account: John Smith, Capital Account; Jas. Williams, Capital Account; Real Estate, Toronto; Expenses; Travellers' Salaries; Insurance; Interest; Cash Discount on Sales; Cash Discount on Purchases; Travelling Expenses; Taxes; Repairs; Advertising; Jno. Smith, Drawings Account; Jas. Williams, Drawings Account; Merchandise; Stores; Wages; Bank Account; Bills Receivable; Bills Payable; Investment in Commercial Cable Stock; Accounts Receivable; Accounts Payable; Trading Account.

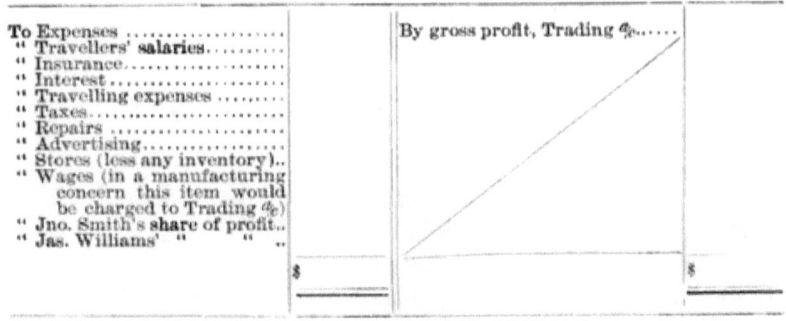

PROFIT AND LOSS ACCOUNT FOR THE YEAR ENDING ——

To Expenses	By gross profit, Trading a/c ......
" Travellers' salaries	
" Insurance	
" Interest	
" Travelling expenses	
" Taxes	
" Repairs	
" Advertising	
" Stores (less any inventory)..	
" Wages (in a manufacturing concern this item would be charged to Trading a/c)	
" Jno. Smith's share of profit..	
" Jas. Williams' " " ..	
$	$

BALANCE SHEET FOR THE YEAR ENDING ——

Liabilities.		Assets.	
Accounts payable		Cash in bank	
Bills payable		Accounts receivable................	
Jno. Smith, Capital %:		Bills receivable	
Investment.		Merchandise	
Deduct drawings		Stores	
Add share of profits.........		Investment in commercial cable	
Jas. Williams, Capital %:		stock	
Investment.....................		Real estate, **Toronto**	
Deduct drawings			
Add share of profits..........			
$		$	

TRADING ACCOUNT FOR THE YEAR ENDING ——

Stock on hand at beginning of year		By Sales.	
Purchases		Less cash discount on sales ...	
Freight and duty		By stock on hand at end of year	
Less cash discount on purchases		(This amount should be deducted from the opposite side, instead of adding to this when percentages are to be calculated.)	
Gross profits transferred to Profit and Loss %..			
$		$	

Question 2.—A Merchant in Midland gives his Book-keeper the following memo:—

Shipped to A. B., Buffalo, Cargo Lumber per "Lothair," Lake Freight, $1.25 per 1,000 feet of Lumber, eight thousand shingles to be counted as equal to 1,000 ft. lumber. Bill of Lading was for 150,000 XX shingles, 600,000 XXX shingles, 232,000 ft. Culls.

Sold shingles to Jno. Smith, Buffalo, XX shingles at $1.05. XXX shingles at $2.05, F.O.B. Buffalo, and delivered the lumber to Jno. Williams, to sell on my account and risk at 2% Commission. Charge the lumber at $6.00 F.O. Vessel, Midland. Open accounts for Lumber and Shingles, and Journalize the transaction so that the Shingle Account will show average price shingles, F.O. Vessel, Midland.

JOURNAL ENTRIES.

John Smith, Buffalo, Dr.		$1,387 50	
To Shingles account			$1,270 31
" Freight " Lothair..........			117 19
Bill of Lading :			
150,000 XX Shingles @ $1 05	$ 157 50		
600,000 XXX " @ 2 05	1,230 00		
	1,387 50		
Freight on Shingles:			
150,000 XX Shingles @ $1.25 per 1,000			
feet lumber........................	23 44		
600,000 XXX Shingles @ $1.25 per			
1,000 feet lumber	93 75		
XX Shingles realized........$ 157 50			
Less........................ 23 44			
	$ 134 06		
XXX Shingles realized $1,230 00			
Less........................ 93 75			
	$1136 25		
Jno. Williams, Commission Account, Dr. ..		1,682 00	
To Lumber			1,392 00
Freight Account, Lothair			290 00
Price at Midland:			
232,000 ft. culls, @ $6 00	1,392 00		
Add freight @.... 1 25	290 00		

LUMBER ACCOUNT.

				1898		
					By J. W., Com. Ac.	$1,392 00

SHINGLES. Showing Credit side of Ledger Account.   Cr.

			XX Shingles.		XXX Shingles.		
1898	By J. Smith	J. F.	150,000	$134 06			$ 134 03
	"	"			600,000	$1,136 25	1,136 25

Question 3.—How would the following errors in Book-keeping affect (1) **The Profit & Loss** Account, (2) **The** Balance Sheet, if not corrected:

(a) A Sum of $125 for freight paid for John Jones on goods purchased by him posted wrongly to Purchases Account.

(b) A Sale of Goods for $500 posted to the debit of Freight Account instead of to the debit of the purchaser.

(c) A Sum of $250 received from a customer entered as a Cash Sale of $250.

A.—(a) The Profit would be decreased by $125.

The Balance Sheet would show the accounts receivable less by $125 than they should be. (If Jones has paid his account at the correct amount, there might be $125 to his credit; then the error would affect Accounts Payable).

(b) The $500 charged to Freight Account instead of to the purchaser would also decrease the profit by this amount, and show the Receivable Accounts in the Balance Sheet less by $500.

(c) The Cash Sales would be credited by $250 too much, which would increase the profit wrongly by that amount. In the Balance Sheet the Accounts Receivable would be too much by $250.

Question 4.—From the following **transactions** make up the Cash Book of Walter Scott, and bring balance down:—

Jan. 1, 1897, Cash on hand, $200, in office and balance at Bank credit, $185; Received John J., $100, including discount, $2; A. W., $50; P. G., $65; W. James, cheque, $50, his note ten days, $200.50. Discounted note and received from Bank proceeds $200. Paid John J $150, which includes cash discount of 5% he allowed. Paid Smith $40 in full. James' note protested and charged back. Costs $1.34. Bank agreed to discount Walter Scott's own note $500, 3 mos., and paid him proceeds, $492.50. Paid Wages, $250;

Insurance, $75. Received Bill of Exchange, £100, Bank allowed at rate of $4.85 for it.

Dr. CASH.   CONTRA. *Cr.*

1897				1897			
Jan. 1	To Cash on hand..	$ 200	00	Jan. 1	By Discount, J. J..	$ 2	00
	" Balance in bank	185	00		" Discount, W. James' note ..	0	50
	" John J.	100	00		" John J.........	150	00
	" A. W.	50	00		" Smith, in full ..	40	00
	" P. G...........	65	00		" W. James note dis. and costs.	201	84
	" W. James......	50	00		" Dis. on W. Scott note.........	7	50
	" Bills rec., W. J. note dis......	200	50		" Wages	250	00
	" Discount J. J...	7	50		" Insurance	75	00
	" Bank, W. Scott note dis......	500	00		" Balance on hand and in bank.	1,116	16
	" W. Scott B/Ex. £100....	485	00				
		$1,843	00			$1,843	00
	" Balance cash on hand and in bank	1,116	16				

MEMO.—We are not informed if W. Scott made the above payments by cheque, or deposited any of his receipts in the bank, so have shown the simplest form of Cash Book. In practice the Cash Book with columns is generally used, and certainly with advantage.

Question 5.—Give form of Sales Book for Manufacturer who has four classes of goods. He wants each kept separate, and part of the goods are to be sold F.O.B. Toronto, part at price delivered in other parts of the Dominion. He wants to show average price of all goods sold as if sold F.O.B. Toronto.

(a) How would you provide for this?

(b) What Journal entries at end of the month would you make of sales posted direct to Ledger?

Names of Customers and Details of Sale	Total Value	Class A		Class B		Class C		Class D	
		Quan.	Value	Quan.	Value	Quan.	Value	Quan.	Value

A.—(a) By adopting a form of Sales Book similar to above, freight on goods to be delivered in other parts of the Dominion, would be charged through the Cash Book to Freight Account in the ordinary way, but a register known as Freight Register would be kept showing the amounts chargeable to each class. At the end of the month the freight paid on each class would be deducted from the total sales of these classes as shown in the Sales Book, the difference being the net selling price, F.O.B. Toronto. The freight thus deducted would be credited to Freight Account, thus closing that account so far as these items are concerned. To arrive at the average price of the goods, add the quantities column and divide into the total value of same class.

JOURNAL ENTRIES.

Sundry Customers, Dr., posted from Sales Book.
To Sales Account .... Class A.
"   "   ....   "   B.
'   "   ....   "   C.
"   "   ....   "   D.
"   Freight Account.
    Transactions for month ending as per Sales Book Fo.

Question 6.—It is required of you as Book-keeper for a manufacturer that you make provision for ascertaining the cost of his Goods.

(a) What books would be necessary?

(b) Give names of accounts you would require to open in General Ledger.

(a) Order Book,
   Wages Book and Time Register,
   Cost Ledger,
   Usual Commercial Books.

(b) Cost Ledger Account, or some similar heading,
   Wages Account,
   Purchases Account,
   Stores.

Question 7.—As Book-keeper you are closing the books for the Financial year. Make the proper Journal entries to Trading and Profit & Loss accounts for

Provision for bad debts	$980 00
Unearned Insurance	95 00
Depreciation, Machinery and Plant	140 00
" Buildings	500 00
Unearned Taxes and Water Rates	85 00
Bills Receivable, under Discount, Unearned Interest	140 00
Bills Receivable, Accrued Interest on Notes bearing Interest	80 00
Mortgages Receivable, Accrued Interest	185 00
" Payable, Interest to date of closing	87 00
Accrued Wages	385 00

Profit and Loss Account, Dr.	$1,707 00	
To Provision for Bad Debts Account (or credit the bad debts, transferring them to a separate ledger)		$980 00
To Machinery and Plant		140 00
To Buildings (or open Depreciation Account for last two items, instead of reducing the Assets)		500 00
To Interest Accrued, Mortgages payable		87 00
Unearned Insurance, Dr.	95 00	
Unearned Taxes and Water Rates, Dr.	85 00	
To Profit and Loss Account		180 00
Unearned Interest on Bills Receivable, Dr.	140 00	
Accrued Interest on Bills Receivable, Dr.	80 00	
Accrued Interest on Mortgages Receivable, Dr.	185 00	
To Profit and Loss Account, Interest		405 00
Trading Account, Dr.	385 00	
To Accrued Wages		385 00

Question 8.— TRIAL BALANCE

James Lewis, 31st Dec., 1897.

	Dr.	Cr.
James Lewis, Capital		$10,000 00
James Lewis, Personal	$ 500 00	
Bank of Nova Scotia	300 00	
Cash in office	45 00	
Merchandise Account	4,300 00	
Repair Account	43 75	
Bills Receivable	3,200 00	
Bills Payable		2,000 00
Real Estate	675 00	
Can. Bank of Commerce Stock	783 00	
General Expenses	930 00	
Freight and Duty	500 00	
Accounts Receivable	4,000 00	
Accounts Payable		5,000 00
Profit and Loss	1,723 25	
	$17,000 00	$17,000 00

The above trial balance is handed to you with the request that you prepare Revenue Account and Balance Sheet.

(a) Could you give the information from the trial balance? If not,

(b) What further information would you require to get?

A.—(a) Not without first ascertaining if there was any Merchandise on hand, and provisions made for such items as Accrued Interest, etc., unless it could be assumed that this was a Trial Balance taken from a Bankrupt's books, and the stock had been wilfully sacrificed or destroyed by fire, or otherwise which is unlikely, judging from the date given.

(b) Inventory of Merchandise on hand; knowledge as to whether balance at Profit & Loss Account included any current charges or was caused by former losses. Accrued Accounts and provisions for losses as mentioned in (a).

Question 9.—Supply the information you are short in Question 8, and make out Revenue Account and Balance Sheet.

A.—Merchandise has been ascertained to be worth $9,000, and Mr. Lewis states there are no provisions for Bad & Doubtful Debts, etc., requiring to be made. P. & L. Balance represents former losses.

TRADING ACCOUNT.

To Balance	$4,800 00	By Inventory	$9,000 00
" Freight and Duty	500 00		
	4,800 00		
" Balance Gross Profit...	$4,200 00		

PROFIT AND LOSS ACCOUNT.

To General Expenses	$ 930 00	By Trading Account	$1,200 00
" Repairs Account.......	43 75		
" Profit for period	3,226 25		
	4,200 00		4,200 00
" Balance brought forw'd	1,723 25	" Balance Profit	$3,226 25
" Balance	1,503 00		
		" Balance	1,503 00

BALANCE SHEET.

Liabilities.			Assets.		
Bills Payable	$ 2,000 00		Bank of Nova Scotia..		$ 300 00
Accounts Payable....	5,000 00		Cash in office		45 00
James Lewis:		$ 7,000 00	Merchandise, as per inventory		9,000 00
Capital %	10,000 00		Bills Receivable.......	$ 3,200 00	
Drawings	500 00		Accounts Receivable.	4,000 00	
		9,500 00			7,200 00
Profit and Loss.......		1,503 00	Real Estate............		675 00
			Can. Bank of Commerce Stock		783 00
		$18,003 00			$18,003 00

Question 10.—

BALANCE SHEET, JOHN WILLIAMS, DEC. 31ST, 1897.

Liabilities.		Assets.	
Creditors on Bills payable	$6,000 00	Cash	$ 4,700 00
" Open Account	5,250 00	Investments	3,500 00
" Loans and Mortgages	2,500 00	Debtors, Bills Receivable	6,900 00
Reserve for bad and **doubtful debts**	500 00	Debtors, Open Account	3,250 00
J. Williams, Personal Acct.	7,000 00	Stock	4,500 00
J. Williams, Capital Acct.	15,000 00	Plant and Machinery ... $4,200 00	
		Less 7% depreciation 290 00	3,910 00
		Freehold land Mortgaged per contra	8,000 00
		Goodwill	1,000 00
		Preliminary Expenses	490 00
	$36,250 00		**$36,250 00**

The above being Williams' Balance Sheet as certified by Jesse James, Chartered Accountant, Williams decides to convert his business into a Joint Stock Company, valuing his Freehold at $11,000, which gives him a surplus of $25,000.

The Company takes the business over on this basis, allotting him $22,000 in stock, and the remaining $3,000 between four others in payment of the purchase.

Make the Journal entry to open the books of the Company.

JOURNAL ENTRIES TO OPEN BOOKS OF COMPANY.

J. Williams .... Dr.	$22,000 00	
Four others................................. "	3,000 00	
To Capital Account		$25,000 00
For Shares issued as follows, etc., etc.		
Cash .... Dr.	4,700 00	
Investments .... "	3,500 00	
Bills Receivable............................ "	6,900 00	
Debtors, Open Account, as per list ...... "	3,250 00	
Stock .... "	4,500 00	
Plant and Machinery .... "	3,910 00	
Freehold Land.............................. "	11,000 00	
Goodwill .... "	1,000 00	
Preliminary Expenses...................... "	490 00	
To Bills Payable...........................		6,000 00
" Creditors, Open Account, as per list......		5,250 00
" " Loans and Mortgages		2,500 00
" Reserve, bad and doubtful debts		500 00
" J. Williams..............................		22,000 00
" Four others..............................		3,000 00
	$39,250 00	$39,250 00

CHAPTER III.

BOOK-KEEPING.

Question 1.—Explain fully the difference between Single and Double Entry Book-keeping and the advantages to be derived from the latter system. Explain how the Profit & Loss for a given period is arrived at under both the Single and Double Entry Systems. How does a Single Entry Balance Sheet differ from one prepared under the Double Entry System?

A.—The difference between Single and Double Entry Book-keeping may be explained as follows:—

(1) That in the former personal accounts only are recorded in the Ledger, whereas in the latter and more modern system, both Personal and Impersonal accounts are kept. By Personal accounts we mean accounts opened in the names of persons, showing the various transactions entered into with them. Impersonal accounts cover all the other accounts of a business and keep a record of all the Profits and Expenses, as well as all the Liabilities and Assets, other than Book Debts. There is certainly a system, if it can be so called, of Single Entry Book-keeping, which besides keeping the Personal accounts, keeps records in its books of such accounts as Bills Payable, Bills Receivable, Merchandise, Capital, etc., but as will be explained further on, this is an incomplete system, only partially adopting the merits of Double Entry Book-keeping.

The difference may also be explained as follows: The Single Entry system only keeps record in its Ledger of the accounts of persons with whom business is done on credit, but the Double Entry system not only does this, but keeps track of all the business done. A well-known axiom of the latter system is, that for every credit there is a debit, which can be explained by an example. We receive a parcel of goods from Sydney Smith, we therefore credit him the value of the goods and debit merchandise or some similar account,—the latter account may show one debit and the creditors may be numerous, but as long as the totals agree the principle is maintained. By adopting this system the total debit balances and the total credit balances agree, remembering that cash on hand is the debit balance of the cash account.

To apply the Double Entry system advantageously a Journal is necessary, though its use is much reduced in modern practice by posting from the subsidiary books direct to the Ledger.

The advantages of Double Entry are numerous and may be briefly summarized as follows:—

(1) By balancing the Ledger, by which we mean taking a Trial Balance, it generally proves that the postings have been correctly made, though it does not prove that an item may not have been posted to a wrong account.

(2) It keeps a record of all the expenses and disbursements as well as receipts and profits.

(3) It enables a full history of all the Assets and Liabilities to be kept, their depreciation or otherwise as may be required.

(4) It affords a satisfactory proof of the correctness of a Balance Sheet and of the profit earned, etc. In Single Entry Book-keeping there is no proof whatever of the correctness of the books or check kept on the expenditure, unless a most elaborate system be adopted of entering details in separate books, which in fact Double Entry Book-keeping does with a minimum of work and a maximum of usefulness.

To arrive at the Profit or Loss under Single Entry, you group together all your Liabilities and Assets, strike a balance, and if the net assets exceed those at the former date of making a Balance Sheet there is a profit, or vice versa.

Under the Double Entry system you obtain the Profit **or the Loss by grouping into one account** the balances of the various accounts that **deal with** the earnings and expenditures of the business. This is done by first crediting **the** Merchandise or Trading **Account** with the value of the **goods or** stock **on** hand and treating **this amount as a balance to be** carried forward. The difference **between the total credits** and debits being transferred to Profit and **Loss Account.** All such items as Rent paid in **advance, Interest accrued,** etc., must be **dealt** with in the **same way and brought forward as** liabilities **or assets.** Then **the credit of** this Profit **or Loss Account** shows a profit, **or** if a debit balance it would **show a loss.**

The Balance **Sheet of any firm should show the same** particulars whether the **books have been kept by** Single or Double Entry.

BOOK-KEEPING. 25

Question 2.—Sketch out the best form of Cash Book to be used where all receipts are paid into the Bank and all payments are made by cheque. Also one where the transactions are not all passed through the Bank. Make a dozen entries on each side and Balance and rule off each book as you would at the end of every month.

Dr. CASH.

Date	Particulars	Folio	Sundries	Bills Rec.	Int.	Bank
1888						
Oct. 1	To J. Smith, Capital a/c	250	$3,000 00			$3,000 00
" 5	" Cash Sales	100	200 00			200 00
" "	" B.R. 1 Dis.			$200 50	$0 50	177 00
" "	" " 2 "			180 00	3 00	36 00
" "	" " 3 "			37 00	1 00	218 00
" 6	" J. Brown	300	18 00			
" "	" Cash Sales	100	85 00			
" 7	" G. Robinson	302	15 00			100 00
" "	" Deposit Bank					
" 8	" Cash Sales	100	98 00			
" "	" B.R. 4			50 00		98 00
" "	" " 5 Dis.			100 00	2 00	178 00
	" Bank Deposit					
			3,416 00	507 50	6 50	$4,007 00
				Fo. 150	Debit entry	
" 8	" Balance		1,316 00			$1,316 00

CONTRA. *Cr.*

Date	Particulars	Folio	Sundries	Mdse.	Bills Payable	Expense	No. of Cheque	Bank
1888								
Oct. 1	By Stationery					$15 00	1	$ 15 00
" "	" Office Furniture	220	$118 00				2	118 00
" "	" Purchases, J. K. & Co.			$1,000 00			3	1,000 00
" 4	" Telephone					22 50	4	22 50
" "	" Petty Cash	90	25 00				5	25 00
" 6	" Wages	80	42 00				6	42 00
" "	" B.P. No. 1				$500 00		7	500 00
" "	" Rent in advance					80 00	8	80 00
" "	" J. Smith, Private a/c	230	50 00				9	50 00
" "	" G. Harris, Office Books					30 00	10	30 00
" "	" T. Jones, note discharged and costs		21 84					21 84
			430 84	1,000 00	500 00	153 50		2,059 34
				Fo. 110	Fo. 160	Fo. 60		1,316 00
	" Balance							$4,007 00

For other forms of Cash Book see Index.

Question 3.—To what use is the Journal now generally put? Is a Journal entry necessary for recording such items as interest, rent, etc., accrued but not due at time of closing books? If not, in what other way would you provide for such items?

A.—The Journal is now generally used to record such transactions as cannot conveniently be entered in the subsidiary books, such as the correction of errors, or the transfering of balances from one account to another. There is a tendency with some book-keepers to pass all such entries through the Cash Book, in fact some systems of book-keeping adopt this method entirely, but it is not a wise plan, as the Cash Book should only record transactions in which cash or its equivalent are concerned.

With reference to the latter part of the question, it is not necessary to record such items as interest, rent, etc., accrued but not due at time of closing books, in the Journal. These items can be conveniently entered in the book containing inventories of Merchandise, etc., and posted direct to the debit or credit of the proper account, carrying the amounts forward as balances to be shown in the Balance Sheet as reserves for expenses accrued, or as assets for items already debited but not chargeable to the period for which the statement is being prepared.

In any business where there are a large number of accounts and several Ledgers are kept, by means of columns in the Journal and Cash Book, or by using subsidiary Cash Books as is done in Banks, each Ledger can be balanced separately and independently. If posting then is done direct to the ledger from the subsidiary books they should be summarized periodically in the Journal.

Question 4.—Explain the various ways in which a Banking account can be recorded in one's books. What advantages and disadvantages may arise from keeping the Bank Account entirely in the Cash Book.

A.—The Banking Account can be kept in various ways:—

(1) By simply treating the balance in the Bank, as shown by the stubs in the Cheque Book and proved monthly by the Bank Pass Book, as part of the balance in the Cash Book, or if overdrawn the Bank balance will tally with the shortage of the receipts in said book. This system cannot be recommended except possibly for small businesses.

(2) Another system is that of recording the Bank transactions in the Cash Book, treating the cheques or withdrawals from the Bank as so much Cash received, and to be accounted for as other receipts. Deposits in the Bank, whether in cash or as discounts, are treated as payments to the Bank. Under this system, which is probably the simplest and best, the balance in the Cash Book shows only the cash on hand. The total withdrawals and the total deposits may be posted direct to the Bank Account in the Ledger and balanced as an ordinary account.

It is not even necessary to open an account in the Ledger for Bank, as the column on the credit side of the Cash Book shows the total deposits, including the previous balance, and the column on the debit side shows the withdrawals, the difference between these totals will therefore show the true Bank balance at the time of balancing the Cash Book, and must be entered in the sundries column on the opposite side to enable the Cash Book to be balanced.

(3) A different method of keeping the Bank Account in the Cash Book is to enter the deposits on the debit side and the withdrawals on the contra or credit side, some accountants contending that the deposits are virtually receipts and should not be entered on the same side as disbursements. To enable this to be done cash columns are arranged and the deposit is entered in the Bank column and a corresponding entry is made to contra in the cash column.

Payments made by cheque or note are entered in the Bank column.

N.B.—See form of Cash Book at end of answer.

(4) Some accountants prefer to keep the Bank Account in a separate book in which the deposits are entered on the left side and the cheques and withdrawals on the right. Special columns similar to those which would be kept in a Cash Book simplify the posting of these cheques to the accounts to which they are chargeable. This relieves the general Cash Book of an immense number of entries and is a good system for a business issuing many cheques. The following form will illustrate the method:—

Dr.   BANK ACCOUNT.   *Cr.*
(Accounts to be charged.)

Date	Particulars	L. F.	Deposits	Date	Particulars	L. F.	Withdrawals	Bills Payable	Mdse.	Etc.

In the above illustration of "Bank Account" the Deposits are taken from the credit side of the Cash Book, and the Withdrawals from the stub of Cheque Book, and the Notes and Dishonors are entered as paid or charged by the Bank.

There are other systems of keeping the Bank Account, but these explained practically include them all.

The advantages of keeping the Bank Account entirely in the Cash Book or in a separate Bank Book instead of posting to the Ledger, are numerous. The Bank Pass Book can be readily checked and compared and the balance can be obtained at any time. The only disadvantages that might arise are where there are a great number of entries, which can be obviated by keeping separate books as shown above.

BOOK-KEEPING.

Dr. CASH.

Date	Particulars	Folio	Cash	Bills Rec.	Int.	Bank
1891						
Oct. 1	To J. Smith, Capital a/c	250	$250 00			$3,000 00
" 3	" Cash Sales	100	200 00			
" 1	" B.R. No. 1 Dis.			$200 50	$0 50	200 00
"	" " " 2 "			180 00	3 00	177 00
"	" " " 3 "			37 03	1 00	36 00
" 6	" J. Brown	350	18 00			218 00
" 8	" Deposit Bank	100	65 00			
"	" Cash Sales	302	15 00			
" 7	" G. Robinson	100				100 00
" 8	" Deposit Bank	100	98 00	90 00		98 00
"	" Cash Sales		80 00	100 00	2 00	178 00
"	" B.R. No. 4, 5 Dis.					
"	" Deposit Bank					
			$400 00	507 50	6 50	4,007 00
	Outstanding Cheque No. 10			Fo. 150	Posted to Dr. of Int.	36 00
						4,043 00
" 8	" Balance					$1,352 00

CONTRA. Cr.

Date	Particulars	Folio	Cash	Mdse.	Bills Payable	Expense	No. of Cheque	Bank
1898								
Oct. 1	By Stationery	230				$15 00	1	$ 15 00
" 1	" Office Furniture					118 00	2	118 00
"	" Purchases, J. R. & Co.			$1,000 00			3	1,000 00
" 4	" Telephone	80				22 50	4	22 50
" 5	" Wages	90				42 00	5	42 00
"	" Petty Cash	90				25 00	6	25 00
" 6	" Bank		$218 00					
" 8	" B.P. No. 1				$300 00		7	500 00
"	" Rent		100 00			80 00	8	80 00
" 7	" J. Smith, Private a/c	230				50 00	9	50 00
"	" G. Harris, Office Bks.					36 00	10	36 00
"	" T. Jones, note dis- charged	304	178 00					
" 8	" Bank							201 84
			$496 00	1,000 00	500 00	153 50		2,030 34
	" Bal. as per Bank Book		Fo. 110	Fo. 160	Fo. 50			1,352 66
								$4,043 00

In the Example no payments except the Bank Deposits are shown made in Cash, as the transactions are the same as shown on page 25 for the sake of comparison.

This is an excellent form of Cash Book, and is here shown to exemplify more particularly the method of keeping the Bank Account therein

Question 5.—Macdonald, a wholesale merchant of Montreal, has a debtor at Barrie named Jones. Jones borrowed, without giving security, from Macdonald $500, and for goods supplied owes $750, this latter amount being guaranteed by a responsible party, on the borrowed money $50 is overdue. Macdonald presses for payment of all his account, and Jones remits $300, and authorizes Macdonald to draw on him at sight for $300, which acceptance he pays.

Presuming you were Macdonald's book-keeper how would you deal with the transactions? Show the account.

Dr.	JONES "LOAN ACCOUNT."		Cr.
To Cash	$500 00	By Cash .... " Part of sight draft	$300 00 200 00

Dr.	JONES. Guaranteed by X.		Cr.
To Goods	$750 00	By Sight draft	$100 00

MEMO.—The book-keeper, looking after his employer's interest, would see that the unsecured liability was first liquidated. It is advisable that the Guarantor should be informed of the steps taken in pressing for payment. In showing the Ledger Accounts no notice has been taken of the interest due on the loan, this of course would come off the $100 credited to the guaranteed account. In the appropriation of the payment here made it has been assumed that Jones gave no directions as to how it was to be applied. If he had done so his instructions would govern the distribution of it.

Question 6.—What method for keeping accounts with its customers do you consider best suited for a Gas or Water Undertaking? Explain fully the working and advantages of such a book.

A.—A good form of keeping accounts with customers of a Gas or Water Undertaking is a Ledger ruled as follows:—

	FIRST QUARTER.				SECOND QUARTER.			
	Date	Gas @ Net amount	Cash received	Balance	Date	Gas @ Net amount	Cash received	Balance
A Accounts arranged alphabetically or according to streets, (the latter plan is the best).								
Total gas accounts, and cash received.								

Allow one line for each account. Charge up the accounts, less discount, if any, from the Register, and credit all accounts from the Cash Book. The accounts when added up will balance with the Gas Account in the Register and with the amounts received as per the Cash Book.

At the end of quarter (or month if the accounts are sent monthly) transfer to overdue Ledger all accounts unpaid adding the discount which will be recorded in the Register. The total of the balances column will agree with the accounts thus transferred. The names will only be required to be written up, say once a year, as with form of Ledger arranged similar to a modern Trial Balance Book; this can be easily done.

Question 7.—From the following particulars prepare Profit and Loss Account for the year showing Gross Profit on Manufacturing and Net Profit on Business, also Balance Sheet as at 31st December, 1895.

		Dr.	Cr.
A.	Capital Account, 31st Dec., '91....		$22,500
A.	Drawings Account...............	$ 4,725	
B.	Capital Account, 31st Dec., '94...		14,650
B.	Drawings Account...............	2,850	
	Bills Payable.......................		2,789
	Bills Receivable....................	496	
✓	Stock, 31st Dec., '94................	17,810	
	Machinery Account.................	16,924	
	Real Estate and Buildings..........	4,926	
✓	Purchases..........................	33,897	
	Book Debts........................	6,600	
✓	Wages..............................	20,929	
	Sundry Creditors...................		1,297
✓	Sales...............................		78,943
	Office Furniture and Fittings.........	1,140	
	Rent...............................	1,500	
	Cash in hand and in Bank...........	426	
✓	Power, Light, Heat, etc.............	1,864	
	Commission........................	1,141	
	Travelling Expenses................	629	
✓	Discount off Purchases..............		496
✓	Discounts to Customers.............	782	
✓	Freight Outwards...................	429	
✓	Rebates allowed to Customers........	376	
	Fire Insurance......................	484	
	Interest and Bank Charges..........	296	
	Horse Keep........................	350	
	Sundry Expenses...................	1,281	
	Royalties paid.....................	462	
	Advertising........................	391	
	Bad debts written off...............	467	
		$120,675	$120,675

Stock on hand 31st Dec., 1895, $18,126.

Provide 5% on Book debts to cover the Bad debts and Discounts.

Write 6% depreciation off Machinery and Office Fittings.

Carry forward Fire Insurance unexpired, $175.00.

Provide for three days wages, $125.00.

Partners entitled to 6% interest on Capital, and Salaries as follows: A., $3,500 a year; B., $2,000 a year, profits divided equally.

A.— PROFIT AND LOSS ACCOUNT.

To Rent........................	$1,500 00	By Gross Profit from Trading Account........	$21,820 00
" Commission................	1,141 00		
" Travelling Expenses..	629 00		
" Freight Outwards	429 00		
" Fire Insurance.$484 00 Less unexp'd 175 00	309 00		
" Interest and Bank Charges...........	296 00		
" Horse Keep...........	350 00		
" Sundry Expenses	1,281 00		
" Advertising...........	391 00		
" Bad debts written off..	467 00		
" Provision for bad and doubtful debts.....	330 00		
" Depreciation on machinery and office fittings............	1,083 84		
" Interest on Capital at 6 %................	2,229 00		
" Salaries................	5,500 00		
	$15,935 84		
" Balance net profit	5,884 16		
	$21,820 00		$21,820 00

BALANCE SHEET.

Liabilities.			Assets.		
Bills Payable............		$2,789 00	Cash on hand and in Bank...............		$ 426 00
Sundry Creditors........		1,297 00	Bills Receivable.........	$ 496 00	
		$4,086 00			
Provision accru'd wages		125 00	Book Debts ....$6,600 00 Less provision for bad and doubtful debts........ 330 00	6,270 00	6,766 00
"A" Capital Account..	22,500 00				
Less drawings..	4,725 00				18,126 00
	17,775 00				
Interest, @ 6 %.....	1,350 00		Stock on hand .. Machinery Account Less 6 % depreciation.	16,924 00 1,015 44	
Salary.............	3,500 00				15,908 56
½ profit............	2,942 08				
		25,567 08			
"B" Capital Account..	14,650 00		Office Furniture and Fittings Less 6 % depreciation.	1,140 00 68 40	
Less drawings. ..	2,850 00				
	11,800 00				1,071 60
Interest @ 6 %.....	879 00		Real Estate & Buildings		4,926 00
Salary.............	2,000 00		Unexpired Insurance		175 00
½ profit............	2,942 08				
		17,621 08			
		$47,399 16			$47,399 16

Question 8.—On Dec. 31st, M's Capital was $25,000; N's Capital, $15,000; and O's Capital, $10,000. They shared profits equally. Their Creditors of $50,000 demanded payment of their debts, and the assets realized $55,000

(a) What were the assets stated at in the firm's books?

(b) What was the loss of each partner?

(c) What became of the $5,000 left?

(d) What has O. to pay M.

A.—We first prepare the Balance Sheet from the information given, which will give the answer to question (a), as the assets will equal the total liabilities in the firm's books.

Liabilities.		Assets.	
Creditors	$50,000 00	Nominal value	$100,000 00
Capital Accounts:			
M $25,000 00			
N 15,000 00			
O 10,000 00			
	50,000 00		
	$100,000 00		$100,000 00

REALIZATION ACCOUNT.

To Assets	$100,000 00	By Cash	$ 55,000 00
		" Loss	45,000 00
	100,000 00		100,000 00
" Loss	45,000 00	" M	15,000 00
		" N	15,000 00
		" O	15,000 00
	$45,000 00		$45,000 00

The loss of each partner would therefore be $15,000, and the Final Balance Sheet will give the answers to questions (c) and (d).

FINAL BALANCE SHEET.

Liabilities.			Assets.	
Creditors		$50,000 00	Cash	$55,000 00
Capital Accounts:			O to pay	5,000 00
M $10,000 00				
N .... nil.		10,000 00		
		$60,000 00		$60,000 00

M. had therefore to receive $10,000, which he would receive as follows:—the $5,000 mentioned in the question and the balance from O.

Question 9.—You are appointed Book-keeper to a firm whose accounts have been kept by Single Entry. You are required to transfer them to the Double Entry System. Explain the process and give an illustration.

A.—The question does not state if the change of system is being made at the time of balancing the books, or during the current year. In the former case the process is very simple, and consists in collecting the items composing the Balance Sheet, and opening the proper accounts in the Ledger. This can be done through the Journal, crediting and debiting the firm's Capital Account as required.

In the latter case accounts would have to be opened, so that all the liabilities and assets may be represented in the ledger as well as the profits and losses, care being taken that the balances therein agree. The best plan would be, first, in the case of a manufacturing or trading business, to open a Trading Account and charge to it the amount of merchandise as per last inventory; the amount of wages paid as per Wages Book; the amount of merchandise bought, from the Invoice Book or other record, since date of last balance; if practicable, amount of discounts, freight and duty should be obtained from the subsidiary books and charged. Credit this account with all sales made, less discounts, the information being obtained in a similar way. The resulting balance will show in your Ledger as Dr. or Cr. to merchandise or Trading Account.

Then take out the balances from the Ledger, supply all the balances representing the known assets and liabilities referred to in the former Balance Sheet, carefully noting if any changes have been made since the date thereof.

If these balances are then added up the difference will be represented by the difference between the totals of the profits and losses of the period.

If the proper record has been kept of receipts and payments or expenses in a statistical form, or in separate columns in the Cash Book, it will not be difficult to form the balances wherewith to open the Profit and Loss Accounts; if this should not be practicable, or would take too much time, the principal sources of income, if any, other than sales, should be picked out and credited and the amount to balance should be charged to Profit and Loss under suitable headings. The following illustration will explain the "modus operandi."

Mr. Smith gives the instructions as set forth, the book-keeper takes out the balances from his Ledger as follows, and obtains after grouping them together the following result:

Accounts Receivable	$1,500 00
" Payable	1,600 00
Jas. Smith, Capital Account	9,000 00

MEMO.—Mr. Smith's drawings have been charged to his account.

The balance of Merchandise Account has been obtained as described above and found to be $350. From the previous Balance Sheet the following particulars have been obtained:

Real Estate	$2,000 00
Office Furniture and Fittings	600 00
Machinery	2,000 00

The book-keeper has made out lists of Bills Payable and Receivable as follows:—

Bills Payable	$1,625 00
" Receivable	3,000 00
Cash on hand and in bank amounts to	615 00

Now, collecting the above information and adding up the balances, the following result is obtained:—

	Dr. Balances.	Cr. Balances.
Accounts Receivable	$1,500 00	
" Payable		$1,600 00
J. Smith, Capital Account		9,000 00
Merchandise	350 00	
Real Estate	2,000 00	
Office Furniture and Fittings	600 00	
Machinery	2,000 00	
Bills Payable		1,625 00
" Receivable	3,000 00	
Cash on Hand and in Bank	615 00	
	10,065 00	
Difference	2,160 00	
	$12,225 00	$12,225 00

This difference, $2,160, is found to consist of

General Expenses	$985 00
Rent	375 00
Salaries	800 00

He opens accounts for these, with the above balances to each account and has his Ledger ready and opened to start the system of Double Entry.

Supposing a case where it is found not feasible to write up the Merchandise Account as described, the book-keeper would ascertain the amount of the merchandise at date of last Balance Sheet and debit this amount to Merchandise Account; proceed then as before and the difference obtained can be posted direct **to Profit and Loss Account, or to a** discrepancy or **adjustment account until** the end **of** the **year,** when it will be **closed to profit** or loss.

The **merchant** will then **at the end** of the year know his net profit or loss, but will not be able **to trace it to** its actual source for **the period prior to** the **date** of changing his **system** of book-keeping.

Question 10.—The accounts **of the firm** of Frederick Whitney and Charles Murray after the **year's trading,** ending December 31st, **1896,** show as under:—

Capital Assets	$85,000 00
Salaries	8,000 00
Merchandise Account, Dr.	36,000 00
Discount on Purchases	500 00
Bank Charges	725 00
Freight on Purchases	1,250 00
Sundry Creditors	28,000 00
Stable Maintenance	350 00
Rents (of sublet premises)	1,000 00
Discount on Sales	1,500 00
Labor	39,150 00
Bills Payable	8,250 00
Sales (less returns)	175,082 00
Travelling Expenses	2,600 00
Rent of Warehouse	3,000 00
Purchases	90,000 00
Sundry Debtors	20,000 00
General Charges	8,100 00
Insurance (used $1,310)	1,810 00
Bills Receivable	6,200 00
Cash on hand	517 00
Partners' Capital	91,400 00

Prepare Revenue Account and Balance Sheet, A's Capital (before the books are closed) being $60,000 **and** B's $31,400. The partners share profits equally and 5% per annum to be allowed **on** extra Capital.

A.—The information given is insufficient, unless it is to be assumed that there is no merchandise on hand. As however, there is clearly an omission in the question (see page 18) the value of the merchandise on hand is assumed to be $30,000. It is also noted that as no mention is made of depreciation, etc., that such provisions must be included in the balances given.

TRADING ACCOUNT.

1895 Dec. 31. Balance....		$36,000 00	By sales $175,082 00 Less discount 1,500 00	173,582 00
1896 Dec. 31. Purchases.. $90,000 00 Less disc't.. 500 00		89,500 00		
Freight ...		1,250 00		
Labor......		39,150 00		
		165,900 00		
Less mdse... on hand..		30,000 00		
		135,900 00		
Bal. being gross profit		37,682 00		
		$173,582 00		$173,582 00

REVENUE ACCOUNT.

To Salaries	$8,000 00	By Trading Account, gross profit	$37,682 00
" Bank charges	725 00		
" Stable maintenance ..	350 00		
" Travelling expenses ..	2,600 00		
" Rent........$3,000 00 less premises sublet.... 1,000 00	2,000 00		
" General charges	8,100 00		
" Insurance... $1,810 00 less unused. 500 00	1,310 00		
" Balance, net profit on business...........	14,597 00		
	$37,682 00		37,682 00
" Interest on extra capital................	$1,430 00	By Balance	14,597 00
" F. Whitney, ½ profits.	6,583 50		
" C. Murray, ½ profits ..	6,583 50		
	$14,597 00		$14,597 00

BALANCE SHEET.

Liabilities.				Assets.			
Sundry creditors	$28,000 00			Cash on hand....			$ 547 00
Bills payable....	8,250 00		$ 36,250 00	Sundry debtors..	$20,000 00		
				Bills receivable..	6,200 00		
Partners' capital							26,200 00
"A" (presumably F. Whitney)				Mdse. on hand ..			30,000 00
				Capital assets ..			85,000 00
Capital %	60,000 00			Unused insur'ce.			500 00
Interest on excess capital, at 5 %.........	1,430 00						
½ profits	6,583 50						
		$68,013 50					
"B" (presumably Charles Murray)							
Capital %	31,400 00						
½ profits	6,583 50						
		37,983 50	105,997 00				
			$142,247 00				$142,247 00

CHAPTER IV.

BOOK-KEEPING.

(For Question 1 see page 45.)

Question 2.—A wholesale fruit concern transacts both a commission and a general business. They sell their own and consigned goods in the same invoice, and do not guarantee consignors against bad debts. Give forms of any special books required and Journal entries to illustrate what may arise in course of dealing with consignments.

A.—*Special Books required.*

    Register of Consignments (a)
    Consignment Ledger   (b)
    Sales Book   (c)

(a) As consignments come to hand they are entered in Register and numbered consecutively, giving full particulars and instructions.

(b) Ordinary Ledger with accounts opened with number of Consignment and Consignor's name.

(c) Sales Book.

Date	Name	Particulars	No. of Consgt.	Fo.	Consgt. Sales	Sales	Total
1898 Nov. 4...	Brown & Scott	10 lbs. Butter 16 " " 15 " "	13 17		$60 00 93 60	 $105 00	 $258 60

JOURNAL ENTRY.

Brown & Scott, Dr.	$258 60	
To Consignment Sales		$153 60
" Sales..		105 00

MEMO.—The two items $60 and $93.60 will be credited to Accounts Nos. 13 and 17 in the Consignment Ledger. The balances in this Ledger will agree with the balance to Consignment Sales Account in General Ledger. Charge Freight, etc., to this account and post in Consignment Ledger in same way.

When a consignment is all sold, first ascertain, by reference to Sales Book, to whom goods were sold, and if paid for, then

JOURNAL ENTRY.

Consignment Sales, Dr	$....	
(Proceeds of sales less charges.)		
To Consignor		$....
" Commission Account		....

Question 3.—A Mining Company is disposing of its Treasury Stock at 15 cents per $1 share. A Development Company which is disposing of its Treasury Stock at 10 cents per $1 share purchases 50,000 shares of the Mining Company's Stock, giving 75,000 shares of its own in payment. When the Mining Company's financial year closes, its stock is selling at 10 cents, and the stock of the Development Company is worth 20 cents. Give Journal entries and open accounts in the books of each Company showing **transactions and adjustments at end of** financial period.

A.—

DEVELOPMENT COMPANY.
JOURNAL ENTRIES.

Mining Company, Dr............	$ 7,500 00	
75,000 $1 shares, @ 10c.		
Discount on shares, Dr.	67,500 00	
90c. per share on above shares.		
To Treasury Stock		$75,000 00

Mining Company's Stock, Dr.... $7,500 00
    To Mining Company $7,500 00
      For 50,000 shares of this
      Company, purchased,
      giving in payment 75,-
      000 shares at selling
      price, 10c. on the $1.

Investment Profits or Losses, Dr.. $2,500 00
    Reduction in value of Mining
    Company Stock.
      To Mining Company Stock. $2,500 00

LEDGER ACCOUNTS.

Treasury Stock,
    To Stock unsold .... $......
                            By Mining Co........... $7,500 00
                                75,000 shares.
                              " Discount on shares... 67,500 00

Mining Company,
    To 75,000 shares 7,500 00
      Our stock.   By Mining Company
                                  Stock 7,500 00

Discount on Shares,
    To Discount on 75,-
      000 shares 67,500 00

Mining Company Stock,
    To 50,000 shares .... 7,500 00   By depreciation in value .. 2,500 00

Profit and Loss Account,
    To depreciation in
      Mining Co. Stock.. 2,500 00

MINING COMPANY.

JOURNAL ENTRIES.

Development Company Stock, Dr. $7,500 00
    To Development Company .. $7,500 00
      75,000 shares purchased @
      10c.

Development Company, Dr......$ 7,500 00
Discount on Shares, Dr......... 42,500 00
    To Treasury Stock $50,000 00
      50,000 shares of Stock ex-
      changed for Development
      Company Stock.

When **Treasury Stock** is sold some adjusting **entry must** be passed so that the **balance** of Treasury Stock **Account shall** agree **with the amount of unsold shares.**

Development Company Stock, Dr. $7,500 00
    To Profit and Loss Account.. $7,500 00

This entry is asked for by the question, but strictly speaking this amount **is not an** earned profit until the Stock is sold, and the wiser course might **be to** treat **this** as a Reserve to meet losses **on other** Stocks. Similarly **it** might be agreed that depreciation on **Stock should not be treated as a** loss until **the Stock** is sold.

LEDGER ACCOUNTS.

Development Co. Stock,
    To 75,000 shares, @
        10c.............$ 7,500 00
    " Increase in value. 7,500 00

Discount on Shares,
    To Discount on 50,000
        shares............42,500 00

Development Company,
    To Mining Co. Stock   By their Stock .... $ 7,500 00
        bought 7,500 00

Treasury Stock,
    To Stock unsold.... $......   By 50,000 shares Devel-
                                              opment Company 7,500 00
                                            " Discount on shares. 42,500 00

Profit and Loss, or Reserve @.
                                            By Increase value Devel-
                                              opment Co. Stock .. 7,500 00

Question 1.—Name and classify (sub-classify when possible) the Ledger Accounts of a manufacturer and wholesale trader, stating the purpose served by each class of accounts.

A.—LEDGER ACCOUNT.	SUB-DIVISION.	CLASSIFICATION.	SUB-CLASSIFICATION. (Showing Purpose Served.)
Capital Account.	Capital Account of Each Partner.	Capital.	
Mr. ———, Loan Account.		Debts and Liabilities of the Firm.	
Bills Payable.			
Names of Debtors.			
Contingent Liability, usually not recorded as a Ledger Account, but should appear under classified heading in Balance Sheet.			Showing Amount of Investment. AMOUNT OF LOANS ON MORTGAGES. AMOUNT OF DEBTS owing by Firm. Debts for which notes or acceptances have been given. Trade Debts on Open Account. CONTINGENT LIABILITIES; Shewing claims against the Firm not acknowledged as debts. Moneys for which the Firm is contingently liable, such as Bills under discount at the Bank.
Reserve Account.	Particular Name of Separate Account.		Reserve Accounts. Amount set aside from Profits to meet contingencies. Undivided profits.
Profit and Loss.	Trading Account; Merchandise, Purchases Account, Sales Account, Wages, Freight, Duty. Expenses; Sub-divided into such accounts as Rent, Salaries, Commission, Interest and Bank Charges, Bad Debts, Depreciation, Provisions for Contingencies, Insurance, &c.	Profit and Loss.	The profit or loss of business.
Name of Property. Merchandise, Plant and Machinery, Furniture and Fittings,	Raw Material, Manufactured Stock, Stock in course of Manufacture. Machinery, Working Tools, Working Plant, such as horses and wagons, &c. Office Furniture, Fittings in Warehouse, &c.	Property held by Firm.	Immovable Property, distinguishing (a) Freehold Land, (b) " Buildings, (c) Leasehold " Movable Property: (d) Stock in Trade, (e) Plant.
Names of Debtors, Name of Principal, Bills Receivable,	Secured, Unsecured, Bad and Doubtful.	Debts owing to the Firm.	Trade debts on open account. Drawings by Principal or Partner. Debts for which the Firm holds Bills.
Cash Account, (where kept) Bank Account, (shown in Ledger and Cash Book). Name of Investment.		Cash and Investment.	Nature of Investment and rate of interest. Amount of cash, where lodged, and if bearing interest.

Question 4.—The management of a social club desires to have prepared, monthly, statements showing profit or loss in conducting its affairs. Membership fees are payable annually in advance, but are not all so paid. Mortgage interest is payable half-yearly, Taxes annually, Water and Light quarterly. What features would you introduce so that the monthly Ledger statement would show the true position? Give Journal entries.

A.—The ordinary Ledger Accounts would show each month:—

        Total Membership Fees received to date,
           " Expenses, paid to date,

To ascertain the true position of the club each month, keep a separate book in Ledger form as follows, writing it up monthly:—

MEMBERSHIP FEES.
                      By Fees accrued due to date $......

EXPENSES.
To Amount expended as per
    Ledger .... $......
" Taxes accrued due ....
    (On basis of previous year).
" Water and Light accrued
    due ....
" Mortgage Interest accrued
    due ....

As long as the expenses, which can include as many accounts as may be required, are less than the Fees accrued due to date, the club is living within its income, and vice versa.

It is not recommended that these accounts be kept in the Ledger, but as the question seems to call for it, the monthly Journal entries would be as follows:

```
Members, Dr....................    $......
    To Membership fees ............         $.......
        Fees due for 1 month.
```

MEMO.—When Fees are received from the Members they are credited to "Members" account, which would really represent a liability, as the Fees are payable in advance.

```
(Mortgage) Interest, Dr ............  $......
    To Mortgage..... ..............         $......
        1 months' interest on debt.

Taxes, Dr...........................  $......
Water and Light, Dr ................  $......
    To City Treasurer...............         $......
        Amounts for 1 month.
```

If the social club, however, derives a revenue from other sources, such as sale of wines, liquors, etc., the profit (or loss) on this department can be estimated monthly, but the only true and satisfactory method is by taking stock.

Question 5.—A manufacturer of machinery who also deals in general supplies sells the former subject to liens until paid in full, and the latter on the usual terms of credit without security. How would you keep the account of a customer who purchases both machinery and supplies, and what precautions would you take from time to time in the interests of the manufacturer, respecting such account?

A.—Two accounts should be opened, one for the machinery, the other for supplies. Care would have to be taken that payments received on account of machinery were not credited to supplies.

It of course follows that the machinery account would be watched from time to time to see that payments were being made as agreed, etc.

Question 6.—A business house borrows from its Bankers upon its own Notes, depositing customers' paper as collateral generally. What transactions are contemplated by this arrangement, and what special books (if any) and accounts must be kept? Give Journal entries.

A.—The transactions contemplated by this arrangement are, that the Bank will allow a standing overdraft and will from time to time repay themselves by collecting and crediting to "The Business House's" account their customers' bills as they mature.

No special Book is necessary beyond the Bills Receivable Book unless bills are very numerous, when a "special register" might be kept, but a "Bank Collateral Account" must be kept to which all bills lodged as collateral security should be charged periodically, and credited when due, and then either debited to cash or the defaulting customer, or treated as overdue.

    Bank Collateral Account, Dr.
     To Bills Receivable,
      Bills for month lodged with Bank,
      and so marked in Bill Book.

    Bank or Cash, Dr.
     To Bank Collateral Account.
      J. Smith's bill paid.

    Overdue Bill Account, Dr.
     To Bank Collateral Account.
      J. Brown's bill dishonored and costs.

    J. Robinson, Dr.
     To Bank Collateral Account.
      Bill dishonored and costs.

Question 7.—A business house has three offices, Toronto, Ottawa, London; each having its own complete set of books. When closing the accounts of all the offices for the purpose of a General Financial Statement, it is found that the balance between offices as shown in their respective books do not agree to the extent of Merchandise, Cash, and Bills then in transit. What entries would you make to adjust these differences in the books and in the Financial Statement?

A.—It would not be necessary to make any special entries in the books to adjust these differences, as the entries would be made in due course upon advice being received of the transactions. In preparing the Financial Statement, however, a careful record would have to be made of the Merchandise, Cash and Bills then in transit, as particulars would have to be given showing the full value of Merchandise, etc., both on hand and in transit. The full information would be obtained by referring to the regular monthly advices which would be interchanged between the offices themselves in a business of this nature. We are not informed in the question if one of these offices is a Head Office, in which case the returns would be so arranged as to readily give the information required.

The Grand Balance Sheet so to speak is a summary of the three balance sheets, but would not include the adjusting Accounts between the offices. So if the Merchandise " in transitu " is added to the several amounts of Merchandise on hand the statement as a whole should balance.

Question 8.—Give Journal entries for the following:—

Reduction of Paid up Capital.

Discount upon Shares Issued.

Dividends upon Paid up Capital.

Trade Discounts upon Goods Sold.

Payments upon forfeited shares which have been re-sold at par.

An endorsement (accommodation) for another.

A.—
Reduction of Paid-up Capital :
Paid-up Capital Account, Dr.
To Deficiency Account.

In accordance with the necessary steps, etc., as set forth in the Act under which the Company is incorporated. (In the Stock

Ledger all the Shareholders must be charged with their Proportion of the reduction.)

Discount upon Shares Issued:
Discount on Shares Account, **Dr.**
To Capital Stock Account.
(Or Treasury Stock Account.)

Memo.—The Capital Stock Account, of course, must be credited as well with the Cash amount at which the shares were sold. In Mining Companies the difference between the nominal value of the Capital and the Cash value is usually very great, and must be represented by some such account as "Discount on Shares." Except under the Mining Act, it is very questionable whether shares can be legally sold at a discount, unless subject to liability to creditors on the amount unpaid.

Dividends upon Paid-up Capital:
Profit and Loss Account, **Dr.**
To Dividend Account.

For amount of Dividend declared by directors. (Memo.—The best method is then to draw cheques for full amount of Dividend, charging same to Dividend Account and remitting them to shareholders entitled thereto. In large concerns it is very common to open a separate Bank Account for Dividend cheques, marking them as such.)

Trade Discounts on Goods Sold:
Trade Discounts, **Dr.**
To Sundry Debtors.

For amount of Trade Discounts. These Debtors are also credited for the net amount of cash received. The items are very commonly passed through the Cash Book, when cash is received.

Payments Upon Forfeited Shares, which have been Re-sold at Par.

Entry in Stock Ledger:
Defaulting Shareholder, **Dr.**
To Forfeited Share Account.
Forfeited Share Account, **Dr.**
To New Purchaser:

Entry in General Journal :
  New Purchaser, Dr.
      (For amount shares realized.)
      To Defaulting Shareholder.
  Cash, Dr.
      To New Purchaser.

Defaulting Shareholder being originally charged, to credit of Capital Account, with call on shares as made, he is credited with the amount such shares realized. By the question he has paid part and there is a surplus which will show to his credit, and to which he is entitled less interest and expenses.

[Extract from Lindley on Companies.]

If the money arising from the sale of a forfeited share is more than sufficient to pay the arrears of calls with interest and the expenses of sale, the surplus is to be paid to the defaulting shareholder.

An Endorsement (Accommodation) for another :
  Contingent Account, Dr.
      To Accommodation Bills Payable.
          For endorsement to accommodate John Brown.

MEMO.—On due date this entry would be reversed, as the liability will either have been removed or will have to be paid.

Question 9.—Hurd & Co., Rogers & Co., and Jno. Williams agree to buy a Steamer, and operate it as a Single Ship Company. Hurd & Co. are to take Bill of Sale for 8-64th, Rogers & Co. 16-64ths, and Jno. Williams 40-64ths. The price paid is $100,000 cash. Jno. Lewis agrees to loan them $50,000 for three years, Interest at 7%, payable half yearly. The members mortgage their individual shares pro rata. But Lewis insists that in addition he must have a "joint and several" Bond, which binds each member to pay the full $50,000. Hurd & Co. and Rogers & Co. are in financial straits, and are unable to pay anything beyond what the boat earns. Williams is a man of means and is obliged to pay interest for Hurd & Co. and Rogers & Co. They run the boat for three years before any division of profits is made; at that time a Dividend of $50 per share is declared, Hurd & Co. and Rogers & Co. agreeing that Williams shall apply their dividend on what he has paid.

(a) How do the accounts stand?

(b) Make Journal entries as Williams' book-keeper, showing his position in the matter.

A.—(a) The accounts stand as follows:

Hurd & Co., Investment 8 shares $12,500 00
    Interest on account loan by Jno.
    Lewis, paid by Jno. Williams...... $1,312 50
    Deduct their Dividend, $50 per share
    on 8 shares 400 00
                                            912 50

    * Present face value of Investment,
      not including liability to Lewis .. $11,587 50

Rogers & Co., Investment 16 shares.......... $25,000 00
    Interest on account loan by Jno. Lewis,
    paid by Jno. Williams $2,625 00
    Deduct their Dividend, $50 per share
    on 16 shares 800 00
                                            1,825 00

    * Present face value of Investment,
      not including liability to Lewis .. $23,175 00

MEMO.—Hurd & Co owe Jno. Williams $912.50, Rogers & Co. owe Jno. Williams $1,825. *They are also liable on the Joint and Several Bond for $50,000, and have mortgaged their individual shares pro rata.

Jno. Williams, Investment 40 shares $62,500 00
    Interest on account loan by John
      Lewis, amount paid $6,562 50
    Deduct Dividend, $50 per share on 40
      shares 2,000 00
                                           4,562 50

    Present face value of Investment, not
      including liability to Lewis........ $57,937 50

MEMO.—Williams has been obliged to pay the interest due by Hurd & Co. and Rogers & Co. under the "joint and several" Bond given to Lewis; he is, therefore, secured for these payments, subject to Lewis' claim, and it is important that he records these entries properly in his books.

He does not treat these payments as amounts lent to Hurd & Co. and Rogers & Co., but as amounts he has been obliged to pay under the Bond.

This is an example of the principle known as the doctrine of subrogation.

(b) Journal Entries made by Williams' book-keeper:

Single Ship Company, Dr........	$32,500 00	
To Cash....................		$31,250 00
" Jno. Lewis		31,250 00

For purchase of 40-64ths Single Ship Co. MEMO.—There is besides a contingent liability to Jno. Lewis of $18,750, as Williams is a Joint and Several Guarantor for the $50,000 advanced by Lewis.

JOURNAL ENTRIES SHEWING INTEREST PAID BY WILLIAMS.

Interest, Dr.....................	$3,562 50	
To John Lewis........		$3,562 50

Being the Interest due on Williams' Mortgage to Lewis. As a matter of fact there were six payments, but it is shown "in globo" as sufficiently illustrating the entry.

Journal Entry showing Interest paid to Lewis under the Bond.

Single Ship Co. Investment, Dr..	$3,937 50	
To Jno. Lewis		$3,937 50
Being interest paid under Bond as follows :		
Hurd & Co..................	$1,312 50	
Rogers & Co................	2,625 00	

MEMO.—In answering a question of this nature, the principle governing it is of more importance than a lot of details. In actual book-keeping all the entries would appear in their proper sequence, and such items as Interest to be charged on the above amounts would have to be considered.

Question 10.—Prepare Trading Account, Profit and Loss Account and Balance Sheet from the following Trial Balance of Joseph Tape, Tailor, etc., as on 30th April, 1898.

Sundry Debtors on Open Account $3,600 00		
Bad Debts Account	195 00	
Credit Sales		$7,110 00
Sundry Creditors on Open Acct..		3,475 00
Bills Receivable	340 00	
Taxes	85 00	
Imperial Bank	430 00	
Bills Payable		1,320 00
Cash Sales		18,080 00
Discounts on Sales	185 00	
Insurance	125 00	
Purchases	14,255 00	
Joseph Tape, Drawings Account	2,000 00	
Cash	90 00	
Sundry Charges	640 00	
Stock, 30th April, 1897	7,570 00	
Joseph Tape, Capital Account		6,400 00
Rent Account	675 00	
Furniture and Fittings Account	750 00	
Wages (Tailors)	4,470 00	
" (Shop)	935 00	
Interest	40 00	
	$36,385 00	$36,385 00

The Stock on hand 30th April, 1898, is $7,160. Write off 10% for Depreciation on Furniture and Fittings. Provide for discount 5% on oustanding Accounts Receivable. Insurance paid for one year $75, of which ⅔ unexpired. Allow for this.

A.— TRADING ACCOUNT.

To Stock, 30th April, '97	$ 7,570 00	By Cash Sales	$18,080 00	
" Purchases	14,255 00	" Credit Sales	7,110 00	
" Wages (tailors)	4,470 00		25,190 00	
" Balance gross profit	5,870 00	Less Discount	185 00	
				$25,005 00
		Stock on hand April 30, '98		7,160 00
	$32,165 00			$32,165 00

PROFIT AND LOSS ACCOUNT.

To Bad Debts Account...	$ 195 00		By Gross Profit, Trading Account............	$5,870 00
" Taxes................	85 00			
" Insurance....$125 00 less unexpir'd 50 00	75 00			
" Sundry charges......	640 00			
" Rent Account	675 00			
" Wages (shop)........	935 00			
" Interest	40 00			
" Depreciation on Furniture and Fittings..	75 00			
" Discount on Accounts Receivable	180 00			
" Net profit	2,970 00			
	$5,870 00			$5,870 00

BALANCE SHEET.

Liabilities.				Assets.			
Sundry creditors on open Account	$ 3,475 00			Cash on hand	$ 90 00		
Bills Payable	1,320 00			Imperial Bank........	430 00		$ 520 00
		$4,795 00		Sundry creditors on open Account	3,600 00		
Joseph Tape :				Less Discount	180 00		
Capital Account.	$ 6,400 00					3,420 00	
Less Drawings &c.	2,000 00			Bills Receivable.......	340 00		3,760 00
	4,400 00						7,160 00
Net Profit for year	2,970 00			Stock on hand........	....		
		7,370 00		Furniture & Flittings Less depreciation	750 00 75 00		675 00
				Unexpired Insusance.	....		50 00
		$12,165 00					$12,165 00

CHAPTER V.

SHAREHOLDERS AND PARTNERS' ACCOUNTS.

Question 1.—How many kinds of partners may there be, and define each?

A.—There are in reality only two kinds or classes of partners, viz., **General Partners** and **Special Partners**.

General Partners, sometimes known as active, silent or nominal partners, are responsible for all the debts of the Company, and directly or indirectly manage the business.

Special Partners, sometimes known as **Limited Partners, are not liable for the debts of the partnership beyond the amount** by them contributed to the Capital. It is **imperative that** they take no part in the management, and their names must **not be** used in the name of the firm, and the partnership **must be** registered, as, if these **points are** infringed **it would render them General Partners**.

Such a limited partnership **in Ontario does not** legally exist **until it has** been duly registered, whereas **a general** partnership **may be registered any** time within six months after its formation.

An Active Partner is a general **partner who takes an** active **part in the** management, and **is known as such by the public**.

*A Silent or **Dormant Partner** is* a general partner who is not known to the public, though **he may** take part **in the** management.

A *Nominal Partner*, is a general partner whose name appears in the business, but takes no part in the management.

Question 2.—What mutual obligations are implied in a simple partnership contract?

A.—A partnership contract implies that each partner, in addition to acting in conformity with the terms thereof,

(a) Will do his utmost to advance the interests of the firm, and do nothing prejudicial thereto, such as making private profits unless authorized by articles.

(b) Will share profits and losses equally if nothing to the contrary has been agreed upon.

(c) Will be bound by the action of each of the other partners in so far as these are not contrary to the scope or nature of the business.

(d) Is liable to creditors for the whole of the debts of the firm, unless he is a limited partner.

(e) Will afford the fullest information as to any and all transactions entered into.

(f) Recognizes the rights of his partner to take part in the management, unless otherwise agreed.

Question 3—How would you deal with the Ledger Accounts of partners (a) in the allotment of profits, (b) assessment of losses, (c) where one partner's personal drawings exceed amounts specified by partnership agreement, and remaining partner's drawings are less than the amount to which he is so entitled?

A.—(a) Credit each partner's capital account with his proportion thereof as specified in the Partnership Articles.

(b) Similarly debit each partner's capital account in the proper proportions.

(c) Charge the drawings of each partner to his Capital Account. If the Partnership Articles make no provision for interest on partner's drawings no further steps can be taken unless the partners mutually agree to some such charge being made.

Where one partner persistently draws more than he should, there is practically only one remedy, and that is to dissolve the partnership.

Question 4.—"A" agrees to give his services in a certain business, receiving in lieu of wages a share in the net profits. Is he, or is he not a partner? What is the principle governing the case?

A.—He is not a partner.

The principle governing the case is that such employee receives a share in the net profits as a salary, or addition thereto, merely as a bonus to encourage him to put forth his best efforts, but he acquires thereby no share in the business and has no voice in the management, except as an agent. In cases like this a contract clearly drawn should always be prepared. Further, an employee's services could always be dispensed with by proper notice, not so if he became a partner through this arrangement.

Question 5.—What is necessary to be done by a retiring partner to free himself from further liability for partnership debts?

A.—He should send notice (or see that it is done) to every customer or creditor, notifying his withdrawal from the partnership. Further, the change in partnership should be properly advertised.

The retiring partner would then not be liable for any future liability for partnership debts.

If this is a trading, manufacturing or mining partnership, such change must be registered to release the retiring partner.

In the case, however, of a silent or dormant partner, who has not been known to the public, the advertising would not be necessary, nor is notice at all required.

SHAREHOLDERS AND PARTNERS' ACCOUNTS.

Question 6.—What forms of books do you consider necessary for the purpose of correctly exhibiting the position of shareholders in an incorporated Joint Stock Company? Give rulings.

A.— MEMORANDUM OF AGREEMENT AND STOCK BOOK.

WE, the undersigned, do hereby severally covenant and agree each with the other to become incorporated as a company under the provisions of "The Ontario Companies Act" under the name of.......................... Company of................(Limited), with a capital of .... dollars, divided into........... shares of........... dollars each.

AND WE DO hereby severally, and not one for the other, subscribe for and agree to take the several amounts of the capital stock of the said company set opposite our respective names as hereunder and hereafter written, and to become shareholders in such company to the said amounts.

In witness whereof we have signed.

Name of Subscriber	Seal.	Amount of Subscription.	Date and Place of Subscription.		Residence of Subscriber.	Name of Witness.
			Date.	Place.		

By keeping a proper record in the index of the Stock Ledger, the names of the Shareholders can be kept alphabetically arranged, as required in the Act.

REGISTER OF TRANSFERS.

To Whom.			Date	No. of Shares.	Paid in.	Unpaid.	From Whom.		Remarks
Name.	Calling.	Address.					Name.	Address.	

Call Register.—This is a form of book that may be ruled similarly to the Stock Book, entering the various calls made with heading CALL No. 1, CALL No. 2, etc., with the list of shareholders underneath, showing number of **shares and amount** of call due.

FORM OF STOCK LEDGER,
(When Shares are Fully **Paid-up**.)

NAME OF SHAREHOLDER.

Date	Name	No. of Shares.			Value of Shares.			Remarks
		Dr.	Cr.	Bal.	Dr.	Cr.	Bal.	
								(Stating when payment was made.

FORM OF STOCK LEDGER, WHEN CAPITAL IS PAID BY CALLS.

MR. JOHN SMITH.

Date.	Particulars.	No. of Shares.			Subscribed Stock.			Amount of Calls Made.			Amount Unpaid.	Remarks showing Date when Call is Paid.
		Dr.	Cr.	Bal.	Dr.	Cr.	Bal.	Dr.	Cr.	Bal.		
1898 Nov. 1.	By subscription, 10 shares @ $10.00		10	10		$100 00	$100 00					
	1st call made of 25 %				$50 00			$12 50				
Dec. 1.	To transfer, J. Brown, 5 shares	5		5			50 00		$25 00	$25 00	$75 00	Call paid on 12 12 90. C.Bk. Fo. 18.
										12 50	37 50	Transfer Bk. Fo.

The forms for Stock Ledger accounts as here shown are in accordance with the requirements of the Ontario Companies Act. When stock is issued fully paid up, or subscribed for with that intention, the entries in the general books would be

> Subscribers (giving names and details), Dr.
> To Capital Stock.

and when the subscribers pay they are credited in the ordinary way through the Cash Book. Similarly when paid by calls the following entry is made for each call.

> Shareholders (individually), Dr.
> To Capital Stock,
> For second call of $5 per share.

At once posting up the transactions in the Shareholder's Account in Stock Ledger. The total balances in Stock Ledger will thus always agree with "Capital Account." To ascertain what is owing by shareholders refer to the Private Ledger, or the part of the General Ledger set aside for their accounts. As the calls on shares are paid, note in remarks column as shown in illustration above.

Question 7.—How is Preferred Stock created, and what are the advantages derivable by shareholders of the same?

A.—Preferred stock is created by by-law. Full answer as to the method of doing this will be found on referring to index.

The advantages derivable by shareholders are, that their dividends, which are at a fixed rate or as agreed upon, are a first charge upon the profits, and that they can appoint a director or directors to represent them on the board.

Question 8.—State under what circumstances shares may be sold at a discount, or allotted in consideration of the transfer of property, or of a patent right, or of good will?

A.—Shares in a Mining Company may be sold at a discount as authorized by by-law, under the Ontario Mining Companies Incorporation Act, also if so provided for by the by-laws of a company under the Companies Act (Dominion); the great distinction being that in the former case there is no liability on shareholders on the shares as regards the discount so allowed, whereas in the latter case if the company did allow a discount the creditors, if the company were forced into liquidation, could demand that the shareholders pay up the shares, which they had subscribed for, in full.

Shares may be allotted in consideration of the transfer of property, or of a patent right, or of good-will on the formation of the company; or under circumstances where the transactions are legitimate, and in the direct interests of the company it could be arranged that cash be paid for the property acquired, and this cash repaid to the company in purchase of its stock.

Question 9.—What is the voting power of a Shareholder at any meeting of shareholders, (a) if holding partly paid shares, (b) if in arrears for calls, (c) if he has hypothecated his shares?

A.—(a) He has a vote for every share, either in person or by proxy.

(b) He cannot vote.

(c) Hypothecating his shares does not affect his right to vote.

Question 10.—Under what circumstances may shares be forfeited? What is the notice and procedure in such cases? What is the rule respecting the disposal of forfeited stock?

A.—If the calls made thereon are not paid within the time provided by the Act under which the company is incorporated, or by its by-laws, the shares may be forfeited.

The call having been made in accordance with the by-laws of the company, and not paid within the prescribed time, the directors, in their discretion, by resolution to that effect, reciting the facts and duly recorded in their minutes, may summarily forfeit any shares whereon such payment is not made.

The shares so forfeited become the property of the company and may be disposed of as by by-law or otherwise the company may ordain.

CHAPTER VI.

SHAREHOLDERS AND PARTNERS' ACCOUNTS.

Question 1.—A. has proposed to join B. in partnership and to put $2,000 into the business, which has been established by B. They agree that B. is to have ⅔ and A. ⅓ of the profits, and that the capital invested by each is to bear the same proportion.

B. owns the right to a valuable patent, and his other assets, as taken from his books are: Cash, $400; Sundry Debtors, $1,600; Merchandise, $1,000. A. has further agreed to the valuation of these other assets, subject to a discount of 15% on the sundry debtors, and asks B. to submit him a Balance Sheet showing the position of the partners, assuming that he has joined him.

B. has asked you as an accountant to prepare this Balance Sheet, and advises you that he does not propose to invest any more cash.

Prepare the Balance Sheet and give any reasons or explanations you may think necessary.

A.—

BALANCE SHEET,
As Prepared by the Accountant.

Liabilities.		Assets.		
"B" Capital Acct..	$4,000 00	Cash	....	$2,400 00
"A" Capital Acct..	2,000 00	Sundry Debtors	$1,600 00	
		Less discount @ 15%	240 00	
				1,360 00
		Merchandise		1,000 00
		Patent right........		1,240 00
	$6,000 00			$6,000 00

B.'s capital is placed at $4,000 in accordance with the agreement, as A.'s is fixed at $2,000. In the memo given no mention is made of the value of the patent right, and as it is clearly intended to be included in the total assets, its value has been determined by fixing it at the amount which would make the assets agree with the total capital.

No mention is made of any trade liabilities, so presumably there are none. If on enquiry the accountant found that the patent right was worth more than $1,240, it being described as valuable, he could enter it at its real value, and credit, say, " Reserve Fund " with the difference.

Question 2.—A. made B. an advance of $2,000 to enable him to start in business, and took from him a promissory note on demand as security.

Six months afterwards A. wrote to one of B.'s creditors telling him that he was in partnership with B.

The following year B. failed; his assets realized $6,000 and he owed sundry creditors $8,000. A. also put in his claim as a creditor for $2,000 on the promissory note referred to above. B.'s private estate is worth nothing. Adjust the accounts of A. and B.

A.—

Liabilities.			Assets.	
Sundry Creditors	$8,000 00		Cash	$6,000 00
A., Loan Account	2,000 00		B., Dr. on note	2,000 00
		$10,000 00	Deficiency	2,000 00
				$10,000 00

A., in putting in his claim for the $2,000 evidently wishes to rank as a creditor, but B.'s trade creditors must rank first, as A.'s admission that he was in partnership with B. would make him liable for the deficiency in the estate. The sundry creditors will be paid in full if A. is worth the $2,000 which the cash is short of their claim.

As between A. and B. they are not partners, so B. would now owe A. $4,000. It has been assumed from the question that A. and B. are not partners, but that A. wrote to B.'s creditors with the object of improving his (B.'s) credit.

Question 3.—A. and B. are partners with $3,000 and $1,000 respectively invested in their business. They share profits equally, but by the articles of partnership A. is entitled to 5% per annum interest on his capital. Through an oversight the interest was not credited A.'s Capital Account for the year ending the 31st March, 1897. At the present date the error is discovered, and it is desired to rectify matters by simply adjusting the partner's accounts. Their present balances are A., Cr. $3,450, and B., Cr. $1,150. Adjust the accounts, allowing A. the amount to which he is entitled.

A.—

A., CAPITAL ACCOUNT.

To Balance	$3,525 00	By Balance	$3,450 00
		" Adjustment for interest on capital	75 00
	$3,525 00		$3,525 00
		By Balance	$3,525 00

B., CAPITAL ACCOUNT.

To A., Capital Account adjustment	$ 75 00	By Balance	$1,150 00
" Balance	1,075 00		
		By Balance	$1,075 00

A. is entitled to receive $150 for one year's investment on his capital. This amount would be chargeable to Profit and Loss Account, and as they share profits equally each would bear half of this, hence to adjust, credit A. $75, and debit B. $75.

Question 4.—A Joint Stock Company consists of five shareholders. One of the shareholders is an employee and is dismissed. He threatens an action for wrongful dismissal, but finally the matter is settled by another shareholder giving him a certain sum of money for his shares, which are duly transferred to said shareholder. In consequence of this arrangement, what is necessary to be done, and why?

A.—It is now necessary to introduce a new shareholder to restore the number to five, because the Act states that a company cannot exist without five shareholders, and, moreover, the shareholders who, knowing this, continue the company after six months from date of such reduction, would be personally liable to the creditors of the company as if they were simply members of a partnership.

Another shareholder can very readily be obtained by one of the shareholders transferring one or more of his shares to some friend.

Question 5.—A. and B. are partners sharing profits as follows: A. ⅔, B. ⅓. They have failed, and the following is their position as taken from their books:

LIABILITIES.

Bills Payable	$1,000 00
Trade Creditors	5,000 00
A., Loan Account	1,500 00
A., Capital Account	2,000 00
B., Capital Account	1,500 00
	$11,000 00
Assets	$11,000 00

Their assets have realized the sum of $6,000. Adjust the partners' accounts.

A.—

Dr.	REALIZATION ACCOUNT.		Cr.
To Assets	$11,000 00	By Cash	$6,000 00
		" A.'s ⅔ loss	3,333 33
		" B.'s ⅓ loss	1,666 67
	$11,000 00		$11,000 00

A., CAPITAL ACCOUNT.

To ⅔ loss	$3,333 33	By Balance	$2,000 00
" Balance	166 67	" Loan Acct. transferred	1,500 00
	$3,500 00		$3,500 00
		By Balance	$166 67

B., CAPITAL ACCOUNT.

To ⅓ loss	$1,666 67	By Balance	$1,500 00
		" Balance	166 67
	$1,666 67		$1,666 67
To Balance	$166 67		

B. owes A. $166.67.

Question 6.—From the following Trial Balance Sheet of A. and B. raise their Capital Accounts, showing profit or loss.

A., Capital Account		$10,000 00
B., Capital Account		15,000 00
Cash	$1,100 00	
Bills Receivable	4,000 00	
Bills Payable		3,000 00
Trade Debtors	6,000 00	
Trade Creditors		5,000 00
Merchandise	9,000 00	
Wages Account		2,000 00
A., Private Account	1,000 00	
B., Private Account	1,500 00	
General Expenses	600 00	
Rent	600 00	
Interest	300 00	
Machinery and Plant	6,900 00	

Merchandise on hand, $15,000; interest accrued on Bills Receivable, $200; allow 10% on trade debtors; allow 5% on partner's capital. A. and B. share profits equally and draw salaries as follows: A., $1,200, and B., $1,400 per annum, 12 mos. salary due them.

A.— TRADING ACCOUNT.

To Balance, mdse........	$9,000 00	By Inventory,	
" Wages	2,000 00	Mdse. on hand	$15,000 00
" Profit (gross)	4,000 00		
	$15,000 00		$15,000 00

PROFIT AND LOSS ACCOUNT.

To General Expenses	$ 600 00	By Balance, Trading Acct.	$4,000 00
" Rent.................	600 00	" Interest (int. accrued).	200 00
" Interest	300 00	" A., ½ loss...........	875 00
" Allowance, 10 % on trade debtors	600 00	" B., ½ loss...........	875 00
" Interest, on Partners' capital, 5 % for 12 mos.	1,250 00		
" Salary, A............	1,200 00		
" " B............	1,400 00		
	$5,950 00		$5,950 00

A., CAPITAL ACCOUNT.

To Drawings	$1,000 00	By Balance	$10,000 00
" ½ loss	875 00	" Interest at 5 %.......	500 00
" Balance	9,825 00	" Salary	1,200 00
	$11,700 00		$11,700 00
		By Balance	$9,825 00

B., CAPITAL ACCOUNT.

To Drawings	$ 1,500 00	By Balance	$15,000 00
" ½ loss	875 00	" Interest at 5 %	750 00
" Balance	14,775 00	" Salary	1,400 00
	$17,150 00		$17,150 00
		By Balance	$14,775 00

Question 7.—Jones and Smith are partners and share profits in proportion to capital invested. Their Balance Sheet is as follows:

Liabilities, Sundry Creditors, $1,200; Jones, Capital Account, $2,000; Smith's Capital Acount, $1,500

Assets, Sundry Debtors, $2,000; Cash in Bank, $700; Sundry Assets, $2,000.

They are desirous and have arranged to amalgamate with Brown, Robinson & White, who are partners having similar amounts to their Capital Accounts and share profits equally, in a business which has no outside liabilities. Their assets consist of Sundry Debtors, $3,000; Cash in Bank, $500; Sundry Assets, $3,000.

The arrangement agreed upon is that the assets are to be taken over by the new Company, but that reserves are to be formed as follows: 10% on sundry debtors, and 20% on sundry assets, the liabilities of Jones and Smith to be assumed.

Make out a Balance Sheet for the new Company, giving each of the aforesaid partners his proper proportion in shares, and showing the balances to the remaining accounts. The expenses of organizing the Company come to $150 and have been paid by the new Company; include this item.

A.— BALANCE SHEET, JONES & SMITH.

Liabilities.		Assets.	
Sundry Creditors	$1,200 00	Sundry Debtors	$2,000 00
Jones, Capital Acct..$2,000 00		Cash	700 00
Smith, " " ..1,500 00		Sundry Assets	2,000 00
	3,500 00		
	$4,700 00		$4,700 00

BALANCE SHEET, BROWN, ROBINSON & WHITE.

Liabilities.		Assets.	
Brown, Capital Account..	$2,166 67	Sundry Debtors	$3,000 00
Robinson, " " ..	2,166 67	Cash	500 00
White, " " ..	2,166 66	Sundry Assets	3,000 00
	$6,500 00		$6,500 00

In the case of Jones and Smith, their capital will be reduced as follows:

$$
\begin{array}{lr}
10\% \text{ on Sundry Debtors} & \$200\ 00 \\
20\%\quad\text{"}\quad\text{Assets} & 400\ 00 \\
& \$600\ 00
\end{array}
$$

Jones is charged with $\dfrac{600 \times 20}{35} = \$342\ 86$

Smith   "   " $\dfrac{600 \times 15}{35} = 257\ 14$

$$
\begin{array}{lr}
\text{Leaving Jones' capital at} & \$2,000\ 00 \\
\text{Deduct} & 342\ 86 \\
& \$1,657\ 14 \\
\\
\text{Leaving Smith's capital at} & \$1,500\ 00 \\
\text{Deduct} & 257\ 14 \\
& \$1,242\ 86
\end{array}
$$

SHAREHOLDERS AND PARTNERS' ACCOUNTS.

In the case of Brown, Robinson and White their capital will be reduced:

10 % Sundry Debtors		$300 00
20 % " Assets		600 00
Each will bear ⅓ of reduction		$900 00

Then Brown's capital will equal	$1,866⅔
Robinson's " " "	1,866⅔
White's " " "	1,866⅔

BALANCE SHEET OF NEW COMPANY.

Liabilities.		Assets.		
Sundry Creditors	$1,200 00	Sundry Debtors	$5,000 00	
Capital Account in $1 shares, see below..	8,500 00	Less reserve of 10 %	500 00	$4,500 00
		Cash in Bank	1,200 00	
		Deduct cash paid for expenses	150 00	1,050 00
		Sundry Assets	5,000 00	
		Less reserve of 20 %	1,000 00	4,000 00
		Expenses organizing Company		150 00
	$9,700 00			$9,700 00

The capital, $8,500, will be divided amongst the aforesaid partners as follows (they would adjust the odd amounts amongst themselves):

Jones	$1,657 14
Smith	1,242 86
Brown	1,866 67
Robinson	1,866 67
White	1,866 66
	$8,500 00

Question 8.—Jones, Smith & Robinson, Limited, are carrying on a business with two branches. The Capital of the Company is

$20,000 paid up, and Robinson has shares therein to the value of $5,000. Robinson is willing to buy one of the branches and the Directors, being dissatisfied with the working of it, are willing to sell on Robinson's terms, viz., that Robinson hands over his shares to the Company, and takes the branch as a going concern. Can this be arranged? If so, show the steps that should be taken, and give the entries you would pass in the books of the Company.

A.—This can be arranged by Robinson surrendering his shares to the Company for $5,000, and taking over the branch at that figure. The entries in the books would be:

   Capital Stock, Dr...... .... $5,000 00
    To Real Estate.............. $5,000 00
    (Or the branch as the case might be.)

for sale of branch to Robinson as per minute, etc.

MEMO.—Entries would also have to be passed to close the Branch Accounts—these would be very simple and would be transferred to Profit and Loss Account.

Before, however, this could be legally done, a general meeting of the Company would have to be called to consider and pass a by-law covering the proposal as mentioned above. This by-law would require to be passed by a vote of not less than ⅔ in value of the Shareholders at the general meeting called, and the by-law would have to be afterwards confirmed by supplementary letters patent, which can be petitioned for within six months after being passed as above, from the Lieutenant-Governor, through the Provincial Secretary.

With the petition the Company must submit proof of the bona fides of such decrease in capital. If this is approved in due course it will be gazetted and the capital can be lawfully decreased, and the sale to Robinson completed.

Question 9.—Joint Stock Companies in Ontario are compelled by statute to keep certain books. Enumerate them, and give form

SHAREHOLDERS AND PARTNERS' ACCOUNTS.

of Stock or Share Ledger, and your reasons for recommending same.

A.—" A copy of the letters patent incorporating the company and of any supplementary letters patent issued to the company; and if incorporated by special Act, the chapter and year of such Act;

The names, alphabetically arranged, of all persons who are or have been Shareholders in the company;

The post-office address and calling of every such person while such shareholder;

The number of shares of stock held by each shareholder;

The amounts paid in, and remaining unpaid, respectively, on the stock of each shareholder;

The date and other particulars of all transfers of stock in their order; and

The names, post office addresses and callings of all persons who are or have been directors of the company; with the several dates at which each person became or ceased to be such director."

" Proper books of account, containing full and true statements

Of the company's financial and trading transactions;

Of the stock-in-trade of the company;

Of the sums of money received and expended by the company, and the matters in respect of which such receipt or expenditure takes place, and,

Of the Credits and Liabilities of the Company; and also a book or books containing minutes of all the proceedings and votes of the company, or of the board of directors, respectively, and the by-laws of the company duly authenticated, and such minutes shall be verified by the signature of the president, or other presiding officer of the company."

For Form of Stock or Share Ledger see pages 60 and 61.

Question 10.—George Welch and John Pole have dissolved partnership, and the following is the Balance Sheet approved by the partners at the date of dissolution.

Liabilities.		Assets.	
Creditors on Open Acct..	$ 375 00	Cash in hand	$ 300 00
Due Bank	600 00	Debtors' Accts, $5,275.00, valued at..............	2,800 00
Capital Account :		Stock	750 00
At W.G. Welch's		Office Furniture..........	400 00
Credit......$3,525 00			
Less same at J.			
Pole's Debit. 250 00			
	3,275 00		
	$4,250 00		$4,250 00

You, as book-keeper for the firm close up the business and realize from all the assets $5,200. You pay the $975 liabilities, and your salary and expenses of $350. Draw up the partners' accounts for final submission.

A.—

Dr.   REALIZATION ACCOUNT.   *Cr.*

To Assets................	$4,250 00	By Cash	$5,200 00
" Salary and Expenses..	350 00		
" Welch, ½ gain	300 00		
" Pole, ½ gain	300 00		
	$5,200 00		$5,200 00

Dr.   W. G. WELCH, CAPITAL ACCOUNT.   *Cr.*

To Balance	$3,825 00	By Balance	$3,525 00
		" ½ gain in realization assets	300 00
	$3,825 00		$3,825 00
		By Balance ..	$3,825 00

J. POLE'S CAPITAL ACCOUNT.

Dr. / *Cr.*

To Balance	$250 00	By ½ gain in realization assets	$300 00
" Balance	50 00		
	$300 00		$300 00
		By Balance	$50 00

FINAL BALANCE SHEET.

W. G. Welch, Capital Acct.	$3,825 00	By Cash (after payment of liabilities and expenses..	$3,875 00
J. Pole, " "	50 00		
	$3,875 00		$3,875 00

CHAPTER VII.

PARTNERSHIP AND EXECUTORSHIP ACCOUNTS.

Question 1.—A. and B. have been in partnership for 10 years. The term is for 14 years and the articles provide for interest on Capital at 7%. A.'s share of the profit is $\frac{2}{3}$. B.'s $\frac{1}{3}$. The accounts of the partnership have not been kept in a very systematic manner. In the books of the firm the Capital has remained from year to year undivided, but each partner has kept a private book wherein he has entered his share of the Capital, also his share of the yearly profits and his drawings. During the whole of the ten years the partners have never taken the question of interest on capital into account. You are called in to adjust the partnership accounts. State what course you would take in connection with this matter and give your reasons for so doing.

A.—From the question the assumption is that the amount of Capital originally invested by A. and B. was placed to the credit of a general Capital Account in the firm's Ledger, and that the profits were yearly added thereto, and the drawings of both partners deducted, thus giving a different Capital at the commencement of each year.

We are told that each partner kept track in a private book, of his share of the Capital, his yearly profits and his drawings, but neglected to take into consideration interest on capital.

The Articles provide for interest on Capital at 7%, and in the absence of any further information on this subject, each partner would be entitled to ten years simple interest on his Capital only, and no allowance could be made on withdrawals unless this were specially provided for.

Then open a Capital Account for each partner, credit him with his original Capital and the interest as described above. Charge A. with ⅔ and B. with ⅓ of the total interest so credited. Then charge each account with the drawings and credit with profits as taken from their private books, which appear to have their endorsement as correct. If, however, there was any doubt as to the correctness of the division of the profits in the proper proportions, this would have to be adjusted year by year. The sums of the partners' Capital balances thus obtained should agree with the Capital Account referred to in the question, as the assumption is that only the partners' accounts have not been kept systematically, and, moreover, the instructions are confined to adjusting these accounts.

Question 2.—A., B. and C. are partners with capital as follows: A., $10,000; B., $20,000; C., $15,000. They share profits in the proportion of A., ⅜; B., ⅜; C., ¼. They wish to form a Joint Stock Company and they have two creditors for money loaned to them amounting to $10,000, who are willing to take stock to the extent of their loans. It is agreed that this stock shall bear a fixed dividend of 7%. The partners have each been drawing a salary of $2,000 a year and interest on their respective capital at 6%. In forming the Company they wish to continue the old arrangements as between themselves so far as the distribution of profits, salary and interest is concerned. What arrangement would you suggest so as to carry out their ideas and at the same time protect each of the partners individually.

A.—In answering this question we first prepare

BALANCE SHEET OF THE PARTNERSHIP.

Creditors		$10,000 00	Assets	$55,000 00
Capital:				
A.	$10,000 00			
B.	20,000 00			
C.	15,000 00			
		45,000 00		
		$55,000 00		$55,000 00

In forming the Joint Stock Company the creditors would receive Preference Stock for $10,000, bearing a fixed dividend at 7%.

The partners wish further to receive equal salary and dividends as formerly, as far as possible. The simplest way to arrive at this would be for them to arrange with the Company to appoint them at their former salaries. Now, they have received 6% on their capital, or respectively,

A	$ 600 00	per annum.
B	1,200 00	" "
C	900 00	" "

and should therefore receive Preference Stock to rank after the stock issued to the creditors. Let this stock be issued bearing fixed dividend at 10% to avoid unduly inflating the capital.

A. would receive stock representing	$ 6,000 00
B. " " " "	12,000 00
C. " " " "	9,000 00
	$27,000 00

Now, in the past profits have been divided as follows:

A. received, ⅜.
B. "   ⅜.
C. "   ¼.

and as there still remains $18,000 capital still unallotted it would be divided as follows, ensuring that the net profits after paying the Preference Stock were divided as formerly:

A. would receive $18,000 × ⅜ = $6,750 00
B.   "   "   "   × ⅜ = 6,750 00
C.   "   "   "   × ¼ = 4,500 00
$18,000 00

Balance Sheet of the new Joint Stock Company would then stand as follows:

Liabilities.		Assets.	
Capital Stock :		As per former balance sheet	$55,000 00
Preference Stock, first claim, say 100 shares, bearing fixed interest at 7 %	$10,000 00		
Preference Stock, second claim, say 270 shares, bearing fixed interest at 10 %	27,000 00		
Ordinary Stock	18,000 00		
	$55,000 00		$55,000 00

MEMO :
    1st Preference Stock.
  100 shares to creditors.
    2nd Preference Stock.
  60 shares to A.
  120   "   " B.
  90   "   " C.
    Ordinary Stock.
  67½ shares to A.
  67½   "   " B.
  45   "   " C.

Total, 550

Question 3.—Explain the different method of treating the surplus of profit or loss in the books of a Joint Stock Company and those of a partnership.

A.—The surplus of profit and loss in the books of a Joint Stock Company, if any remains after payment of a dividend, should be either carried to a Reserve Fund or left as a balance at Profit and Loss Account; whereas in the books of a partnership such surplus is merged into the Capital Accounts as a general practice.

The principle involved is that the Capital of a Joint Stock Company cannot be altered except as provided for in the statutes;

whereas, in a Partnership the Capital is increased by such surplus or decreased in case of losses.

In a Joint Stock Company's books the balance at credit of Profit and Loss Account is always available for dividends; if it is a debit balance caused by losses, such balance should be paid off before any future profits are divided, said losses could meanwhile be transferred to, say a "Deficiency Account," or could be wiped off by transferring to the debit of Reserve Account, if such reserve had been provided.

Question 4.—A. dies, bequeathing to B. life interest in all his estate (with remainder to G. and H.) with the exception of certain pecuniary legacies and some freehold property which he bequeaths absolutely to C. At the time of A.'s death there is three month's rent due from this property, amounting to $300. A. had also paid a full year's insurance premium in respect of it, amounting to $200, of which nine months is still unexpired. At the time of A.'s death there was cash in the house $35.45. In the bank on current account, $476.55; ditto on deposit, $10,000, with three months interest at 4%. There was also due to the testator, on mortgages: John Jones, $6,000, with 1½ months' interest at 6%; Sam Smith, $4,000, on which 3 months' interest at 6% was paid in advance; Tom Brown, due on note of hand, $700, with 7 months' interest at 7%, from which the executors only realized in all $525. Life insurance and bonuses amounted to $5,685. Testator's horses and carriages realized $475.

The executor's payments were: Funeral expenses, $125; testator's debts, $560; testamentary expenses, $200; executorship expenses, $300; pecuniary legacies, $500; legacies to executors, $1,000. Testator also died possessed of $10,000 bank stock of the market value of $14,750, upon which a six months' dividend at 7% per annum was paid three months after the death. B., the life tenant died three years after the testator, and during her life the executors paid over to her regularly the income from the estate with the exception that at her death there was still due her $275. B. also during her life had the use of the testator's residence and furniture, which at her death were sold and realized $6,000 and $2,000 respectively. The bank stock was sold for $14,100.

Prepare abstract statement of the executor's accounts showing the amount divisible between the residuary legatees, G. and H.

A.— VALUE OF CORPUS OF ESTATE AT TIME OF DEATH.

Assets :

Freehold property bequeathed to C.
Rent on above 3 months		$ 300 00
Insurance premium unexpired, value of 9 months		150 00
Cash in the house		35 45
Cash in the Bank		476 55
Cash on deposit	$10,000 00	
3 months' interest	100 00	
		10,100 00

Due on Mortgages :
John Jones	$6,000 00	
1 month's interest at 6 per cent	45 00	
		6,045 00
Sam. Smith	$4,000 00	
Less 3 months' interest paid in advance	60 00	
		3,940 00
Thos. Brown, note of hand $700 and interest realized		525 00
Life Insurance and Bonus		5,685 00
Horses and Carriages		475 00
Bank Stock, valued at		14,750 00
Residence and Furniture, estimated at		8,000 00

Value of Corpus		$50,482 00
Deduct $650, reduction value of Bank Stock when realized	$ 650 00	
Deduct payments made by Executors	2,685 00	
		3,335 00
Forward		$47,147 00
Deduct due to B.'s heirs		275 00
Amount divisible between G. and H., the residuary legatees		$46,872 00

Executors' Payments.

Funeral expenses	$ 125 00
Debts	560 00
Testamentary expenses	200 00
Executorship "	300 00
Pecuniary legacies	500 00
Legacies to Executors	1,000 00
	$2,685 00

Question 5.—A. bequeaths to B. life interest in his estate with remainder over to C. Among his assets were $5,000 4% City Debentures, interest payable half yearly, on the 30th June and 31st December. The testator died on the 4th April. The life tenant died on the following 15th November. On the 20th December the executors sold the Debentures at 104, the market price of the day. Show, by raising accounts with this investment, the amount coming in respect thereof to the deferred legatee C.

A.—The account showing the investment of the City Debentures could be kept as follows:

Dr. INVESTMENT ACCOUNT. Cr.

Apr.	4	To 4 % City Debs.	$5,000 00	June 30	By Dividend	$	100 00
June	30	" B., life tenant	48 07	Dec. 20	" Sale debentures.		5,200 00
		" Capital Acct.	51 93				
Dec.	21	" transferred to Capital Acct.	200 00				
			$5,300 00				$5,300 00

Dr. CAPITAL ACCOUNT. Cr.

To C., amount due him, deducting therefrom interest from 30th June to 15th Nov. due to life tenants' heirs	$5,251 93	Apr. 4	By investment	$5,000 00
		June 30	" interest thereon to Apr. 4.	51 93
		Dec. 20	" profit, sale of debentures.	200 00
	$5,251 93			$5,251 93

Question 6.—A testator, whose estate eventually realized much less than he anticipated it would, made various bequests as follows: To A., his household furniture and effects, valued at $2,500; to B., his horses and carriages valued at $500; to C., the amount he had on deposit with his bankers, which was $2,000; to E., $1,000; to F., 50 bank shares, valued at the date of the death at $2,000; to G., H. and J., $3,000 each; to various charitable institutions pecuniary legacies amounting to $5,000, and finally, to R., S. and T., $\frac{1}{3}$ each of the residue of his estate.

The estate did not realize sufficient by $5,000 to pay all the above legacies. Show how much each legatee would receive.

A.— Bequeathed to A. his household furniture and effects.
" " B. " horses and carriages.
" " C. " balance in Bank.
" " F. " 50 Bank shares.

The value of these bequests need not be considered, as they would not be realized, and A., B., C. and F. would duly receive their legacies.

Bequeathed to E.............................	$1,000	00
" " G...........................	3,000	00
" " H.............................	3,000	00
" " I.............................	3,000	00
Charitable Institutions	5,000	00
	$15,000	00

Bequeathed to R., S. and T. one-third each of the residue of his estate.

The value of the cash realized by the statement above is $10,000, which would be divided as follows, being proportionately divided, viz.:

To E., 1-15th............................	$ 666	66⅔
" G., 3-15ths	2,000	00
" H., 3-15ths	2,000	00
" I., 3-15ths............................	2,000	00
Charitable Institutions	3,333	33⅓
	$10,000	00

The residuary legatees would receive nothing.

Question 7.—A. bequeaths to his widow a life interest in his estate which at her death is to be divided equally between all his children. Among his assets were the following: Note of John Jones for $1,000 payable on demand, with interest at 8% unsecured; 100 $50 shares fully paid in the Greenland Colonization Co., Ltd.; 50 $100 shares in the Fleeceum L. & I. Co., Ltd., $4,000 Bank Stock worth at death 140, and $2,000 4% Government debentures, market value at death, 105.

The executors deal with the above assets in the following manner: They allow the note of John Jones to run on for 3 years, the interest in the meantime being regularly paid. Finally Jones assigns and the executors receive a dividend of 12c. on the dollar. The Greenland Colonization Co. had been paying dividends for the two years previous to the testator's death at the rate of 15% per annum and the Executors, at the request of the life tenant, retained possession of this stock. Four years after the testator's death the Company went into liquidation and the shareholders recovered nothing of their capital. Shortly after the testator's death the Fleeceum Stock was quoted on the exchange at par, but after this it gradually fell and in two years the Co. suspended payment. A call was made for the whole of the unpaid capital amounting to $2,500. The executors realized on the Bank stock at 160 and sold the debentures at 97.

Who would be entitled to the profit and who would have to bear the losses on the above transactions? Give your reasons. What entries would you make in the executors' accounts to record these various transactions?

A.—In answering this question it is assumed that the accountant called in has taken over the Executor's books, which have been written up specially to record the transactions as here given, showing the accounts as affected thereby

INVESTMENT ACCOUNT.

Dr.		Cr.	
John Jones, note payable on demand, with interest at 8%, unsecured	$1,000 00	By John Jones, 12c on dollar on note	$ 120 00
Greenland Colonization Co., Ltd., 100 850 shares paid up (estimated)	5,000 00	" Executors, for loss on this as per report	880 00
Fleeceum L. & I. Co., Ltd., 50 $100 shares, $50 per share, paid up	2,500 00	" Executors for loss on Greenland Coloniza-tion Co. Stock (esti-mated)	5,000 00
Bank Stock, $4,000, worth at death 140	5,600 00	" Executors for loss on Fleeceum Co. Stock	2,500 00
Government Debentures, marked value at death, $2,000 4%, at 105	2,100 00	" Bank Stock sold at 160	6,400 00
Profit on Bank Stock trans-ferred to Capital	800 00	" Govt. Debs. sold at 97.	1,940 00
		" loss on Debs., amount transferred to Capital	160 00
	$17,000 00		$17,000 00

CAPITAL ACCOUNT.

Dr.		Cr.	
To loss on debentures	$ 160 00	By John Jones, note	$1,000 00
" Balance	16,840 00	" Greenland Colonization Co., Ltd	5,000 00
		" Fleeceum L. & I. Co., Ltd	2,500 00
		" Bank Stock	5,600 00
		" Government Debs.	2,100 00
			16,200 00
		" Profit on Bank Stock	800 00
	$17,000 00		17,000 00
		" Balance	$16,840 00

EXECUTORS' PERSONAL ACCOUNT.

Dr.		Cr.	
To loss on J. Jones' note	$ 880 00	By Balance	$10,880 00
" " " Greenland C. Co., Ltd	5,000 00		
" " " Fleeceum Co., Stock	2,500 00		
" call paid on Fleeceum Co. Stock	2,500 00		
	10,880 00		$10,880 00
" Balance	$10,880 00		

CASH ACCOUNT.

Dr. | | *Cr.*

	Income.	Capital.		Income.	Capital.
To Cash, J. Jones " Bank Stock sold at 160 " Govt. Debentures sold at 97		$ 120 00 6,400 00 1,940 00	By Call paid on Fleeceum Co. Stock and charged to Executors " Cash on hand		$2,500 00 5,960 00
		8,460 00			$8,460 00
" Cash on hand		$5,960 00			

On the transactions named the beneficiaries, viz., the children, would be entitled to the profit made. The loss would be borne as follows:

>The Executors would bear $10,880 approximately.
>" Estate " " 160

As detailed in the repective accounts for the following reasons:

As regards the Greenland Colonization Co., it was an unsuitable investment from an executor's standpoint, and should have been sold within a reasonable time from date of the testator's death, the widow's request being no authority to retain it. The Executors would be charged with its market value at date referred to. In the accounts it has been assumed as worth par value.

As regards the Fleeceum Stock. Surely the name of the Company might have warned the Executors of the risk they ran, besides the fact that there was a further liability equal to the amount paid on the stock. The Executors have to pay all this loss, viz., $5,000.

The loss on the debentures would be borne by the Estate as it was a legitimate investment, though it appears that the Executors would have done far better not to have sold it, and certainly got a poor price. If, however, 97 was below the market value when sold, they must be further charged with a loss in realization.

The loss on Jones' note must also be borne by the Executors, as by continuing it on they virtually endorsed it as an authorized investment.

It is noted that no mention is made of expenses, funeral charges, etc., in this Estate. The Executors would of course be entitled to set off any lawful disbursements made by them in the management of the estate, in accounting for the Cash Balance on hand, and further, if they could prove that they had tried to realize the objectionable investments and failed, it would relieve their responsibility.

The Estate will now stand as follows:—

To credit of Capital Account.....		$16,840 00
Cash on hand	$ 5,960 00	
Owing by Executors	10,880 00	
		$16,840 00

subject as aforesaid to value of the Greenland Colonization Co. Stock and Disbursements belonging to the Estate.

A further liability would also require to be adjusted, viz., the liability of the Executors to make good, in addition to the Capital, the loss in income apparently sustained by the widow, or owing to the Estate, through their mismanagement.

Question 8.—A., B. & C. are in partnership under the usual form of Articles and contemplate forming a private Joint Stock Company to carry on the business. Explain how this change will affect the position of the partners (a) as between themselves, (b) as to outsiders.

Will this change necessarily improve the position of each of the partners personally as distinct from the firm?

A.—In answering this question the point arises what is meant by the term "A Private Joint Stock Company." In Canada such description of a company is not generally known, and most certainly would have no status except as a partnership, or as a Joint Stock Company duly incorporated. However, in England, the term "private Joint Stock Company" is commonly used to describe Joint Stock Companies when the Shareholders are very few in number, and such companies are often further described as "one man" companies, meaning thereby that one shareholder holds nearly all the stock and the other shareholders merely hold shares, so that the Act, which requires a certain number of shareholders to be in the company, is complied with. In England also, Joint Stock Companies are formed and the by-laws may provide that no shares can be sold to the public by one shareholder without first allowing the other shareholders to purchase them at a given price. It is also argued that a company formed without appealing to the public to subscribe for shares may be considered a private Joint Stock Company, but the law only recognizes such companies as duly incorporated under their respective Acts. With this explanation then this question may be answered as follows:—

(1) Assuming that A., B. and C. contemplate forming new Articles of Partnership based on what may be termed Joint Stock Company principles and thus allowing the partners to sell their interest, when disposed, such interest being represented as so many shares. It might be agreed that as between themselves they could withdraw from the partnership, without the other partners having the power to dissolve the partnership, as is the law under ordinary partnership agreements; but this would not remove the liability of the partner selling out, as regards existing creditors. As to outsiders, the partners' liability would in no way be altered, and they would continue jointly and severally liable for all debts. Even if such an agreement be made binding at law, it is very doubtful what advantages would arise; certainly the capital could not be withdrawn from the business, but the change in the "personel" of the firm might be very injurious to the conduct of the business, as presumably the incoming members would be entitled to a voice in the management of the business.

(2) Answering the question, probably as it is intended and assuming that the formation of a Joint Stock Company to be duly incorporated is proposed with the introduction of new shareholders, as without five shareholders this cannot be done, and possibly obtaining new capital, the points under headings (a) and (b) would be:

(a) As between the partners. They would have their powers limited in accordance with the by-laws and the number of shares held, also as to the appointments they held in the new company. A. might be appointed Manager, B. one of the Directors, and C.

remain merely a Shareholder. Then A. and B. would practically manage the business and the latter would only have a voice in General Meetings. Further, the withdrawal of one partner by selling out or assigning his interest or shares to a stranger would not affect the continuity of the business, as in a partnership.

(b) As to outsiders. The liability of A., B. and C. would be limited to the amount of the shares held by them in the new company. They would have the status of limited partners with this important exception, that they could manage and take part in the conduct of the business.

The change will necessarily improve the position of each of the partners, as their unlimited liability is removed, but whether it will improve the position of the firm itself, as the risk may be that it will not be so well managed in the future, is another matter. Certainly, if the profits in consequence fall off, it might equally be argued that the position of the partners was injured.

In cases like this the status and business of the firm must be considered. Some businesses grow too large with an increasing liability, and require too much fresh capital to be advantageously handled by partners, and in such cases when the necessary capital is found by the public the advantages of incorporation are obvious. In small companies it is a very debatable point.

Question 9.—A., B. and C. have been in partnership for 10 years dividing profits equally. At the end of the term the partnership is continued on but under a new arrangement as to division of profits, A. getting ⅜, B. ⅜, and C. ¼. After continuing thus for another year C. dies, and you are called in to wind up the business and adjust the partnership accounts. The business is sold out as a going concern to a Company formed for the purpose, realizing $10,000 more than the assets stood at in the books of the firm. This represents the value of the good-will and certain patent rights not taken credit for in the books.

How should you divide up this $10,000? Give reasons.

A.—From the question it would appear that these assets belonged to the firm, when the new arrangement for profits was made, and unless the Partnership agreement provides otherwise, the $10,000 should be equally divided between A., B. and C.'s estate.

In a partnership where no provision is made for division of profits, such profits are divided equally, and similarly where no mention is made of the respective amount of each partner's capital it is divided equally.

The latter provision as regards profits made would only affect the division of profits for the last year, and would not affect the distribution of the $10,000 unless perhaps it could be shown that their value had changed in that period, and this point would be ascertained when making the division.

Question 10.—What are the rules as to the distribution of Intestate estates both in the case of real and personal property?

A.—

INTESTATE ESTATES.

TABLE OF DISTRIBUTION IN ONTARIO,
Since July 1st, 1886.

PERSONAL ESTATE.

IF THE INTESTATE DIE LEAVING:	HIS PERSONAL REPRESENTATIVES TAKE AS FOLLOWS:
Wife and child or children ..	One-third to wife, rest to child or children; if children dead, then to their representatives (that is their lineal descendants), except such child or children (not heirs at-law) who had estate by settlement of intestate or were advanced by him in his life-time, equal to the other shares.
Wife only	Half to wife, rest to next of kin, in equal degree to intestate, or their legal representatives, or **if no next of kin**, to the Crown.
No wife or child.............	All to the next of kin **and to** their legal representatives.
Child, children, **or** their representatives.	All to him, her or them.
Children by two wives	**Equally** to all.
If no child, children or representatives	**All** to next of kin in equal degree to intestate.
Child or grandchild by deceased child	Half to child, **half to** grandchild, who takes by representation.
Husband only	Half to him **and half** as if he had predeceased intestate.
Husband and child or children	Third to husband and two-thirds to children.
Father and mother	Equally to both.
Father, mother, brother or sister.	Equally to **all.** (See R. S. O. c. 108, ss. 5, 6).
Mother and brother or sister...	Whole to them equally.
Wife, mother, brother, sister, and nephews or nieces... ..	Half to wife, residue to mother, brothers, sisters, nephews and nieces, but nephews and nieces take *per stirpes*.

Wife and father	Half to wife, half to father.
Wife, mother, nephews and nieces	Two-fourths to wife, one-fourth to mother, and one-fourth to nephews and nieces.
Wife, brother or sister and mother	Half to wife. Half to brothers, sisters and mother equally
Mother only	The whole (it being then out of the statute).
Wife and mother	Half to wife and half to mother
Brother or sister of whole blood, and brother and sister of half blood	Equally to both.
Posthumous brother or sister, and mother	Equally to both.
Posthumous brother or sister, and brother or sister born in lifetime of father	Equally to both.
Father's father and mother's mother	Equally to both.
Uncle's or aunt's children, and brother's or sister's grandchildren	Equally to all.
Grandmother, uncle or aunt	All to grandmother.
Two aunts, nephew and niece	Equally to all.
Uncle and deceased uncle's child	All to uncle.
Uncle by mother's side, and deceased uncle's or aunt's child	All to uncle.
Nephew by brother, and nephew by half-sister	Equally *per capita*.
Brothers or sisters, and nephews or nieces	Equally (but the nephews or nieces take *per stirpes*).
Nephew by deceased brother, and nephews and nieces by deceased sister	Equally *per capita*.
Brother and grandfather	All to brother.
Brother's grandson, and brother or sister's daughter	All to daughter.
Brother and two aunts	All to brother.
Brother and wife	Half to brother and half to wife.
Mother and brother	Equally.
Wife, and mother, and children of deceased brother or sister	Half to wife, one-fourth to mother, one-fourth *per stirpes* to deceased brother's or sister's children.
Wife, brother or sister, and children of deceased brother or sister	Half to wife, one-fourth to brother or sister *per capita*, one-fourth to deceased brother or sister's child *per stirpes*.
Brother or sister, and children of a deceased brother or sister	Half to brother or sister *per capita*, half to children of deceased brother or sister *per stirpes*
Grandfather and brother	All to brother.

REAL ESTATE.

Real and personal estate of all persons dying on or after the first day of July, 1886, devolves upon the legal personal representatives, whether the deceased died testate or intestate. In case of intestacy to be distributed in the same way as personal estate, subject to the following modifications:

A widow is entitled to elect whether she will take dower, or a distributive share of her deceased husband's real estate.

A husband entitled to curtesy may, by deed executed within six calendar months of his wife's death, elect to take curtesy in lieu of a distributive share.

The father, mother, brother and sisters of an intestate dying without issue are to share equally in real and personal estate, to the exclusion of grandfather and grandmother.

The real and personal estate of every man dying after the 1st day of July, 1895, intestate, and leaving a widow but no issue, shall, in all cases where the net value of such real and personal estate does not exceed $1,000, belong to his widow absolutely and exclusively. Where the net value of the real and personal estate of any person, who shall die intestate as above mentioned, shall exceed the sum of $1,000, the widow of such intestate shall, after payment of debts, be entitled to $1,000 part thereof absolutely and exclusively. The provision for the widow intended to be made as above shall be, in addition and without prejudice to her share in the residue of the real and personal estate of the intestate remaining after payment of the sum of $1,000 as aforesaid, in the same way as if such residue had been the whole of the intestate's real and personal estate.

CHAPTER VIII.

PARTNERSHIP AND EXECUTORSHIP ACCOUNTS.

Question 1.—What do you understand by " Articles of Partnership?" Give the essential features of the Articles required, should you and another agree to practice together as Chartered Accountants.

A.—" Articles of Partnership," or Partnership Agreements are synonymous terms, and simply mean the agreement made by partners at the time of forming their partnership, and which contains the terms and conditions under which the partnership will be carried on.

The essential features of such an agreement should be as follows:—

Name of firm;

Nature of business, and where carried on;

Names of the partners;

Capital contributed (if any);

The duties of the partners;

Period at which partnership commenced, and period at which to terminate;

How the profits are to be divided, or losses (if any);

Method of valuing retiring partner's share, and his position relating to good-will.

Question 2.—When a partner has assigned his share in a partnership, has the assignee any, and if so, what right to require accounts of the partnership transactions either before or after dissolution?

A.—The assignee, either before or after dissolution, has the right to require accounts of the partnership transactions.

A partner may assign his interest in a partnership without the consent of his co-partner, but he cannot by transfering his share, force a new partner on him.

If a partner does assign his share, he thereby confers upon the assignee a right to payment of what, upon taking the accounts of the partnership, may be due to the assignor. But the assignee acquires no other right than this; and he takes subject to the rights of the other partner.

Question 3.—Ogilvie of Winnipeg, White of Montreal, Grey of Liverpool, have a joint adventure in wheat. Their shares of the adventure are equal. Ogilvie buys wheat for $20,000 and pays freight, $1,800, Insurance $100, and Storage, $100. White advances $10,000 to Ogilvie. Ogilvie invoices the wheat to Grey at $22,000 and draws on him for $15,000. Grey sells the wheat in Liverpool for $25,000, and sends Ogilvie a remittance for $9,200, being the balance of the price received for the wheat less Ogilvie's and White's shares of the expenses paid by him, and commission charged by him $800. Later, however, Grey agrees to refund to the venture Commission charged by him amounting to $600.

What is the total profit, and how should the balance in Ogilvie's hands be divided among the adventurers?

Draw up the Ledger accounts of the three adventurers, but do not take either interest or discount into consideration.

A.—

	The wheat cost	$20,000 00	
	Freight	1,800 00	
	Insurance	100 00	
	Storage	100 00	
	Commission	200 00	
		22,200 00	
	Sold for	25,000 00	
	Profit	$2,800 00	to be divided equally.

Ledger accounts as follows:

OGILVIE, OF WINNIPEG.

Dr.   VENTURE WHEAT, **Self**, White & Grey.   *Cr.*

To Wheat	$20,000 00	By White	$10,000 00
" Freight	1,800 00	" Draft on Grey	15,000 00
" Insurance	100 00	" Grey	9,200 00
" Storage	100 00		
" White, ⅓ share profit and repayment loan	10,933 33		
" Grey, ⅓ share profit less $600 refunded and in his hands	333 33		
" Balance profit	933 34		
	$34,200 00		34,200 00
		" Balance profit	$933 34

WHITE, OF MONTREAL.

Dr.   VENTURE WHEAT, **Self**, Ogilvie & Grey.   *Cr.*

To Advance, Ogilvie	$10,000 00	By Ogilvie	$10,933 33
" Balance profit	933 33		
	$10,933 33		10,933 33
		" Balance profit	$933 33

GREY, OF LIVERPOOL.

Dr.   VENTURE WHEAT, **Self**, Ogilvie & White.   *Cr.*

To Draft, Ogilvie	$15,000 00	By Sale wheat	$25,000 00
" Remittance, "	9,200 00	" Refund commission	600 00
" Commission, "	800 00	" Ogilvie	333 33
" Balance profit, "	933 33		
	$25,933 33		25,933 33
		" Balance profit	$933 33

PARTNERS AND EXECUTORS' ACCOUNTS.

Question 4.—Munroe and McKay are partners in business. Munroe, who takes ¾ of the profits has $50,000 at the credit of his Capital Account, while McKay, who receives ¼ of the profits has to the credit of his Capital Account $40,000. The Assets of the Partnership consist of:—

  Factory and Machinery $75,000 00
  Stock, as per Inventories 30,000 00
  Book Debts 15,500 00

And the Liabilities are:—

  Sundry Creditors on open account $15,000 00
    " " on Bills Payable 10,000 00
  Due Imperial Bank of Canada 5,500 00

and there are current Bills Receivable discounted by the firm at the Imperial Bank of $9,800. Munroe retires from the business, McKay taking over the Liabilities as above shown and the Assets at the undernoted amounts after valuation.

  Factory and Machinery $70,000 00
  Stock as per Inventories 26,000 00
  Book Debts 14,000 00

An arrangement is made whereby McKay receives $500 from Munroe for accepting full liability for the discounted Bills.

Make up statement showing the amount that Munroe should receive.

Losses on Capital are borne by the partners in the proportion in which the profits are divided.

A.—

Dr. BALANCE SHEET OF MUNROE & McKAY. Cr.

Liabilities.			Assets.	
Sundry Creditors, on open account	$15,000 00		Factory and Machinery	$75,000 00
Sundry Creditors, on Bills Payable	10,000 00		Stock as per Inventories	30,000 00
		$25,000 00	Book Debts	15,500 00
Due Imperial Bank of Canada		5,500 00		
Munroe, Capital Acct.	50,000 00			
McKay, " "	40,000 00			
		90,000 00		
		$120,500 00		$120,500 00
Contingent Liability.				
Bills discounted		$9,800 00		

SETTLEMENT ACCOUNT.

Assets	$120,500 00	By Factory	$70,000 00
		" Stock	26,000 00
		" Book Debts	14,000 00
		" Loss on settlement	10,500 00
	$120,500 00		$120,500 00

Of this loss

    Munroe bears ⅔ = $7,000 00
    McKay   "   ⅓ = 3,500 00

Dr. MUNROE'S CAPITAL ACCOUNT. Cr.

To ⅔ loss	$ 7,000 00	By Capital	$50,000 00
" Balance	43,000 00		
	$50,000 00		$50,000 00
		By Balance	$43,000 00

Dr.	McKAY'S CAPITAL ACCOUNT.		Cr.
To ⅓ loss	$ 3,500 00	By Capital............	$ 40,000 00
" Assets taken as arranged.....	110,000 00	" Liabilities taken as arranged	30,500 00
		" Balance.....	43,000 00
	$ 113,500 00		$ 113,500 00
To Balance............	$ 43,000 00		

McKay pays Munroe $43,000 less $500, which he receives for accepting full liability for the discounted bills.

Question 5.—Grant, Pember & Co. started business as Meat Packing Exporters on 1st July, 1895, under Articles drawn between Thomas Grant and William Pember.

T. Grant's Capital consisted of the surplus of $50,000, shown on a Balance Sheet of his then business, consisting of Assets, $141,100, less Liabilities, $91,100. On 15th July, 1895, Pember pays $25,000 to the credit of his Capital Account, and the business is carried on to 30th June, 1896, when the firm's first Balance Sheet is drawn up. The books are kept on the Single Entry system. The Trial Balance of that date shows as under:—

Liabilities.		Assets.	
Sundry Creditors	$58,000 00	Factory...................	$20,000 00
Bills Payable............	27,400 00	Machinery and Plant......	32,000 00
T. Grant, Cap. Acct., less $12,000 drawings..	38,000 00	Office Furniture...........	1,000 00
		Stock.....................	35,000 00
W. Pember, Cap. Acct., less $8,000 drawings...	17,000 00	Sundry Debtors............	84,600 00
		Imperial Bank............	15,000 00
		Cash on Hand.............	200 00

Adjust the Partner's Accounts and show final Balance Sheet. Interest in favor of Grant, $2,000, and of Pember,, $1,000. Depreciate Buildings by 10%, and Machinery and Plant by 20%. Provide for Taxes, $800, Wages, $2,200; due but unpaid. The Articles of Partnership provide that the Profit and Loss shall be shared as under:—

Grant, two-thirds.   Pember, one-third.

A.—Under the Single Entry System the profit or loss is ascertained by comparing the capital at the date of balancing with the capital at the preceding date of balancing, the increase or decrease showing a profit or loss.

Provisions to be made—
Depreciation Buildings			$ 2,000 00
" Machinery			6,400 00
Provide for Taxes	$ 800 00		
" " Wages	2,200 00		
			3,000 00
Charge Interest Capital			3,000 00

The Assets then amount to—
Factory	$20,000 00	
Less	2,000 00	
		18,000 00
Machinery and Plant	32,000 00	
Less	6,400 00	
		25,600 00
Office Furniture		1,000 00
Stock		35,000 00
Sundry Debtors		84,600 00
Imperial Bank		15,000 00
Cash on hand		200 00
		179,400 00
Liabilities		85,400 00
		94,000 00
Deduct provisions to be made and interest on Capital		6,000 00
Present Capital		88,000 00
Former Capital less drawings		55,000 00
Profit		33,000 00
Grant takes ⅔		22,000 00
Pember takes ⅓		11,000 00
		$33,000 00

BALANCE SHEET (Showing Final Entries).

Liabilities.				Assets.	
Sundry Creditors	58,000 00			As per list	$179,400 00
Bills Payable	27,400 00				
		$85,400 00			
Provision for Taxes, &c.		3,000 00			
T. Grant, Capital Account	50,000 00				
Less drawings	12,000 00				
	38,000 00				
Add interest	2,000 00				
⅔ profit	22,000 00				
		62,000 00			
W. Pember, Capital Account	25,000 00				
Less drawings	8,000 00				
	17,000 00				
Add interest	1,000 00				
⅓ profit	11,000 00				
		29,000 00			
		$179,400 00			$179,400 00

Question 6.—A Trustee under a Will, being short of funds, paid a legatee to whom $1,000 was bequeathed, $50 per year as interest for two years from the death, and then paid the legacy in full. How would you debit the two payments of interest, and why?

A.—Pecuniary legacies, as a general rule, bear interest from the expiration of twelve months from the death of the testator, but are not entitled to any interest prior to then.

The question is not explicit enough, as the legatee might have been entitled to interest,

(1) By the terms of the will ordering the legacy to be paid earlier.

(2) The legatee might be entitled to such interest as a child of the testator, or that it was in satisfaction of a debt (possibly a debt of honor).

Answering the question generally, the legatee should only have been paid one year's interest. One payment should be charged to the estate and the other to the Trustee as paid wrongly.

Question 7.—The Executors of John Shewsbury find amongst other Assets of the Estate investments in several Loan and Trading Joint Stock Companies. The Capital in each is only partly called and paid up. So far, the businesses have been prosperous and dividends regularly paid.

The children of the deceased being all minors and the mother being only life-tenant with reversion of the whole of the Estate on her death to the children should they be of age at her death. How would you as an Executor deal with these investments, the deceased giving the Executors full discretionary powers?

A.—Where moneys are left by will to be invested at the discretion of the executor or trustee, the discretion so given cannot be exercised otherwise than according to law, and does not warrant an investment in personal securities or securities not sanctioned by the Courts. Spratt v. Wilson, 19 O. R. 28.

The investments should be realized and the proceeds invested in a safe and proper manner, consistent with the income obtainable, and as far as possible on the statutory rules as to the nature of such investments.

Power as to Investment by Trustees in Ontario.

Trustees or executors having trust money in their hands which it is in their duty, or which it is in their discretion, to invest at interest, shall be at liberty at their discretion, to invest the same in any stock, debenture or securities of the Government of the Dominion of Canada, or of this Province; or in securities which are a first charge on land held in fee simple, provided that such investments are in other respects reasonable and proper, and such trustees or executors shall also be at liberty, at their discretion, to call in any trust funds invested in any other securities than as aforesaid, and to invest the same in any such stock, debentures or securities aforesaid, and also from time to time, at their discretion, to vary any such investments as aforesaid, for others of the same nature; and any such moneys already invested in any such stock, debentures or securities as aforesaid, shall be held and taken to have been lawfully and properly made: R. S. O. 1897, c. 130, s. 2.

It shall also be lawful for a trustee, unless expressly forbidden by the instrument (if any) creating the trust, to invest any trust funds in his hands in terminable debentures or debenture stock of certain societies and companies mentioned in the said Act, provided that such investment is in other respects reasonable and proper, and that the debentures are registered and are transferable only on the books of the society or company in his name as the trustee for the particular trust estate for which they are held in such debentures or debenture stock as aforesaid: R. S. O. 1897, c. 130, s.5.

Question 8.—A Trust Estate is to be divided at 30th June, 1897. The funds remaining for division amount to $107,500. The Beneficiaries' shares of the whole Estate are:—

A., 2-5; B., 2-5; C., 1-10; D., 1-10. The following payments have been made on account:—

A. $20,000 on 31st December, 1896.

B. $15,000 on 30th September, 1896.

C. Nil.

D. $8,000 on 30th June, 1896.

Calculate interest at 4% and draft in proper form the division of the remaining funds as on 30th June, 1897.

A.—	A. has had advanced $20,000 00		
	Interest thereon, 6 mos. at 4 %........ 400 00		
		$20,400 00	
	B. has had advanced 15,000 00		
	Interest, 9 mos. at 4 % 450 00		
		15,450 00	
	D. has had advanced 8,000 00		
	Interest, 12 mos. at 4 % 320 00		
		8,320 00	
	Funds remaining for division	107,500 00	
	Value of Trust Estate...........	$151,670 00	
	A. receives 2-5ths of estate $60,668 00		
	Less advanced 20,400 00		
		$40,268 00	
	B. receives 2-5ths of estate 60,668 00		
	Less advanced 15,450 00		
		45,218 00	
	C. receives 1-10th of estate	15,167 00	
	D. receives 1-10th of estate 15,167 00		
	Less advanced 8,320 00		
		6,817 00	
	Amount to be divided	$107,500 00	

Question 9.—In the partnership of White & Moore, Grocers, White having died, it is found by his Executors that the firm of which he had been a partner for twenty years had not made up any Balance Sheet or ascertained the profits made. The deceased had drawn from the firm at the rate of $1,500 per annum, while his partner had drawn at the rate of $2,000 per annum The Trustees having brought an action at law for the purpose of ascertaining the rights of the parties re the Partnership Assets a reference is made by the Judge to you as an expert Accountant to enquire into and report as to the state of the partnership accounts. State the procedure you would adopt in making the investigation, and give an outline of your report.

A.—A statement should be prepared showing the value of the assets and liabilities, as on the day of White's death. This would give the value of the present capital.

Ascertain then the amount of capital originally invested by the partners. We are informed that the amounts withdrawn by them amounted to $30,000 and $40,000 respectively. Add this $70,000 to the present capital and compare with the original capital to ascertain the gross profit for the period.

We are not informed if there are Articles of Partnership, if so, this may settle the division of profits as, unless the contrary be stated, they would be divided equally.

If there are no Articles of Partnership, and it was originally a verbal agreement, the question of the division of profits would have to be settled, and the Accountant would ask for instructions, probably suggesting that their steady and consistent withdrawals would seem to point out, in absence of other evidence, the proportions in which the profit is to be divided, viz., White 3-7 and Moore 4-7.

Assuming that there are Articles, no mention being made of rate of division, then these profits would be divided equally between them, and as this would probably cause a considerable sum to be due the deceased, it may explain the action at law.

This being done, the partners' accounts would be drawn up as follows:—

Credit each partner's account with the original capital invested, debit him with his withdrawals and credit him with his share of the profits. The resulting balance will give his share of the present capital. No mention has been made of interest on partners' capital, and unless mentioned in the Articles this would not be taken into consideration.

The report would explain how the profits had been arrived at on the basis of the single entry system; the division of such profits in the proportion to be decided, and the deductions for withdrawals made in the respective accounts.

Question 10.—William Child died on 30th September, 1880, leaving a Will wherein he conveyed his whole Estate to Trustees for the purposes therein set forth.

His four daughters, Maud, Polly, Susie, and Martha survived him and he directed his Executors to divide his Estate equally among them on the youngest attaining her majority.

Until that time the net revenue from the Estate was to be equally divided among the surviving daughters.

Power was given to the Trustees to advance a sum out of the Capital to each of the daughters on their marriage, which sums were to be taken into account upon the division of the Estate. No mention of interest was made.

Maud was married on 30th June, 1882,

Polly was married on 30th June, 1883,

Susie was married on 30th June, 1884,

and each received on the day of her marriage the sum of $10,000 in respect of the power given to the Trustees.

The Executors made a further payment of $2,000 on account of Capital to each of the married daughters on 30th June, 1885, and on each 30th June thereafter until and including 30th June, 1890.

Martha became of age on 31st December, 1890, on which date the Capital in the hands of the Trustees was $80,000. All the income from the Trust funds had been equally divided among the four daughters to 31st December, 1890. No Interest had been charged by the Trustees upon any of the advances to the Beneficiaries.

Prepare the accounts of division at 31st December, 1890, and charge interest where you consider that should be done at the rate of 5%, the net earning power of the Estate.

PARTNERS AND EXECUTORS' ACCOUNTS.

A.— Maud received $10,000 00
      Polly   " 10,000 00
      Susie   " 10,000 00
      The married daughters received since their marriage 6 payments each of $2,000 .... 36,000 00
      They should be charged interest thereon, which would amount to, at 5 % 5,400 00
      Capital in hands of Trustees, 31st Dec., 1890.... 80,000 00

      Total Value of Estate $151,400 00

Maud's share ¼		$37,850 00	
Deduct on marriage................	$10,000 00		
" advances	12,000 00		
" interest......................	1,800 00		
		23,800 00	
			14,050 00
Polly received same amount..			14,050 00
Susie " " "			14,050 00
Martha "			37,850 00
			$80,000 00

CHAPTER IX.

JOINT STOCK COMPANIES.

Question 1.—(a) What are the qualifications for the office of Director of a Company incorporated under the provisions of the "Companies Act"?

(b) How far may these provisions be varied by a By-law of the Company, or otherwise?

A.—(a) The persons named as such in the letters patent are the First Directors of the Company, until replaced by others duly appointed in their stead.

No person shall be elected or appointed as a director thereafter, unless he is a shareholder, owning stock absolutely in his own right, and to the amount required by the By-laws of the Company, and not in arrears in respect of any call thereon; and at all times the majority of the directors of the Company shall be persons resident in Canada.

Further, the person appointed must consent to act. A Shareholder who has agreed to act as a Director and does not possess the proper number of shares, must have the same allotted to him before his election to render the same valid.

(b) The Directors may pass a by-law altering the Stock qualification, the number of Directors, etc., as long as the number of the latter is kept between three and fifteen.

Such by-law would only have force (unless confirmed at a general meeting of the Company, duly called for that purpose) until the next annual meeting of the Company, and in default of confirmation thereat, would cease to have force.

Question 2.—What restrictions or conditions require to be observed in seeking incorporation under the "Companies Act" or the Ontario "Joint Stock Companies Letters Patent Act" respectively as to

(a) Capital Authorized.

(b) Capital Subscribed.

(c) Capital paid in.

A.—(a) *Capital authorized, under the "Dominion Companies Act."*

(1) There is no provision made for the issue of Preference Stock.

(2) One-half of the proposed Capital Stock must be subscribed for by not less than five shareholders, and 10% in cash paid in thereon. If a Loan Company this amount of cash must not be less than $100,000. The cash also must be deposited in some chartered bank in Canada to the credit of the Receiver-General of Canada, and shall be standing at such credit, and the applicants shall, with their petition, produce the deposit receipt for such amount. If the object of the company is one requiring that it should own real estate, any portion not more than half of the cash referred to, may be taken as paid in, if bona fide invested in real estate suitable to such object, and such real estate is by a valid and sufficient registered deed, duly held by trustees (at least two in number) for the Company, and being of the required value over and above all incumbrances thereon. Charter will not be granted for the construction and working of railways, or to banking or insurance companies. Under each Act the application would show:

The amount of capital stock of the company.

The number of shares and the amount of such shares.

Under the Joint Stock Companies Letters Patent Act.

(1) Preference Stock can be issued.

(2) There are no special stipulations as to capital, except that the application must be signed by five persons at least, who are shareholders.

Memo.—If no business is started within three years under the Dominion Companies Act, or within two years under the Ontario Companies Act, the charter will be forfeited by nonuser.

(b) *Capital Subscribed.*

As shown above, under the Dominion Companies Act, half of the capital stock must be subscribed for, whereas under the Ontario Act there is no amount fixed beyond limiting the number of applicants to five, who might only hold one share each, but all the petitioners must have subscribed for share or shares. In case any amount has been paid in or shares taken, by transfer of property to a trustee, the Provincial Secretary may require such evidence as is necessary as to its value, and kind or nature of property, etc.

(c) *Capital paid in.*

The "Companies Act" provides, as shown above, for a certain amount to be paid in when incorporated, viz., ten per cent. of the Stock subscribed, and leaves further calls at the discretion of the Directors.

The Ontario Act,

Provides that not less than ten per centum upon the allotted shares of Stock of the Company shall by means of one or more calls formally made be called in and made payable within one year from the incorporation of the Company; the residue when and as the by-laws of the Company direct.

Apart from the above differences in the Acts themselves, applicants for incorporation must comply with regulations as follows:

UNDER THE DOMINION COMPANIES ACT.

The applicant for letters patent shall give at least one month's previous notice, in the Canada Gazette, of their intention to apply for the same, stating therein,—

(a) The proposed corporate name of the company, which shall not be that of any other known company, incorporated or unincorporated, or any name liable to be confounded therewith, or otherwise, on public grounds, objectionable;

(b) The purposes for which its incorporation is sought;

(c) The place within Canada which is to be its chief place of business;

(d) The proposed amount of its capital stock—which, in the case of a loan company, shall not be less than one hundred thousand dollars;

(e) The number of shares and the amount of each share;

(f) The names in full and the address and calling of each of the applicants, with special mention of not more than fifteen and not less than three of their number, who are to be the first or provisional directors of the company, and the majority of whom shall be residents of Canada.

At any time, not more than one month after the last publication of such notice, the applicants may petition the Governor-in-Council, through the Secretary of State, for the issue of such letters patent.

Such petition shall state the facts set forth in the notice, the amount of stock taken by each applicant, the amount paid in upon the stock of such applicant, and the manner in which the same has been paid in, and is held for the company.

UNDER THE ONTARIO COMPANIES ACT.

The applicants for incorporation, who must be of the full age of twenty-one years may petition the Lieutenant-Governor, through the Provincial Secretary, for the issue of letters patent. The petition of the applicants shall show:

(a) The proposed corporate name of the company with the word "Limited" as the last word thereof; and such name shall not on any public ground be objectionable, and shall not be that of any known company, incorporated or unincorporated, or of any partnership, or individual, or any name under which any known business is being carried on, or so nearly resembling the same as to deceive; provided, however, that a subsisting company, or partnership, or individual, or the person carrying on such business may consent that such name, in whole or in part, be granted to the new company.

(b) The objects, simply stated, for which the company is to be incorporated.

(c) The place within the Province of Ontario where the head office of the company is to be situated, and where its principal books of account and its corporation records are to be kept and to which all communications and notices may be addressed.

(d) The amount of capital stock of the company.

(e) The number of shares and the amount of each share.

(f) The name in full, the place of residence and the calling of each of the applicants.

(g) The number, and the names of the applicants, not less than three, who are to be the provisional directors of the company.

The following information, though not strictly answering the question, will show the procedure in other provinces:

R. S. MANITOBA, CH. 25.

4. The Lieutenant-Governor in Council may, by letters patent under the Great Seal of the Province, grant a charter to any number of persons, not less than five, who shall petition therefor, constituting such persons and others who may become shareholders in the Company thereby created a body corporate and politic, for any purposes or objects to which the legislative authority of the Legislature of Manitoba extends, except the construction and working of railways and the business of insurance.

5. The applicants for such letters patent must give at least one month's notice, to be inserted once in the Manitoba Gazette, of their intention to apply for the same, stating therein:—

(a) The proposed corporate name of the Company, which shall not be that of any other known company, incorporated or unincorporated, or any name liable to be unfairly confounded therewith, or otherwise on public grounds objectionable;

(b) The object for which the incorporation is sought;

(c) The place or places within the Province of Manitoba, where the operations are to be carried on, with special mention, if there be two or more such places, of some one of them as its chief place of business;

(d) The amount of its capital stock;

(e) The number of shares and the amount of each share;

(f) The names in full and the address and calling of each of the applicants, with special mention of the names of not less than three, nor more than nine of their number, who are to be the first directors of the Company.

6. At any time, not more than one month after the publication of such notice, the applicants may petition the Lieutentnt-Governor, through the Provincial Secretary, for the issue of such Letters Patent.

7. (a) Such Petition must state the facts required to be set forth in the notice, and must further state the amount of stock taken by each of such applicants, and also the amount, if any, paid in upon the stock of each applicant;

(b) The Petition shall also state whether the amount is paid in cash or transfer of property, or how otherwise;

(c) The Petition may ask for the embodying in the Letters Patent of any provision which otherwise under the provisions hereof might be embodied in any by-law of the Company when incorporated.

(8) In case the Petition is not signed by all the shareholders whose names are proposed to be inserted in the Letters Patent, it shall be accompanied by a Memorandum of Association, signed by all the parties whose names are to be so inserted, or by their attorneys duly authorized in writing; and such memorandum shall contain the particulars required by the next preceding section (sec. 7).

QUEBEC REVISED STATUTES, 1888.

"THE JOINT STOCK COMPANIES' INCORPORATION ACT."

4696. The Lieutenant-Governor may by letters patent under the Great Seal, grant a charter to any number of persons, not less than five, who petition therefor.

2. Such charter constitutes the petitioners and all others who may become shareholders in the company thereby created a body politic and corporate for any of the purposes within the jurisdiction of this Legislature, except for the construction and working of railways and the business of insurance.

3. It is not necessary that an order in council be passed for granting any such charter, but the Lieutenant-Governor may grant any charter upon a favorable report from the Attorney-General.

4697. The applicants for such letters patent shall previously give notice of their intention to make such application.

Such notice shall be published during four consecutive weeks in the Quebec Official Gazette and contain:—

1. The corporate name of the proposed company, which shall not be that of any other company, or any name liable to be confounded therewith or otherwise on public grounds objectionable;

2. The object for which the incorporation is sought;

3. The place, within the limits of the Province, selected as its chief place of business;

4. The proposed amount of its capital stock;

5. The number of shares and the amount of each share;

6. The name in full and the address and calling of each of the applicants, with special mention of the names of not less than three or more than nine of their number who are to be the first directors of the company. The major part of such directors shall be resident in Canada and be subjects of Her Majesty;

7. In the case of the incorporation of a railway company, the notices shall also be inserted during four weeks in English and

French in two newspapers published in the district through which the proposed line is intended to pass.

The notices shall be published in the English and French newspapers in each district, if there be any published in these two languages, if not, then in newspapers in the same language published in the neighboring districts.

Such notices shall make known the starting point of the proposed road, the districts through which it is intended to run and the terminus.

4698. At any time not more than one month after the last publication of such notice, the applicants may petition the Lieutenant-Governor through the Provincial Secretary for the issue of such letters patent.

2. Such petition must recite the facts set forth in the notice, and must further state the amount of stock taken by each applicant, and by all other persons named therein, and also the amount paid in upon the stock of each applicant, and the manner in which the same has been paid in, and is held for the company.

3. The aggregate of the stock so taken must be at least one-half of the total amount of the stock of the company.

4. The aggregate so paid in thereon must be at least ten per cent. thereof, or five per cent. of the total capital; unless such total exceed five hundred thousand dollars, in which case the aggregate paid in upon such excess must be at least two per cent. thereof.

5. Such aggregate must have been paid in to the credit of the company, or of trustees therefor, and must be standing at such credit, in some chartered bank within the Province, unless the object of the company is one requiring that it should own real estate, in which case, not more than one-half thereof may be taken as invested in real estate suitable to such object, duly held by trustees therefor, and being fully of the required value over and above all incumbrances thereon.

6. The petition may ask the embodying in the letters patent of any provision which otherwise under this section might be embodied in any by-law of the company when incorporated.

Question 3.—State clearly what a Company may and may not do in the matter of dealing in, or acquiring its own shares. What authorities govern?

A.—A Company may not purchase its own shares.

It cannot deal or trade in its stock, certainly as far as acquiring its own stock is concerned. Under certain circumstances, however, a Company might sell its shares by a legitimate trading transaction, which was for its benefit. The proper method then would appear to be to charge the person for the shares issued, and then credit to his account the cash paid for the work done or the property acquired as a legitimate trading transaction. The cheques in payment might actually pass through the books.

Companies, however, have the power to forfeit shares for non-payment of calls, and they become the Company's property, and can be disposed of by the Company, but this does not effect the holders' liability in any way, unless of course, they are resold at a sufficient figure to cover the unpaid calls.

The authorities which govern are the Act or Acts under which the Company or Companies are incorporated, and which are laid down in the Acts themselves or provided for by special by-law.

Question 4.—What are the successive steps necessary to render a By-law for the creation of Preference Stock legal and operative?

A.—The Directors first make a by-law to issue such stock. A general meeting of the Company must then be duly called for considering and passing the same. The by-law shall not have any force until after it has been unanimously sanctioned by a vote of the shareholders present in person or by proxy at a general meeting of the Company duly called for considering the same, or unanimously sanctioned in writing by the shareholders of the Company; provided, however, that if the by-law be sanctioned by three-fourths in value of the shareholders of the Company, the Company may petition the Lieutenant-Governor in Council for an order approving the by-law.

Question 5.—What, if any, are the limitations upon the powers of Directors relating to the payment of calls on shares by transfer of property or goodwill?

A.—The Directors are bound to see that all calls are paid for in cash, subject to any provisions made by special by-law, or incorporated in the Letters Patent, providing for shares issued fully paid up.

Subject to this, and after the Company has started business, it might arise that the Directors desired to acquire property or goodwill necessary for the profitable working of the business, and that the persons from whom such property was to be acquired were incidentally shareholders, and further, that a call on shares had been made. Under such circumstances the set off would be justifiable, but probably the wiser course would be for the Directors to pay the cash, as it is assumed they would have done if the vendor had not been a shareholder; and for the shareholder to pay his calls when due.

The intention of the Acts is to compel payment in cash, and to prevent the Directors allowing payments of calls in other ways than cash (possibly property not required by the Company), and thus prejudice the rights and the securities of the Company's creditors.

Question 6.—What is the procedure necessary to enable a creditor of a Company to compel payment of uncalled or unpaid capital for his benefit?

A.—The creditor must first obtain judgment against the Company the execution thereon must have been issued and returned unsatisfied in whole or in part, this all being done in due form. He may then proceed, having failed to collect his debt from the Company, against the shareholder whose shares have not been fully paid for. All enforced payments thus made by the shareholders will be considered as on account of what is due on their shares.

Should the Company be wound up, the proceedings of the creditor against the shareholder may be stayed, and such creditor would then receive his dividends, in common with the other creditors, in due course.

Question 7.—(a) What obligations are assumed by persons acquiring partially **paid shares either by** transfer or **by sale** under execution?

(b) What obligations remain upon **persons parting** with shares in these ways?

A.—If the transfer has been duly approved by the Directors and entered in the books of the Company, then the Transferor is released and the Transferee becomes responsible for all the future calls. But if the Directors are not satisfied as to the Transferee's position and means, or, in other words, refuse to allow the transfer to be entered in their books, then the transfer would only be valid as exhibiting the rights of the parties thereto, and as rendering the **Transferee liable "ad interim"** jointly and severally with the Transferor to the Company and its creditors until entry thereof has been made in the books of the Company.

In the case of transfer of shares made by sale under execution, or under the order or judgment of some competent court, it would be valid, and the Transferee or purchaser of such Stock would assume all the liabilities thereon, and the original holder would be released, and such transfer need not be approved by the Directors.

Question 8.—(a) What takes place if the number of Shareholders in a Company falls below the number required to secure incorporation?

(b) What takes place if there are not sufficient shareholders in a Company eligible for re-election as Directors?

A.—(a) That every person who is a shareholder in the Company during the time it **carries on business, with** less than **five** shareholders, after a period of **six months** after the number has been so reduced, and is cognizant of the fact that it is so carrying on business with less than five **shareholders, shall be** severally liable for the payment of the whole of the debts of the Company contracted during such time, and may be sued for the same without the joinder in the action or suit of the Company or of any other shareholder; but any shareholder who has become aware that the Company is carrying on business when the number of its shareholders is less than five, may serve a protest in writing on the Company, and may, by registered letter, notify the Provincial Secretary of such protest having been served, and of the facts upon which it is based, and such shareholder may thereby, and not otherwise from the date of his said protest and notification, exonerate himself from liability; and if after notice from the Provincial Secretary the Company refuses or neglects to bring the number of its shareholders up to five, such refusal or neglect may, upon the report of the Provincial Secretary, be regarded by the Lieutenant-Governor in Council as sufficient cause for the revocation of the Company's charter.

(b) The Directors continue in office until their successors are appointed, the time of which and the qualifications are set forth in the By-laws. Under the circumstances detailed in the question the Directors should amend their By-laws to meet the case, either by reducing the number of Directors or by reducing the share qualifications necessary to render a shareholder eligible. The general meeting of shareholders could then confirm this By-law and proceed to elect the new Board of Directors.

Question 9.—What liability or penalty is incurred by an Accountant for false or insufficient information supplied by him for purposes of a Prospectus, and so used?

A.—" He shall be liable to pay to all persons so subscribing or applying on the faith of such prospectus, compensation for the loss or damage they may have sustained by reason of any untrue statement in the prospectus," unless it could be shown that the Accountant had acted in good faith and believed his statements to be true, and could show reasonable grounds for this defence.

See Revised Statutes of Ontario, 1897, cap. 216, "An Act respecting the Liability of Directors."

Question 10.—A Company desires to acquire the name and business of another Company without becoming liable for the debts owing by the latter. How would you advise that this be done?

A.—First, the assent of both Companies to this would be required as obtained in their respective general meetings properly convened.

The latter Company would then pass a by-law to go into voluntary liquidation under the Ontario Winding-up Act (Chap. xvii., Q. 1), and when all their creditors had been paid, application would be made to the Court to stay proceedings and allow the Company to resume business, with the object of amalgamating with the former Company. If, however, the latter Company found that, after all, they would not settle with their creditors, they would complete the winding-up. Then in due course the former Company could apply as provided for in the Ontario Companies Act for power to change its name, and would naturally adopt the name of the latter Company, no one's property, but it is presumed that its business would then be worth little.

The shareholders in the latter Company would receive a certain number of shares in the new Company thus formed as would be arranged.

The question seems to infer that the debts of the latter Company were heavy, if not, the Companies might arrange to pay off the debts by the issue of new stock.

The procedure for amalgamation of companies is given in the R. S. O. 1897, cap. 191, section 103.

The Directors of each Company may enter into a joint agreement under the seal of each Company for such amalgamation, prescribing all the terms, etc., the name of the new Company, number of Directors, in fact, giving its new By-laws.

This agreement must then be submitted to the shareholders of each Company at General Meeting separately called in accordance with their By-laws. If it is carried by a two-thirds majority of all the shareholders of each of such Companies at their respective meetings, this will then be certified under the Companies' seals, and due application can be made through the Provincial Secretary for the necessary power to carry same into effect. With the joint petition, an original of the agreement must be submitted, the new Company to be liable for either of the former Company's liabilities of every sort.

This may be taken as a brief outline of the proceeding and the student should refer to the Act for further details.

CHAPTER X.

JOINT STOCK COMPANIES.

Question 1.—" A." lends to a Loan Corporation $10,000 on Debentures. It turns out that the Company had previously borrowed up to the limit of the powers conferred by Statute. In what position is the Debenture as to the Assets of the Company, and how does the lender stand in relation to the individual members of the Company?

A.—Debentures are generally secured by hypothecating or pledging any or all of the real or personal property of the Company to secure the sums borrowed on them.

In the case in question it would appear that the Directors had acted " ultra vires " in allowing this issue of Debentures and would consequently be held personally liable in the case of any loss to " A " ; the only exception would be that of any Director who could show that he was not a party to the transaction and knew nothing about it at the time the issue was made, and refused to adopt or ratify the same.

It is certain that A. would have recourse against the Directors, and further, that on learning the true facts of the case he could demand from the Company and enforce that his $10,000 be repaid immediately, provided it was bona fide applied in discharging debts of the Company which could have been enforced against it, or bona fide applied for any other legitimate purpose for which it might have come under liability, as he had lent the same in good faith believing (as is assumed) that the debentures were secured by mortgage on the assets of the Company.

There is no liability on the part of the individual members of the Company if their shares are fully paid up.

Question 2.—A Joint Stock Company is about to be formed for the purpose of making advances on goods and chattels and the promoters are applying to the Ontario Provincial Secretary for a Charter. Under which Act will this be granted, if at all? Explain the reasons in your answer.

A.—A Charter would be granted under "The Ontario Companies Act," subject to a satisfactory application being made.

Under the Dominion Act it could not be applied for as it is therein provided that Loan Companies shall only lend on the security of real estate, or of the public securities of Canada, or of any of the Privinces thereof, or Debentures as specified.

It might perhaps be here noted that Loan Companies cannot obtain a Charter under the Ontario Companies Act, and this Company would have to point out that it was not a Loan Company in the meaning of the Act.

Question 3.—What are the conditions that require to be fulfilled before the Charter of a Company can be surrendered?

A.—The Charter of a Company incorporated by letters patent may be surrendered if the Company proves to the satisfaction of the Lieutenant-Governor in Council:

(a) That it has no debts existing or other rights in question, or,

(b) That it has parted with its property, divided its assets rateably amongst its shareholders, and has no debts, or liabilities, or,

(c) That the debts and obligations of the Company have been duly provided for or protected, or that the creditors of the Company or other persons holding them consent; and that the Company has given notice of the application for acceptance of surrender as required by the Act.

Question 4.—Draw up a short prospectus for a Company to be formed to acquire the business of a grocer. Give forms for allotting shares, also forms for Instalment Script and Stock Certificate.

A.—

Prospectus of the Middleton Grocery Company, of Toronto, Limited.

Capital $200,000 in 2,000 shares of $10 each.

PROVISIONAL DIRECTORS.

Here follow the names of the men chosen.

Then would follow the various officers, etc., etc.

    Secretary.
    Bankers.
    Lawyers.
    Auditor.

The Middleton Grocery Company, Limited, is being formed with the object of amalgamating three businesses in the City of Toronto, which have already good connections, and whose accounts and trade have been carefully examined and reported upon by the well-known Accountant, Mr. ―――――. He has based his report, which is appended hereto, by taking an average of their trade and profits for the last five years.

Owing to the steady growth of Toronto, and with the facilities afforded for the successful establishment of this Company, with a clientele already at hand, there is little doubt but that a profit of at least 15 per cent. can be safely relied on.

The Company proposes to retain the three businesses to be purchased, details of which are given in the Accountant's report, establishing the store on Yonge Street as the Head Office, remodelling and replenishing the buildings as may be deemed advisable.

As ample capital will be furnished to conduct the new Grocery Company, several prominent men having already undertaken to subscribe, early application for shares is required. It might here be mentioned that Messrs. Brown, Jones and Robinson, the respective proprietors of the businesses, having such faith in the success of the undertaking, have agreed to accept payment for their premises and goodwill in shares, the book debts, store fixtures, stock, etc., to be taken at a valuation, the Company assuming no liability.

The premises, which are under lease, and the goodwill have been valued by competent experts at $18,000.

It is proposed to apply for a Charter under the Provincial Act, and when it is obtained, to make calls as follows,—20 per cent. on that date, and 20 per cent. three months after, and a further 10 per cent. six months after date of Charter. The balance of calls, if any are required, to be at the discretion of the Directors, but no calls to exceed 10 per cent., or at less intervals than three months.

Application for shares may be addressed to the Secretary, Mr. ————, at his address, ————.

Here follows the Accountant's report,—

To the Provisional Directors of the Middleton Grocery Company, of Toronto, Limited:

Gentlemen,—

Please allot me one hundred shares in this Company, for which I enclose you marked cheque for $200.

                        Yours truly,

                        ....

FORM OF ALLOTTING SHARES.

THE MIDDLETON GROCERY COMPANY, OF TORONTO, LIMITED,
YONGE STREET, TORONTO.

                                      1st December, 1898.

Sir,—

The Provisional Directors of this Company have this day allotted to you One Hundred Shares of their stock, in accordance with your application, with 20 % paid up thereon.

                    Yours truly,

                      ... .

                                           Secretary.

To............................
                Toronto.

FORM OF INSTALMENT SCRIP.

SCRIP.

Number................
Shares................
$................ of $10 each.

The Middleton Grocery Co., of Toronto, Limited.

Received from Mr.................................... the sum of .... being first call of twenty per cent. on .... shares of the Capital Stock of the Middleton Grocery Company, of Toronto, Limited, which said shares have been allotted and reserved in accordance with the Act under which the Company is incorporated.

In witness whereof we have hereunto subscribed our names at the City of Toronto, this.................... day of .... 189........

.... Secretary. [Seal.] .... President.

STUB.

THE MIDDLETON GROCERY CO., OF TORONTO, Limited.

Instalment Scrip.

No. ....

Date ....

Name ....

1st Instalment, 20 per cent.

$.................... .... President.

.... Secretary.

FORM OF STOCK CERTIFICATE.

STUB.

No.

Shares

Dated to

Issued

Received this Certificate.

CERTIFICATE.

Number............................Shares............................

Capital, $200,000 of 2,000 shares of $10 each.

This certifies that............................is entitled to............................shares of the Capital Stock of the **Middleton Grocery Company, of Toronto, Limited**, on which the full amount of............................Dollars per share is hereby acknowledged to have been paid. The said shares being transferable on the books of the Company only by............................ or............................Attorney duly constituted.

Dated at............................189......

............................Secretary. [Seal.] ....President.

Question 5.—(a) What are the rules as to voting at (1) Shareholders' meetings, stating who may vote. (2) Directors' meetings?

(b) Supposing Directors have been elected improperly, how does it affect transactions completed by them?

A.—(1) *Shareholders' Meetings.*

Every shareholder who is not in arrears in respect of any calls is entitled to as many votes as he holds shares in the Company, and may vote either personally or by proxy.

Every executor, administrator, guardian or trustee shall represent the stock in his hands, at all meetings of the Company, and may vote accordingly as a shareholder; and every person who pledges his stock may nevertheless represent the same at all such meetings, and may vote accordingly as a shareholder.

If stock be held jointly by two or more persons, any one of them present at a meeting, may, in the absence of the other or others, vote thereon, but if more than one joint stock holder be present or be represented by proxy, they shall vote together on the stock jointly held.

Unless a poll is demanded, a declaration by the chairman that a resolution has been carried, and an entry to that effect in the proceedings of the Company shall be prima facie evidence of the fact without proof as to the number or proportion of votes recorded in favor of or against such resolution.

If a poll is demanded, it shall be taken in such manner as the by-laws prescribe, and in default thereof, then as the chairman may direct.

In the case of an equality of votes at any general meeting, the chairman shall be entitled to a second or casting vote.

(2) *Directors' Meetings.*

The rules governing such meetings are:

That the Directors have one vote each and can only vote in person.

That the quorum as fixed by by-law must be present.

The chairman usually has a casting vote in case of a tie, which is also regulated by by-law.

As to third parties at least, it does not affect the validity of any transaction completed by them while acting as Directors in good faith, but it would clearly be the duty of such Directors as had been improprly elected to at once retire, and the vacancies thus created could then be filled in accordance with the by-laws.

Question 6.—State briefly the difference between "The Ontario Companies' Act" and "The Companies' Act" as affecting the formation of a new Company. What are some of the special circumstances which would lead you to advise seeking incorporation under either Act respectively?

A.—The conditions to be fulfilled in applying for Letters Patent under "The Companies' Act" are more restrictive than under "The Ontario Companies' Act." In the former the application must be advertised in the Canada Gazette, and the stock taken or subscribed for must be at least one-half of the proposed Capital Stock of the Company; and ten per cent. of such stock so taken must be paid in cash and deposited to the credit of the Receiver-General of Canada and shall be standing at such credit in some chartered Bank in Canada, and the applicants shall, with their petition, produce the deposit receipt, unless the Company is required to hold real estate, then half the cash may be thus represented, subject to conditions as to value, etc., as laid down in the Act. On the other hand, the Ontario Companies Act lays down no such conditions, excepting requiring where paid-up shares are given for property, that satisfactory evidence of such be shown when making the application, but it does not restrict the number of shares which can be thus acquired. It also requires ten per cent. of the subscribed Capital to be paid up within the first year.

The special circumstances which would influence the choice of Act would be, whether the undertaking or business was of a purely local character or not.

Even a Company intending to do business in other provinces, having its headquarters in Ontario, might wisely elect to obtain the local Charter, but where an extended business was in contemplation, with branches to be opened in the other provinces, it would be best probably to obtain the Dominion Charter. The Company would have a better position in dealing with many cases that might affect its branches, etc.

There is another point also which would have to be considered in applying for Charter. The Company might not have the cash qualification required under the Dominion Legislation. Many Companies being formed to acquire businesses with practically little cash required, the vendors accepting shares in payment, such Companies would probably elect to be incorporated under Provincial Legislation.

Question 7.—Give definitions of the following:—

Common Stock;

Deferred Stock,

Watered Stock,

Over-issued Stock,

Preferred Stock,

Treasury Stock.

A.—*Common Stock,*

Means the shares or stock of a Joint Stock Company, which shares rank equally as to dividend; but the holders of which are not entitled to any preference or privilege as a class over any other shareholders.

Deferred Stock,

Means stock where the payment is deferred until another class of stock has received its dividend, or such dividend may be deferred until a fixed date, or until some transaction has been completed, etc.

Watered Stock,

Is stock which is shown in the books as fully paid up, but for which its equivalent in cash or value has not been actually received and must therefore be representative of some fictitious asset.

Over-issued Stock,

Is stock illegally issued above the amount authorized by the charter of the Company. Such stock is void.

Preferred Stock,

Is stock that is entitled to dividends as arranged out of the profit before common stock holders receive any dividend.

Treasury Stock,

Represents stock that is authorized to be issued and has been set aside for sale by the Company, the proceeds to be used in carrying on its business.

Question 8.—A., B., C., D., are Directors in a Joint Stock Company. It is found that the Company is unable to meet its liabilities. All the Stock is paid up, and the only Assets are Patents and Office Furniture. The Patents have been assigned to the Bank, and the Landlord has seized the Office Furniture for Rent. The list of Creditors is as follows:—

John Smith, Rent	$ 500 00
A. Brown & Co., Advertising	310 00
John Williams, Books and Stationery	75 00
Union Bank, Advanced	2,000 00
John James, Salary as Bookkeeper	135 00
John Brown, Wages	75 00
J. Robinson, Wages	40 00
A. Smith, Legal Services	100 00
	$3,265 00

The Stock being all paid up, what liability, if any, is upon the Directors or Shareholders in respect of these claims, or any of them?

A.—There is no liability upon the Shareholders, as the Stock is paid up.

If there is no surplus after the rent and the Bank have been paid, the Directors would be liable for the wages and salary due.

The clause in the Act referring to this point is as follows:—

"The Directors of the Company shall be jointly and severally liable to the laborers, servants and apprentices thereof for all debts not exceeding one year's wages due for services performed for the Company while they are such Directors respectively; but no Director shall be liable to an action therefor, unless the Company has been sued therefor within one year after the debt became due, nor yet unless such Director is sued therefor within one year from the time he ceased to be such Director, nor yet before an execution against the Company has been returned unsatisfied in whole or in part; and the amount due on such execution shall be the amount recoverable with costs against the Dirctors." R. S. O. 1897, c. 191, s. 85.

Question 9.—What are the powers of Companies:

(a) to issue shares at a discount.

(b) to issue shares and accept payment other than in cash.

(c) to hold real estate.

(d) to restrict transfers of shares.

A.—(a) Companies have power to issue shares at a discount under the "Dominion Companies' Act," but it is conceived that the liability on these shares, as between the holders thereof and the creditors of the Company, would still remain on any portion not actually paid for in cash or its equivalent, even though the shares appeared in the books of the Company as fully paid up.

A Mining Company can issue shares at a discount, without further liability, under the Ontario Mining Act.

Companies under the Ontario Companies' Act cannot issue shares at a discount.

(b) In the formation of Companies, shares are often issued representing value for services rendered or property, and this is perfectly legitimate. The Dominion Companies' Act limits the number of shares which can be issued in return for real estate, and the Ontario Companies' Act requires that the real estate be properly valued. Apart from this, Companies have no power to issue their shares for other than cash, although where this payment was not cash but represented the cash price of the shares, and was a legitimate transaction, it would merely be a matter of intelligent book-keeping to make the sales of shares perfectly legal.

(c) The Company under the Ontario Companies' Act has power to acquire by purchase, lease or other title, and to hold, sell, alienate and convey any real estate necessary for the carrying on of its undertaking, and the Company shall upon its incorporation become and be invested with all the property and rights, real and personal, theretofore held by or for it under any trust created with a view to its incorporation, provided however that unless other statutory enactments apply, no parcel of land or interest therein at any time acquired by the Company and not required for its actual use and occupation, or not held by way of security, or not situate within the limits or within one mile of the limits of any city or town in this Province, shall be held by the Company or by any trustee on its behalf, for a longer period than seven years after the acquisition thereof, but shall be absolutely sold and disposed of, so that the Company shall no longer retain any interest therein unless by way of security; and if such land is held for a longer period than seven years, it shall be forfeited to the Queen.

Under the Dominion Companies' Act every Company incorporated under that Act may acquire, hold, sell and convey any real estate requisite for the carrying on of the undertaking of the Company.

(d) Transfer of shares, to be valid, requires to be recorded in the books of the Company in accordance with its by-laws. The Directors can refuse to allow this to be done when shares are not fully paid up, and whenever any entry is made of any transfer of such stock, if the transferees are not of apparently sufficient means, the Directors present when such entry is authorized are personally liable if they allow such transfer to be made. No share can be transferred until all previous calls have been fully paid up.

Question 10.—What Companies are required to make annual returns of their affairs, and what are substantially the nature of these returns?

You find, in compiling a return, that certain shareholders have pledged their holdings as collateral to advances made to the Company. How should these appear in the return? How would the lender proceed to realize upon his collateral should it be necessary to do so?

A.—The Ontario Companies' Act requires that the Company shall on or before the first day of February in every year, make out a summary, duly verified, containing as of the 31st day of December preceding, the following particulars:—

(a) The corporate name of the Company;

(b) The manner in which the Company is incorporated, whether by special Act or by Letters Patent.

(c) The place where the head office of the Company is situated.

(d) The place or places where, or from which the undertaking of the Company is carried on;

(e) The name, residence and post-office address of the President and the Secretary, and of the Treasurer of the Company;

(f) The name, residence and post-office address of each of the Directors of the Company;

(g) The date upon which the last annual meeting of the Company was held;

(h) The amount of the capital of the Company and the number of shares into which it is divided;

(i) The number of shares subscribed for and allotted;

(j) The amount of stock (if any) issued free from call; if none is so issued, this fact to be stated;

(k) The amount issued subject to call;

(l) The amount of calls made on each share;

(m) The total amount of calls received;

(n) The total amount of calls unpaid;

(o) The total amount of shares forfeited;

(p) The total amount of shares which have never been allotted or subscribed for.

(q) The total amount for which shareholders of the Company are liable in respect of unpaid stock held by them.

The summary shall also contain a list of persons who, on the 31st day of December previously, were shareholders of the Company, and their addresses and occupation and the amount of stock held by each, and the amount, if any, unpaid and still due by each. R. S. O. 1897, c. 191, s. 79.

The above section shall not apply to any Company not having gain for its purpose or object, where such Company by its charter of incorporation is declared to be exempt from the provisions thereof, or to any Company not having gain for its purpose or object which, on proof thereof being shown to the Lieutenant-Governor-in-Council, is, on and after a date to be set forth in the order of the Lieutenant-Governor-in-Council in that behalf, declared to be exempt.

Every other Company is subject to the requirements of this section.

The shares pledged by shareholders as collateral to advances made to the Company, should appear in the return in the names of these shareholders, as they are entitled to vote thereon. The lender to realize his collateral must proceed in the usual course of law; he could not sell or transfer the stock, even if transferred into his name by way of security.

CHAPTER XI.

AUDITING.

Question 1.—You are asked to act as Auditor for a Joint Stock Company.

What books and information would you require for the first Audit?

A.—The Auditor would require for his first audit:

To see all the books and have a list of same handed to him,—(The Stock or Share Ledger would be one of the books to be audited).

To examine the Articles of Incorporation and the by-laws; also the minutes of the Directors, where it may be necessary.

To ascertain who was entitled to receive and make payments on behalf of the Company, and order goods.

To generally investigate the system under which the books were kept, and note what internal check (if any) was kept as to the correctness of the work, etc.

To carefully note the sources of receipts with a view to guarding against fraud. All vouchers, including Invoices, Bank Cheques, etc., would also be required.

The above may be considered as answering the question, though the experienced auditor would be guided by circumstances as to the exact methods of gaining the necessary information, and the work to be done. For instance, in auditing the Stock Ledger, if shares had been issued during the period under the audit, it would be his duty to see that the value given therefor was properly accounted for in the financial books, and that this Ledger represented the amount of capital as shown to be invested in the business or subscribed for. Transfers of shares are made under the authority of the Directors and it is their duty, possibly through their officers, to see that these are correctly made.

The Auditor, however, will see that all the calls are properly made and accounted for, as such a transaction affecting the cash receipts would come under his audit.

Question 2.—What system would you recommend to a Trading Company doing a general business through the Dominion, as being the best for keeping a proper check on all cash receipts, part of their collections being made by the travellers?

A.—Probably the best check on cash receipts is to use printed receipt forms bound up as a Cheque Book and numbered consecutively. Statements of accounts rendered should have a memorandum thereon, stating that only receipts on the firm's printed form will be recognized.

The responsible person who received the remittances coming to hand by mail, might enter the amounts and names on the stub of Receipt Book, thus affording a good safeguard, a clerk duly filling out the receipts, after the cashier had initialed said stubs.

The traveller could be furnished with such a Receipt Book, and the stub or carbon copy should on his return be compared with the cash remitted or paid in by him.

A very useful check on cash receipts is to compare a few of the deposits made into the Bank (from copies kept) with the receipts of the same period. The cheques paid in should be recorded on the debit side of Cash Book unless possibly one might have been cashed.

Question 3.—In a Manufacturing Business what method would you propose for the protection of the Company in the purchase of materials and supplies in connection with the business and for the payment of the same?

A.—The success of a Manufacturing business so much depends on the knowledge and experience shown in the purchase of materials and supplies that it is a "sine qua non" that first class men be employed to manage the Company. Apart from this, and to ensure that market prices are paid for the goods, proper registers should be kept known as Stock Books, wherein are entered all materials and supplies purchased and the person receiving the goods should also initial the invoice accompanying them and their costs. Where practicable, Ledger Accounts could be kept of quantities, charging when bought and crediting when given out. The person who orders the goods should not be the one who passes the account for payment. The Directors also, noting that their goods were bought from first class houses, could ensure reasonable protection. As to protection in the payment of accounts, a proper system of Book-keeping, combined with regular auditing of the invoices, etc., and internal checking of the quantities of the goods purchased, would ensure that no payments were made, unless for value received, as under such proper system, one officer is a check on the work done by another.

The purchases themselves would be checked from the credit side of the Account in the Purchase Ledger through the Subsidiary Book to the invoice itself, showing the nature and cost of the goods bought.

In conclusion, the Company, to be successful, would have to exercise judgment in engaging their managers, and also in the system of Book-keeping adopted, etc., without which no "method proposed" would be of much avail.

Question 4.—What, in your opinion, would be an adequate system of checking the amounts due and payments for wages in a large Factory?

A.—First a proper system of Registers must be kept for checking the time worked by the employees. For piece work the Pay Sheets would have to be certified to by the foreman.

The Wages Sheet should be then made out from the Registers by a separate clerk and handed to the cashier after it has been duly checked. The cashier, or some other responsible person then pays the wages to the employees, and if possible, occasionally a Director or an Auditor should be present. Some factories give each employee a voucher for the wages due, which he hands in, such voucher operating as a receipt.

The Auditor should check the Wages Book and Pay Sheets and see that the totals agree with cheque drawn for "wages," and also might impress upon the management the importance of internal check on this part of the expenditure.

The best practical check after all is having the Wages Sheet checked by several persons, each department's wages being certified, as experience shows that collusion in fraud is rare amongst responsible officers in a firm.

Where a proper system of costing is adopted—the cost of wages is added to the Material used in the manufacturing of goods, the total cost of wages on the work done can then readily be ascertained, and this should tally with the total of the Wages Sheet for the same period.

Question 5.—In checking the Bank Account in a firm's books you find the balance agrees with the Bank Pass Book at the end of a certain period.

Would you consider any further examination necessary? Give reasons for your answer.

A.—Further examination would certainly be necessary. The Bank Account must always be checked, both receipts and payments. Although the balance happened to agree with the Bank Pass Book, there might be an error in the firm's books, and further, there might be outstanding cheques marked as good and charged, which would require verification.

The Bank Balance should also be ascertained from the Bank in addition to comparing the accounts with the Bank Pass Book.

This can be well illustrated by a case which actually occurred.

A firm accepted a Draft at sight, which was duly charged to their account by the Bank on the 31st of the month, but which was omitted to be charged by the firm to their customer, not being entered in the Bills Payable Book. On the 30th of the month a cheque for a similar amount was drawn and sent to another customer. The Bank Account was balanced in due course. The Auditor, however, on checking the items in the Cash Book with the Bank vouchers found that the Bill referred to was not entered. The mistake as above was discovered and the Bank Balance had to be altered to its correct amount by a correcting entry. The cheque given on the 30th was outstanding, and had not been paid by the Bank as the book-keeper supposed on the 31st.

Question 6.—What do you mean by Depreciation and in what manner, if at all, should it affect these accounts: "Buildings," "Leases," "Stocks and Shares," "Plant and Machinery."

Depreciation,

A.—Is that lessening in the value in assets through wear and tear, or change of fashion, or effluxion of time, and must not be confused with "Fluctuation in value," which also affects the value of such assets as land, stocks, etc. The object of setting aside an amount annually for Depreciation is to equalize the payment over a series of years—otherwise any one year would have to bear a heavy expense, which might be detrimental to the concern.

Buildings,

The Depreciation would depend on the quality of materials employed. The time the building will last should be estimated and a percentage written off each year sufficient to amount to the original cost thereof by the end of the period. Repairs will have to be charged to Revenue Account.

Leases,

The time a Lease has to run is known, and each year a sufficient amount must be written off as Depreciation, so that when the Lease expires, the asset will simultaneously disappear, by such credits, from the books of the firm.

There are several ways of treating this account:—

(1) To write off a fixed proportion of the Lease each year.

(2) To write off a percentage of the balance each year—in this plan the amounts written off steadily decrease.

(3) To write Account off on the Annuity System, adjusting the amount so as to allow for interest on the investment. This is the best way of dealing with Leases as a general rule.

(4) By investing a certain amount each year, sufficient to replace the Lease when it expires.

This would require the smallest amount to be set aside each year, but would take the cash out of the business. However, it has many advantages which would compensate for this, one being that at the end of the period a fund was provided to replace or renew the Lease.

Stocks and Shares,

Are not subject to Depreciation, though they fluctuate in value. A Company trading exclusively in Stocks and Shares might probably, to ascertain their profit or loss, estimate their value periodically, but then there would be seen both a Depreciation and Appreciation in value, and these could be adjusted through some Suspense or Adjustment account.

Plant and Machinery,

The Depreciation in Plant and Machinery is always a most difficult subject to treat exactly, as Machinery is so subject to Depreciation, not only from wearing out, but from becoming obsolete through later inventions. Especially is this noted in Machinery worked by electricity. Some principle of depreciation in value however, must be arrived at, based on the life of the Machinery; unless the Plant and Machinery is revalued each year, where practicable, and the reduction charged to "Depreciation Account," or a reserve set aside for the purpose, which is perhaps the better way.

Question 7.—A Company has Agencies established in different sections with a separate account in the Ledger for each Agency, in which is charged all of the goods shipped it.

At the end of the financial year they (the Agencies) still have some stock on hand.

How would you treat these accounts?

A.—Each Agency should be instructed to carefully prepare an inventory of all goods as on hand at the end of financial year. The information thus obtained would be embodied in the general " inventory of stock," and entries posted, giving each Agency credit for the amount thus advised.

As separate accounts are kept for each Agency, the profit or loss of each can be easily ascertained, and when carrying forward the balances for the new year, the stock on hand would be included in each balance.

Another way is to prepare a Trading Account, with a column on each side allowed for each Agency.

On the Dr. side the first entry would show the total Merchandise on hand, at date of previous balance—the Agency columns showing Stock at each one.

The next entry would show the Purchases for the financial year, showing cost of goods shipped to each Agency.

In a similar manner, credit all the Sales, also credit Total Merchandise on hand, showing also Stock on hand at each Agency.

The balance gives the gross profit of the business—and each column with its corresponding column will give the gross profit of each Agency.

To expedite matters, each Agency Account can have separate columns for Purchases and Sales, etc.

The Total Stock on hand will be carried forward to Merchandise Account, and to each Agency as the case may be.

Question 8.—What proof would you require as to the correctness of the value in the stock taking of a Trading Company?

A.—The Stock Sheets should be signed by the person taking the same. The extensions and additions must be checked, and the basis upon which the stock is valued must be enquired into to see what allowances have been made for depreciation, if any. The auditor cannot vouch for the absolute correctness of the inventory with the stock itself, though specific items should, occasionally, be checked and compared with the original invoices.

The reliability of this valuation depends upon the reliability to be placed upon the persons who take out the inventory and value the same.

Question 9.—In a Balance Sheet you find an entry "Interest and Investments."

Explain this and state what action you would take before passing it as being correct?

A.—The entry "Interest and Investments" would refer to the investment as an asset and the interest accrued thereon to date of Balance Sheet. Before passing this as correct, it would have to be ascertained if the investment was a paying one; and in considering this the auditor would be guided by its "market value" or its previous history as shown in the books.

In the case of Companies loaning money where interest earned though not received is a very important and correct form of revenue, especial care has to be exercised that revenue is not created by loading up and charging bad advances. Charging up interest accrued due is very different from interest charged up periodically on bad advances, the same not being collectable.

The auditor should also require to have some proof as to the investment itself, and would have to see the scrip, etc., according to the nature of such investment.

It might be observed that the entry referred to seems a very unusual one—probably "Interest on investments" is meant, if so, the answer is included as above.

Question 10.—How would you satisfy yourself that all the liabilities which should be included in a balance Sheet were in it?

A.—Some responsible officer or Member of the firm should certify that all the outstanding accounts had been included.

The auditor should examine salaries, wages, rent, etc., and see that all have been provided for to date of balance. Also that provisions have been made for all interest, etc., accrued due, and such items as auditor's fees, etc. The matter of Contingent Liabilities, such as Bills under Discount, or Disputed Claims or guarantees must not be overlooked. The invoices entered after date of Balance Sheet might also with advantage be examined to see if any should have been included therein.

CHAPTER XII.

AUDITING.

Question 1.—What is the object and scope of an Audit?

A.—Dicksee, in his book on Auditing, divides this into three headings:—

(1) The detection of fraud.

(2) The detection of technical errors.

(3) The detection of errors of principle.

To answer this question fully would be impossible here. The Auditor's responsibilities vary under different circumstances and in accordance with the instructions given him. Briefly summarized and covering the headings quoted, it may be stated that the usual object of an audit is that the periodical Balance Sheet may be vouched for as correct; and in the same way the scope of an Audit may be looked upon as any investigation or checking which the Auditor considers necessary to enable him to so vouch that the Balance Sheet shows the true position of the Company or Firm. In the case of a Joint Stock Company, the responsibility of the Auditor is more defined than when acting for a firm, where his duties may be specifically detailed and his responsibilities limited.

Question 2.—You are appointed Auditor for a new Trading Company, and are asked to draft some general instructions for the guidance of the office staff with a view to having everything in proper shape when you begin the audit. Give an outline of what would be embodied in your memorandum.

A.—The general instructions thus asked for might be to the following effect:—

(1) That a list of all the books in use be prepared.

(2) That the books be regularly balanced each month.

(3) That all the vouchers of payments made and invoices be kept carefully in the order in which entered in the books, and that no voucher be filed away until initialed or marked by the Auditor.

(4) That all cash received be deposited in the bank, and that all payments be made by cheque, excepting Petty Cash payments, which are to be recorded in a Petty Cash Book.

(5) That receipts be given for all cash and remittances received, and that particulars of same be duly entered in stub of Receipt Book. This would not apply to a Retail Trading Company, where a proper system of checking cash sales would have to be asked for in addition to above.

(6) Other instructions might be given according to the nature of the business and also depending upon the completeness or not of the system of Book-keeping adopted by the Company.

Question 3.—(a) What do you understand by the term "Voucher"? (b) For what entries would you require them? (c) In what books would items be found for which Vouchers should be produced?

A.—(a) A "Voucher" is any document which vouches or certifies as to values received or values parted with.

(b) For all entries where cash had been paid, or persons credited or charged with goods, and as far as practicable for cash received.

(c) The Cash Book,
    Journal or Day Book,
    Invoice Book.

Question 4.—What steps would you take to verify the following Assets of a Manufacturing Company: Cash, Bills Receivable, Stock, Machinery?

A.—*Cash,*

This would be counted, taking care, where the balance is large, that a deficiency had not been made good, by cashing some cheque intended for some other purpose, or using some remittance for the same purpose. In a periodical audit, the cash should be counted at irregular periods.

Bills Receivable,

By comparing list of the Current Bills with the Bills themselves.
(See answer to next question.)

Stock,

This question is answered under another question, see page 142.

Machinery,

This question is answered under another question, see page 157.

Question 5.—You are auditing the books of the Brown Furniture Co. State what steps you would take to ascertain whether there was a sufficient sum charged against Revenue to meet the probable loss in Book debts.

A.—An Auditor is not expected to be infallible, but he is expected to take reasonable precautions and care that proper provisions for loss are made.

In this case, if he went through the Accounts and Bills Receivable with the Manager, carefully scrutinizing each account, being guarded largely by the age of the debt, and the payments received, and seeing that provision was made for all doubtful debts, the bad debts having been written off, he would have taken sufficient steps. Probably the best plan is, after writing off the bad debts to set aside a percentage of the Book Debts each year to provide for doubtful debts, the amount of such percentage to be fixed by past experience.

The Auditor also, in checking the Ledger Accounts, would know in many cases which were bad or doubtful, but it is the duty and business of the Company to conduct their own affairs.

Question 6.—(a) How would you determine the propriety of a dividend?

(b) How would you satisfy yourself that the dividends had been paid to those entitled to them?

A.—(a) It is not the Auditor's duty to determine the propriety of a dividend. In the case of a Joint Stock Company the responsibility rests with the Directors, who doubtless act on the report of the Auditor.

The propriety of a dividend may be determined by considering the following points:—

(1) The amount of profit;

(2) Whether this profit is available in cash or has been "locked up" in assets of another nature;

(3) Whether the cash, if available, could not be far more profitably left in the business.

(b) By referring to the list of shareholders on the date of paying such dividend, which would show number of shares held by each, and thus the proportion of dividend to which each was entitled. Also by checking the voucher signed for dividend by each shareholder, or the endorsed "Dividend Cheque," which had been sent and was returned by the Bank in due course.

Question 7.—In auditing the accounts of a partnership you find that Green's dishonored note forms part of the balance of Bills Receivable. Is this correct? If not, state fully what should have been done with it?

A.—This is not correct.

When Green's note matured or became due, it should either have been charged to "Overdue Bill Account" or charged back to Green's account, and Bills Receivable credited.

Bills Receivable Account should only include current Bills Receivable on hand, and on the due date of every bill, whether paid or not, it must be credited to this account and charged to

Cash or some other account. In the case of an endorsed note, where proper notices of dishonor must be sent promptly, the necessity of this can be readily seen.

Question 8.—What procedure would you follow in auditing the Capital Account of a Manufacturing Company, no previous audit having been made?

A.—The Auditor should ask for the previous Balance Sheet, see that all items composing the same are recorded in the Ledger, and that the balance to Capital Account at the beginning of the period to be audited, agreed in the same way.

It would also be necessary to ascertain "generally" that the Assets in the Balance Sheet referred to were correctly stated as far as could reasonably be done, though the auditor could not be held responsible for the correctness of same.

The Capital of the Company represents the value of the Assets after deducting therefrom all the Liabilities, so to certify as to the correctness of this an audit of the business would have to be made. As far as the Account itself is concerned, the balance to credit thereof must be ascertained to agree with the balances showing the Assets minus the balances representing the Liabilities. There is no practical difference in auditing the Capital of a Manufacturing Company unless perhaps the values of the Merchandise, in its process from the raw material to the finished article, with the costs incurred, require some special consideration.

Question 9.—What is an Income and Expenditure Account? Point out in what respect, if any, it differs from an Account of Receipts and Payments?

A.—*An Income and Expenditure Account,*

Shows the value of whole Income, whether actually received in cash or not, and the whole Expenditure for the same period, whether paid in cash or due. It is practically a synonomous term for "Profit and Loss."

An Account of Receipts and Payments,

Is usually a summarized statement taken from the Cash Book and only shows cash transactions. *The latter account therefore, as compared with the former,* shows only the Cash received or disbursed. There is also a further minor difference. The latter account is in reality the Cash Account or "Cash Book," so the receipts appear on the left hand side—the Income and Expenditure Account appears as a Ledger Account or accounts, so the receipts are on the right hand side.

Question 10.—In auditing the books of a Manufacturing Establishment, what voucher would you require for Wages paid, and how would you satisfy yourself that the Wages List did not contain the name of fictitious employees?

A.—The answer to this question may be obtained by referring to page 139.

The only satisfactory proof that the Auditor can obtain that Wages are correctly paid, is, where possible, by seeing it done himself, or by insisting that a proper system of internal check is adopted.

The Voucher for Wages paid is primarily the Wages Sheet, confirmed by the cheque drawn on the bank, and strengthened by the evidence that the employees, whose names appear thereon, actually received the cash.

In small establishments the men commonly sign for their Wages, in large ones this is not usual. Sometimes vouchers are given the employees, and these are handed in when they are paid.

CHAPTER XIII.

AUDITING.

Question 1.—Under what circumstances do you consider "Goodwill" or "Patent Rights" Legitimate Assets? As an Auditor how would you advise such Assets being dealt with year by year?

A.—"Goodwill" as an asset, is one which is never or rarely considered as an available asset, in considering the value of the assets of a Company. It may, however, be considered as a "Legitimate Asset" when it represents the cost of the "Goodwill" paid when acquiring a business, even if the shares of the Company then starting have to be considerable "watered" in consequence of the exorbitant or fancy value at which this "Goodwill" has been placed. Frequently, when a partner is retiring, the firm has to pay a sum for his "Goodwill," which then usually appears as an item in the future Balance Sheets. The item "Patent Rights," to be a Legitimate Asset, should represent the amount, less possibly reduction, paid for the Rights of any Patent.

The Auditor would always prefer to see such assets reduced from profit year by year, on the principle that they do not usually represent their actual value. But Assets like these are difficult to value; the "Goodwill" of a business may actually be increasing in value, and on the other hand a Company may be formed to sell goods covered by "Patent Rights" with the understanding that when these Rights terminate their business will cease, so the Shareholders prefer to draw all the profits as they are earned.

The real principle seems to be that with a Company intended to carry on a permanent business, when they have acquired such assets as "Patent Rights" that they should be written off or reduced yearly, so as to expire when the Rights run out.

Question 2.—Explain fully the items entering into Costs Account in a Manufacturing Business consisting of three Departments, each semi-dependent on the other. Give full particulars as to the method you would pursue to arrive at the Net and the Gross cost of production.

A.—The object of the Costs Account is to enable the Manufacturer to ascertain the cost of manufacturing his goods, and their value when finished.

The various items which have to be considered in arriving at this cost are as follows:

(1) Wages or Labour;

(2) The Material used;

(3) The Expenses of the Factory incidental to their manufacture.

What may be called the practical method of ascertaining this cost is now receiving some attention at the hands of our Manufacturers. It is admitted that it is only a crude way to take a sample article and to value it by ascertaining the cost, from the report obtained from foremen and expert workmen, and then thereafter to take that as its future value or cost. There are many who keep their books in the most crude way, and look upon high-class Book-keeping as a fad; yet the firm who adopts the best way will hardly be content to go back to old methods.

Most merchants arrive at their gross profit by adding to the cost of the Raw Material the other items mentioned as above, and then deducting therefrom the Material on hand, etc.

The system of Costs Accounts is a practical and accurate method of ascertaining the cost of each article manufactured. As to ascertain the details of "Accounts Receivable" we refer to the Accounts Receivable Ledger, so to ascertain the details of the manufactured goods we turn to the Costs Ledger.

To answer this question fully would not be possible here, and all that can be attempted is to sketch the outline of the system followed avoiding as far as possible any technical terms.

The books required to collect the items Wages and Material, showing the cost of converting them into the manufactured article are

    An Order Book.

    A Wages Register—Stores Register.

    A Costs Ledger.

Certain goods are to be manufactured. Each workman keeps a record of his time and shows on a slip the number of hours expended on each job (except he is working on the piece-work principle). Each job is numbered in the Order Book, and it is known by its number. This information, viz., the time on job, is recorded in a Register, and if there are a number of men employed thereon, for convenience sake, a column in Register will be set apart for its use, or it is taken direct from the slips. By this means we arrive at the cost of the Wages.

Similarly when the foreman starts the job he calculates what Material he will require and apportions such to the workmen. This Material is duly charged.

Now, to find the value of item (3): The Expenses of the Factory—this is not as exact an item as the two former, as it can readily be seen that if the Factory is busy the percentage will be lower than if the contrary be the case. A Factory can turn out 10,000 articles at a lower cost than 5,000.

This expenditure must then be estimated and may be understood as follows: If one day's expenditure be estimated at $10.00, and three jobs have been completed with 50, 25 and 25 hours of labour expended on each job, one would be charged $5.00 and the others $2.50 each, this is the principle, though the basis is not a perfect one, and it is hard to find one, as one man's one hour may be worth, from the work he turns out, another's one and a half hours.

Now, to focus these items and bring them into the books, again not full details but the principle can only be shown.

When the Material is bought it is charged to Merchandise in the General Ledger and charged to Stores in the Costs Book—similarly with the other items. *Now let us charge up our jobs in the Costs Ledger.* Turn to the Wages Register and charge job with wages, showing time and cost from it. Any other orders can also be charged if we are posting up for a period.

When charging these accounts credit Wages Account.

Similarly charge up items (2) and (3). Let us then assume that the Factory is handing over this work to the Warehouse. The goods will in the Costs Ledger be severally credited to their accounts at the figures therein shown and charged to the General Ledger Account.

The Cost Ledger being kept on the principles of double entry will always balance.

In the General Ledger charge manufactured goods and credit the Costs Ledger Account or Merchandise.

The following entries will explain—purely fanciful figures are used to show how the items are treated:

COST LEDGER ACCOUNTS.

Dr.	GENERAL LEDGER ACCOUNT.		Cr.	Dr.	MATERIAL.		Cr.
To Job 1......	$26 00	By Material.	$100 00	To G. L. ℅..	$100 00	By Register.	$45 00
" 2......	26 00						
" 3......	26 00						
Balance......	22 00				WAGES.		
	$100 00		$100 00			By Register.	$30 00
		By Balance..	$22 00				
	JOB NO. 1.				FACTORY EXPENSES.		
						By Register.	$3 00
To Wages	$10 00	By G. L. ℅..	$26 00				
" Material..	15 00						
" Factory	1 00						
	$26 00		$26 00				
	JOB No. 2.				JOB No. 3.		
To Wages	$10 00	By G. L. ℅..	$26 00	To Wages....	$10 00	By G. L. ℅..	$26 00
" Material..	15 00			" Material..	15 00		
" Factory ..	1 00			" Factory ..	1 00		
	$26 00		$26 00		$26 00		$26 00

GENERAL LEDGER ACCOUNT.

	COST LEDGER ACCOUNT.						
To Purchase Book...	$100 00	By Manufacturing ℅	$ 78 00				
		" Balance..	22 00				
	$100 00		$100 00				
To Balance..	$22 00						

This account is ruled off to show how it corresponds with the Adjusting Account in Costs Ledger. At the end of the period when Wages, etc., are charged to it, the corresponding entries will be passed in the Costs Ledger and will close the Wages Accounts, etc., showing as above credit balances.

Now the question asks how a business with Three Departments semi-dependent on the other will be kept. We are not told how they are semi-dependent, but for illustration will assume an instance:

Take a Gas Company—where the making of the gas involves a necessary outlay in coal—after the gas is made, from the material left most valuable products can be obtained, and it is also valuable in itself as coke. Let us suppose that the gas is made at a loss in Department No. 1. Department No. 2 makes a handsome profit out of the Dyes manufactured. Department No. 3 treats the coke and likewise pays.

It is simply a matter of book-keeping to charge Departments No. 2 and 3 for the material used and credit Department No. 1.

Similarly in Furniture Making.

Material over and useless in one department could be used with profit in another department—charge second Department for material, or treat the profit made as belonging to Department No. 1.

The terms Net and Gross Cost of Production are difficult to define. Authorities have hardly yet fixed terms so clearly as in Book-keeping pure and simple.

The Net Cost would be plus the Factory charge as explained. The Gross Cost—with only Wages and Material.

Question 3.—In taking Stock what valuation is a Manufacturer justified in placing upon goods in the process of manufacture, finished stock, unsold and finished stock sold but not delivered? Give reasons for your answer.

A.—The Manufacturer is justified in valuing his unfinished stock at what it has cost him to bring it to its present condition, and his finished stock at the actual cost of production, plus the Manufacturer's profit; he should not however anticipate his trade profits, and occasionally might have to make allowances for depreciation in values.

Dicksee states, "The only point to remember is that, while a manufacturing profit is earned only when the manufacture is completed, a trading profit is only made when a sale is completed. Neither profit must be anticipated, but it does not appear to be invariably essential that manufacturing profit should be held over until a sale has been effected."

As regards "finished stock sold but not delivered": Surely it is usual to charge the purchaser when goods are sold and not to wait until they are delivered. The Manufacturer would not include such items in stock, even if the goods were sold C.O.D., and it was not considered prudent to anticipate the profit, this would be provided for in another way. The value of this "sold stock" would be included in his assets under the heading of "Book Debts," or possibly as "Goods Sold C.O.D."

If, however, we are to understand that this item "finished stock sold but not delivered," means that the goods are sold, but to be delivered at a future fixed date, the Manufacturer should value them as "finished stock" only, as the trading profit will belong to the period in which they are actually delivered.

Question 4.—What do you consider the best system for arriving at the depreciation to be written off or provided to redeem the following assets:—

(a) Fixed or Permanent Machinery.

(b) Loose Machinery, Utensils, Tools, Implements, etc.

(c) Office and Shop Furniture and Fittings.

(d) Horses.

(e) Leasehold Property.

(f) Goodwill.

A.—(a) *Fixed or Permanent Machinery.*

Charge all repairs and renewals of parts to Revenue. Write off annually to Depreciation from $7\frac{1}{2}$ per cent. to $12\frac{1}{2}$ per cent. from the reducing balances, the rate depending on the nature of the Machinery. In the case of Boilers, 10 to $15\frac{1}{2}$ per cent. should be written off, as they wear out more rapidly. Regard also should be had as to the adaptability of the Machinery to its requirements, and if it is becoming obsolete, it must be thoroughly revalued and the difference written off, see page 141.

(b) *Loose Machinery, Utensils, Tools, Implements, etc.*

These should be revalued annually. A good method is to keep a Stock Ledger Account of these, and always insist on the old Tools being handed up before fresh ones are given.

A hard and fast rule cannot however be laid down where conditions may be so entirely different and dependent also upon the size of the factory.

(c) *Office and Shop Furniture and Fittings.*

Deduct say 7 per cent. on the reducing balances.

(d) *Horses.*

No percentage rate of depreciation can be laid down; experience alone will give this for the particular business. The safest plan is to revalue the Horses periodically, and this should not be a difficult matter.

(e) *Leasehold Property.*

If the lease is a short one, the amount to be written off annually is a simple matter. In the case of a long lease, the amount to be written off each year is virtually an annuity, which will replace the investment, or the cost of the lease and interest thereon, at the end of the period. It would be a wise precaution to create a sinking fund for the purchase of fresh property, but this is not usually done. Where there are buildings on the property, this depreciation, or a part of it, will be charged as rent, see page 140.

(f) *Goodwill.*

Is an Asset that is usually of most uncertain value, and as such it is always satisfactory to see it written off by surplus profits. But it cannot be said that it depreciates necessarily in value; on the contrary, it may be steadily appreciating.

In valuing the Assets on a Balance Sheet, generally speaking, it would not be considered, and would not be looked upon as an available Asset. Under these circumstances then, the Auditor is not called upon to ask that any sum be set aside to meet the depreciation of "Goodwill," it is entirely in the discretion of the Management to deal with this Asset.

Question 5.—A Joint Stock Company whose Capital has become greatly impaired but which is at last making a small profit wishes to write off half its Subscribed Capital in order that it may be able to pay a 6 per cent. dividend. The Stock is fully paid up. What steps are necessary to be taken in order to do this, and what entries would you make in the books to record the transaction? How will this affect each Stockholder's liability?

A.—Only an outline of the procedure is here given, full details can be obtained by referring to the Act R. S. O. cap. 191, sections 18 to 21.

A special general meeting must be duly summoned for the purpose of passing a by-law, which must be carried by a majority of two-thirds in value of the Shareholders present. A proper petition would then be made through the Provincial Secretary for the authority of the Lieutenant-Governor to reduce the Capital as proposed. If this is granted, then the entries in the books would be as follows:—

Debit Capital Account to the credit of "Impairment and Deficiency Account." The debit balance to Profit and Loss Account can then be written off to this Deficiency Account.

In the Stock Ledger each Shareholder will have his holdings reduced by 50 per cent.

The 6 per cent. on the reduced Capital will then be paid in the ordinary way.

The question asks how this will affect each Shareholder's liability. The shares being fully paid up, there was no liability before, and there is none after the reduction. The Company's liability to its creditors is not altered, and if the 6 per cent. dividend is being improperly paid the Directors would be responsible.

Question 6.—To what extent do you consider it an Auditor's duty to examine into and report upon the Stock Inventories and the mode in which the Stock has been taken and valued?

A.—For the answer to this question see page 142; adding thereto: The Auditor would also be guided by noting the percentage of Gross Profits as compared with previous years. If this showed any marked increase it might tend to show that the present valuation was excessive.

Question 7.—Set out in detail the form of Balance Sheet (without figures) you consider best suited to show the position of an ordinary manufacturing Joint Stock Co.

BALANCE SHEET OF THE............MANUFACTURING CO.,
As on............1898.

Liabilities.		Assets.	
Nominal Capital....shares of $....each................	$.....	Cash on hand	$.....
		Cash in Bank	$..... $.....
Subscribed Capital....shares of $....each, $....per share called up................	$.....	*Trade Debtors—* Bills Receivable............ Accounts Receivable	$..... $.....
Less calls in arrears..........	$..... $.....		$.....
Creditors, trade— Bills Payable .... Accounts Payable...........	$..... $.....	Less provision for discount and bad debts	$..... $.....
	$.....	*Stock on Hand—*	
Other Creditors, if any .... *Reserve Account,* if any.... *Profit and Loss Account—* Balance available for dividend	$..... $..... $.....	Raw Material .... Manufactured, incomplete .. " finished ...... Stores	$..... $..... $..... $.....
		Plant and Machinery— At cost.................... Less depreciation at say 10 % per annum.................	$..... $.....
			$..... $
		Office Furniture and Fittings— Less depriciation at say 7 % per annum................. Freehold Land and Buildings.. Leasehold Property less depretion	$ $ $.
		Other assets .... Preliminary expenses (if not written off)	$..... $.....
	$.....		$.....

Question 8.—Should the following items be Capitalized or charged to Revenue for the year?

(a) Premium given for a Lease.

(b) Costs attending a Mortgage.

(c) Commission on an Issue of Debenture Stock.

(d) Brokerage on the Purchase of an Investment.

(e) Accrued Interest or Dividend included in the Cost Price of an Investment.

(f) Preliminary Expenses on the formation of a Company.

(g) Minimum Royalties Paid but Unearned, Recouperable out of Future Workings.

(h) Cost of Removing a 6-inch Gas Pipe to another locality and replacing it with a 9-inch pipe.

Give your reasons fully in each case.

A.—(a) *Premium given for a Lease.*

Should be Capitalized, and an amount written off yearly for Depreciation, as each year this asset decreases in value.

(b) *Costs attending a Mortgage.*

Should be charged to Revenue, whether paid in Cash or included in the Mortgage. It might be argued that the cost could be spread over the term of the Mortgage, but this would be far-fetched and not practical.

(c) *Commission on an Issue of Debenture Stock.*

Should be charged to Revenue, but it might be distributed over so many years, on the principle that the Capital thus introduced into the business was required and worth the cost of obtaining. If the Debenture were "permanent," the amount might be treated as an Asset.

(d) *Brokerage on the Purchase of an Investment.*

Might be included in the Cost of the Investment. In this case one would have to be guided by circumstances.

(e) *Accrued Interest or Dividend included in the Cost Price of an Investment.*

The best plan would be to charge the Investment pro tem. with the amount paid, adjusting the account to its value, ex dividend, when the Dividend or Interest was actually paid.

(f) *Preliminary Expenses on the Formation of a Company.*

Should be Capitalized and should afterwards be reduced from Profits, so as to distribute this expense over say two or three years. This is not however compulsory, as it appears this may remain as an Asset, though certainly a most unsatisfactory one.

(g) *Minimum Royalties Paid but unearned, recuperable out of future workings,*

May be charged to Capital Account and repaid by being charged to Revenue Account when the "future workings" are realized.

(h) *Cost of Removing a 6-inch Gas Pipe to another Locality and replacing it with a 9-inch Pipe.*

Charge the cost of removing 6-inch pipe and replacing same to Revenue Account. Capitalize the difference in value between the 9-inch pipe and the 6-inch pipe.

When 6-inch pipe is placed in new position it **can also** be capitalized at its value. If this is done simultaneously with putting in the 9-inch pipe, it will be sufficient to capitalize value of latter only.

The Asset is increased in value, and this increase in value may be Capitalized, but the costs are a charge upon Revenue for the year.

Question 9.—Explain the difference between a "Sinking Fund" and an ordinary "Reserve Fund." How are each created and for what purposes? Many persons contend that a Reserve Fund to be of any value should always be specially invested. State your opinion fully on this point. Are these Funds Assets or Liabilities? And why?

A.—A "Sinking Fund" is a fund set aside and specially invested. The object of this fund or investment is to meet some known Liability coming due, such as debentures, or to replace some depreciating Asset, such as a leasehold property. While a Sinking Fund is formed for a definite purpose, and is taken from Revenue or Profits; a Reserve Fund, which is created from Profits, is formed to provide for unforseen contingencies and Trade losses.

In considering what a Reserve Fund is, care has to be taken to distinguish between Undivided Profits and Reserves set aside for specific purposes, such as depreciation, provision for doubtful debts, etc. The latter should be always shown in the Balance Sheet as far as possible, deducted from the Assets they refer to.

As to whether a Reserve Fund should be specially invested or not depends largely on the nature of the business. In the case of Financial Institutions it would unquestionably be of advantage that the Reserve Fund should be represented or set off by gilt-edged investments.

In a Trading Business it is usually treated, and in the opinion of the best authorities wisely so, as so much extra Capital to be retained therein. The larger profit it would thus enable the business to earn seems to show a self-evident proof of the wisdom of this course. It might, however, be assumed that extra funds were not required, then some suitable investment would naturally be looked for.

"Reserve Fund Account" is a Liability, being so much due out of the Assets of the proprietors, and appears as such in the Balance Sheet. The Sinking Fund is an Asset and appears in the Balance Sheet, showing the investments thus set aside and "ear marked" for some specific purpose, corresponding with the amount to a Sinking Fund Account.

Criticise the following statement:

Liabilities.		Assets.	
Loan and Debentures	$289,476 00	Land and Buildings	$293,864 00
Bank Overdraft	4,891 00	Rents accrued and unpaid	2,917 00
Sundry Creditors	946 00	Sinking Fund	6,000 00
Invested by Treasurer—Surplus Fund	7,924 00	Unexpired Insurance	365 00
		Cash in Hand	91 00
	$303,237 00		$303,237 00

A.—The position of the Company thus shown is very involved. First, looking at what might be termed their "Liquid Liabilities," assuming that the Loan and Debentures are not due for some time, we note: That there is an Overdraft at the Bank, and Sundry Creditors, and no Liquid Assets to meet same, or to provide interest on the Loan, etc.

The "Asset," "Land and Buildings" might realize 50 per cent. on forced sale.

The Sinking Fund valued at $6,000 may or may not be well invested, we are not told.

The Unexpired Insurance can scarcely be valued at anything.

The Surplus Fund Invested by the Treasurer: This cannot be explained—Where are the Investments? certainly not amongst the Assets. It is rather difficult to criticise such a statement, one feels more inclined to criticize the person who prepared it.

A noticeable feature also in the business is that there appears to be no Capital represented, unless it is to be supposed that this has all been wiped off by losses, which have been charged to "Capital Account" itself.

The statement has been criticised and it is somewhat satisfactory to feel that it is not a real one the Auditor has been asked to pass an opinion on.

Question 10.—How would you treat in the Balance Sheet:

(a) Provisions for Bad and Doubtful Debts.

(b) Contingent Fund (which is the amount charged against Profit and Loss on account of Depreciation of Plant).

(c) Partners' Capital Account.

(d) Unused Premiums of Fire Insurance.

A.—(a) *Provisions for Bad and Doubtful Debts.*

This amount should be deducted from the Asset showing "Accounts Receivable" and "Bills Receivable."

(b) *Contingent Fund.*

In a similar way deduct this amount from the balance of " Plant Account," on the Asset side of Balance Sheet.

The student might note the answer to Question 9 in this paper, referring to "Reserves," which is exemplified here, and under heading (a).

(c) *Partners' Capital Account.*

Either show the Net Balance taken from the Ledger after all the entries have been passed, or set each Partner's account out as follows:—

    Balance............................ $ ....
    Less Drawings for period ....
                                                      ————————
    Add Interest on Capital (if any).... $..........
    Add Profit or Deduct Loss ....
                                                     ———————— $..........

(d) *Unused Premium of Fire Insurance,*

Would appear as an Asset on the Balance Sheet.

CHAPTER XIV.

AUDITING.

Question 1.—You are appointed Auditor for a Limited Company which has just commenced business. What books and documents, if any, would you call for, in addition to the regular books of account, and for what purpose would you require them?

A.—Those known as the Statistical Books, which consist of:—
 1. Book containing copy of Letters Patent.
 2. Register of Shareholders, giving particulars as to shares issued, calls made, etc., also addresses of Shareholders.
 3. Register of Directors, giving date of appointment, names and addresses.
 4. Register of Transfers.
 5. Stock Ledger.
 6. Minute Books.

The object of requiring to see these books would be to ascertain that the necessary steps and records required by the Act under which the Company was incorporated, had been properly attended to as far as these concerned his audit. It would be sufficient if the first five books enumerated were all included in one book.

Further, he would require to refer to these books in auditing the Stock Ledger, to see that the shares had been properly allotted, and issued according to the deed of incorporation, and also that all the shares issued had been paid for as specified, etc.

Question 2.—State in detail what evidence you would require of the accuracy of the books of a Savings & Loan Company, as to the accounts of Mortgagors, Depositors, and Debenture Issues. What irregularities would you expect to find in such accounts?

A.—All the items composing these accounts should be compared and checked with the original Books of Entry, and the Accounts themselves should be added up to prove their correctness. In the case of Mortgagors' Accounts, evidence would have to be obtained of advances made, viz., that the Mortgagor obtained the loan. The Mortgage would have to be examined to see that it had been prepared and registered by the Company's solicitors, and that the deeds were with it. The Policy of Insurance, if any, should be examined to see if the Mortgage is recorded thereon and that the policy is in force. The valuation of the property mortgaged should be ascertained from the valuator's report.

Some evidence should be required as to payments made by the Mortgagor, whether on account of principal or interest. A periodical statement sent to the Mortgagor, asking for his reply, is the best form of check on these Accounts, as irregularities have usually consisted in not crediting Mortgagors with payments made by them. Where Mortgagors have a pass book supplied them this would form a basis of check.

In checking Depositors' Accounts, the Pass Books would be regularly inspected, compared and initialed, noting if deposits are regularly made, as the case may be, care being taken that all the books are exhibited. The Auditor should look to the Management to examine these books as they come to hand direct from the Depositors. In cases where deposits are made for a fixed period and a receipt, known as a Deposit Receipt, is given therefor, the Auditor will carefully examine the stubs of the Receipt Book with the Company's books, especially comparing the matured receipts therewith and noting that there are no missing receipt forms. In this form of deposit where fraud has been effected, the receipt issued was for the correct amount, but the stub only recorded the amount passed through the books. In Depositors' Accounts, irregularities would consist in wrong charges being made, or credits omitted ,and if there are irregularities and the books all agree, the

Depositor himself, by being asked to examine his Pass Book, affords a check, which is the only conclusive one, apart from the Company's books. Some Depositors, where a monthly payment is due, pay in advance, this requires careful examination.

As regards Debenture Issues, the Auditor would require evidence that the amount that the Debenture realized was entered in the books, which would not necessarily be their face value. The interest upon the Debentures would have to be checked, and vouchers for payments produced, etc.

As part of this audit, when a fresh issue of Debentures was made, the Minute Book would be referred to for the purpose of ascertaining the authority therefor. In the case of Loan Companies, where the Issue of Debentures is limited in proportion to their Capital, it would have to be seen that this limit was not exceeded.

Where Debentures are issued from a book the stubs would be carefully examined, etc. Stubs should always be initialled by the men signing the Debentures or Receipt issued.

Question 3.—In auditing Municipal Accounts how would you satisfy yourself that all amounts paid in on account of Taxes, had been duly entered in the Cash Book? Suggest any forms of Accounts or Voucher that would be conclusive on this point.

A.—In auditing Municipal Accounts, the general principles governing all audits must be observed, and it might be here noted that no audit can be worth much unless the Auditor is, or makes himself, thoroughly acquainted with all the details appertaining to the Accounts and Books and the method of procedure of the business or institution he may be auditing. He would also require to know the laws or regulations governing such business or institution, and in this question it is observed that the particular class of Municipality is not indicated. While the principle remains the same, a different procedure might be necessary in the case of a large city Municipality or a rural one, etc.

In ascertaining then whether all the Taxes had been entered in the Cash Book, the procedure would be to trace them to their original source as far as possible. In this instance, the information can be obtained from the Collectors' Rolls, which contain the complete list of taxes to be collected, and which are prepared from the Assessment Rolls after revision and after all appeals for alteration in Taxes have been duly settled and the Rates struck. The Collectors have to hand over the Taxes collected at stated intervals to the Treasurer, whose duty it is to enter them in the Cash Book, giving the Collectors a receipt therefor. These acknowledgments would afford additional vouchers to check the Cash Book with. The following points may then arise:—

(1) That the Treasurer had or had not entered all the Cash received by him from the Collectors.

(2) That the Collectors had not accounted to him for all the Taxes collected by them.

The Auditor's duty is to ascertain that all the Taxes collected have been accounted for. The question says to " satisfy yourself," It is feared that the majority of Municipal Auditors easily satisfy themselves on this important point, and in fact never audit such receipts beyond merely checking the additions of the Cash Book. This tracing of Taxes moreover is not an easy matter and involves a great deal of work. In all audits it is far more difficult to trace a Cash Receipt which has been omitted to be entered in a Cash Book than it is to audit the payments, though unfortunately few Auditors attach the importance to this that should be given. When the Cash is received, a stub giving the details of the Receipt given should be kept, and these stubs consecutively numbered can be compared with the Rolls; and apart from this, to ensure a practical proof of the correctness of the Taxes received, the following procedure could be adopted with advantage.

(a) From the Cash Book note the total amount of Taxes received.

(b) From the Collectors' Rolls make out the total of Taxes to be collected.

(c) From the Collectors' Report of Taxes which they are unable to collect, make out Taxes in arrear for current year.

Then (a) + (c) should = (b). If (c) is not available no conclusive proof can be given that all the Taxes as collected are accounted for.

Further, the Auditor should be satisfied that the arrears are correctly carried forward into the Collectors' Roll for the following year.

Although the Act prohibits the Treasurer from mixing such Receipts with his personal cash, it is too often done through carelessness. In fact, Treasurers have lost money by crediting too much to the Municipality, though certainly it is often the other way. A clear system of arriving at the total Taxes to be accounted for, as has here been attempted to be explained, would be a boon to most Treasurers, and should be permanently recorded.

Question 4.—The accounts of an Executorship Estate, comprising Cash, Mortgages, Shares and Real Estate, are presented to you for audit. You find that a Cash Book only has been kept. You are handed the Vouchers for payments, the securities and the Bank Pass Book. What are the successive steps to be taken to satisfy yourself that the Trust has been faithfully executed.

A.—A copy of the will should be examined and a memorandum made of all legacies, annuities, specific bequests, and other directions contained therein.

In auditing the Cash Book, the Auditor would have to ascertain that all amounts due to the Testator at the date of his death had been collected, or accounted for; that all the interest on the Mortgages and Shares and Rents had been accounted for; that all the legal debts owing by the estate had been paid, and that they agreed with the vouchers handed in; and, further, that the corpus represented the true amount. The Auditor would also ascertain that the terms of the will had been carried out, the proper legacies paid, etc., and that all duties had been paid.

As a matter of course, all the items in the Cash Book would be checked and compared with the vouchers. He would also see that the Securities and the Balance in the Bank Pass Book represented the undistributed portion of the estate.

The apportionment of the estate between Corpus and Income would have to be carefully examined, if there were residuary legatees.

Question 5.—What may occur to throw suspicion on the accuracy of alleged balances in the Bank, and what conclusive tests would you apply?

A.—It is somewhat difficult to know what is meant by this question.

Has a want of confidence arisen in the Cashier from his mode of life, etc? or has the Auditor in the course of his work noted discrepancies when checking the Bank Pass Book with the firm's books. Again, he might have noted that the Pass Book had been altered, or that the dates of entries did not correspond. Whether his suspicions were aroused or not, the conclusive tests he would apply would be as follows:—

To compare the Receipts and Payments with the Bank Pass Book and Bank Vouchers, and see that the balances agreed with his client's books, allowing for and scrutinizing all outstanding cheques right up to date. He would verify the correctness of the Bank Book by taking it himself to the Bank to see that it had not been tampered with.

An Auditor counts the cash, not that he suspects fraud, but that he may be enabled to verify as to its correctness, and so right through his audit.

Question 6.—Your are required by the Inspectors of an Insolvent Trader's Estate to verify the Trustees's Accounts. Stocks of Merchandise and Real Estate have been sold, Book Accounts collected, and there have been Losses upon discounted paper. There are disputed claims, both preference and ordinary. Dividends have been declared and paid. Detail your audit and what would your report to the Inspectors specifically mention?

A.—The Accounts would be audited first as to their clerical correctness; then the vouchers would be examined for all payments made, and care taken that they were all properly authorized. The Receipts would be carefully examined to see that they included the proceeds of the Stocks and Merchandise and Real Estate sold; that the proceeds of the Book Accounts realized have been all properly accounted for, in other words, that the Assets of the Insolvent Estate are represented by the payments made, including the Dividends, the Cash on hand and the Deficiency or Loss incurred in realization.

The Auditor, too, would examine the disputed claims, and possibly might throw some light thereon, though it might not be his duty to adjudicate thereon.

In his report he would state whether or not a fair sum, in his opinion, had been realized on the sale of the Assets, and would certify as to the correctness or not of the Accounts as handed to him, stating further that he had examined the Cash on hand set aside for the disputed claims, and found it correctly deposited or not in the Bank, and that it was sufficient for the purposes retained. He might also recommend a course to be adopted as to these disputed claims, showing how they should be properly classified and the precedence to be observed in settling the same.

Question 7.—What Check would you have upon Fictitious Entries showing purchases, also returns of goods sold?

A.—The examination of the Invoices themselves, with the entries in the Invoice Book, specially noting that they were initialled by a responsible officer or member of the firm as vouching for the receipt of the goods.

The same principle would apply in checking returns of goods sold. A register of such goods returned should be kept, and the person receiving back the goods should acknowledge the same.

In considering the question of Fictitious Entries, the matter of collusion should be looked into. Where different departments are conducted by different men the risk is much minimized. In large establishments properly conducted, the Cashiers have little opportunity of passing Fictitious Entries and getting them "properly" certified to.

In cases where duty is paid, this affords a check on the purchases, also freight charges, etc., but in actual practice this is difficult to apply. When fraud is known to have existed and the Auditor is specially looking therefor, it is a different matter.

Question 8.—What precautions do you deem necessary in ascertaining the list of Shareholders entitled to vote at an annual meeting of a Company?

A.—The list of Shareholders, as on date of annual meeting, may be described as the Trial Balance of the Stock Ledger, and the total thereof, will, or should, if correct, agree with the Capital Subscribed.

By comparing the Stock Ledger, first with the original shares issued, and calls (if any) subsequently made, seeing that none of these were in arrears, and checking all transfers made, sufficient precaution would have been taken.

Consequently, calling off the list with the Stock Ledger and checking the additions, would be sufficient check.

Question 9.—In a Private Banking Institution, how would you ascertain the amount for which checks had been charged to Depositors' Accounts, but not presented for payment.

A.—The only way this could be ascertained would be by calling over the Depositors' Accounts with the Cash Books, carefully noting the cheques which were not "ticked" in the Ledger. The cheques thus charged, and shown to be unpaid as far as the Banker was concerned, could be summarized and recorded.

This total would enable the balances in the Depositors' Ledger to be balanced with the Depositor's Account in General Ledger.

Question 10.—You are required to audit branch accounts of a Trading Company so far as practicable without visiting the branches. Can this be performed so as to ensure substantial accuracy, and if so, what would be your instructions respecting the information to be furnished?

A.—It can in certain businesses, especially where the selling price of goods is fixed; but there should be some system of check inaugurated by the Company itself, such as a periodical inspection of Stocks by their Inspector, proper record of sales kept, etc.

The Auditor would instruct that each Branch furnish daily or weekly returns, showing the exact business done, on a form to be specially prepared. The return would also show Receipts and Expenditure, which would be embodied in the Branch Account.

In the Head Office Ledger a separate account is opened for each Branch, and with advantage, in column form. Each Branch should be instructed to remit periodically to the Head Office all the Cash received. They would be allowed a certain standing amount of Cash for Expenses, and when sending forward the Cash for their Receipts, would also submit a statement for their Expenditure (as authorized for Expenses, Wages, etc.) with the Receipts, in return for which the Head Office would send them their cheque, thus replacing their Cash on hand to the proper amount. By this means each Branch Account would show in the Ledger on the Credit side all the Cash received, subdivided into suitable headings, and on the Debit side the amount of cheque remitted, also subdivided into Merchandise, Expenses, etc.

When Merchandise was sent to a Branch, the Branch would be charged under Merchandise column, and they would respond by crediting the Head Office, etc. Under this system, which by the way is not a theoretical one, but one in actual practice and working well, the Auditor can practically check the Accounts at the Head Office.

Careful scrutiny into the Accounts themselves will show if the results at the end of the year, or period, fairly tally with the business done.

CHAPTER XV.

INSOLVENCY.

Question 1.—State the main provisions of the statute governing the Winding up of the Estates of Insolvent Traders in Ontario?

A.—*The main provisions of the statute, viz., the Assignments and Preferences Act, are as follows:*

That confessions of judgment, cognovits, etc., in fraud of creditors, are void.

That assignments, etc., in prejudice of creditors, are void.

That all assignments for benefit of creditors are under the Act.

That property improperly disposed of can be recovered for the creditors.

Providing for the ranking of claims of creditors, appointment of assignees, steps to be taken, etc.

Providing that assignments take precedence of executions.

As to meetings of creditors, voting, proofs of claims, accounts and statement, what claims are preferential, etc.

As to dividends and remuneration of Assignee and Inspectors.

As to examination of Assignor, his affairs and accounts.

Question 2.—A trader places his estate in your hands, consisting of the following: Real Estate $10,000, mortgaged for $6,000, and interest overdue $300, interest accruing $120. Merchandise $8,000. Fixtures $250. Merchandise in Warehouse, $1,000, hypothecated for $300. Book Accounts, good, $1,500, doubtful $500, bad $3,000. Bills Receivable held by Bank $1,400, subject to an advance of

$1,050. Cash $25. His liabilities in addition to the above secured claims are: Rent $200, Taxes $70, Wages $125. Unsecured or Ordinary Claims (A.) $4,700, (B.) $3,200, (C.) $3,050, (D.) $1,850, (E.) $800, (F.) $650, (G.) $225 (H.) $40. There is also an Unsecured Disputed Claim of (K.) for $300. Prepare a statement for the meeting of creditors.

STATEMENT FOR MEETING OF CREDITORS.

Gross Liabilities.	Liabilities. (As stated and Estimated by Debtor.)		Expected to Rank.	Assets. (As Stated and Estimated by Debtor.)		Estimated to Produce.
	UNSECURED CREDITORS			PROPERTY.		
	A............	$4,700 00		A. Cash on hand.... $ 25 00		
	B............	3,200 00		B. Mdse..... 8,000 00		
	C............	3,050 00		C. Fixtures.. 250 00		
	D............	1,850 00				$8,275 00
	E............	800 00		BOOK ACCOUNTS,		
	F............	650 00		Good, as per list......		1,500 00
	G............	225 00		Doubtful, $500 ; estimated say		200 00
	H............	40 00		Bad, $3,000.		
			$14,515 00			
	K., disputed claim..	300 00		SURPLUS FROM SECURITIES in the hands of Creditors fully secured per contra.		
	SECURED CREDITORS,		$14,515 00			
	ADVANCE ON MORT'GE	6,300 00				
	Int. overdue accrued	120 00		Real Estate ..$3,580 00		
	Estimated value of Security, Real Estate	10,000 00		Merchandise.. 700 00 Bills Rec'v'ble 350 00		
						4,630 00
	Balance to contra ..	3,580 00				14,605 00
	ADVANCE ON MDSE ..	300 00		Deduct Creditors for distrainable rent, taxes and wages		
	Mdse. in Warehouse hypothecated	1,000 00				395 00
	Balance to contra ..	700 00		Net Assets (subject to realization)		14,210 00
	ADV'CE DUE TO BANK			Deficiency, as per statement................		305 00
	Secured by Lien on Bills	1,050 00				
	Amount of Bills Receivable	1,400 00				
	Balance to contra ..	350 00				
	Creditors for Rent, recov'ble	200 00				
	" " Taxes ..	70 00				
	" " Wages..	125 00				
	Deducted contra	395 00				
			$14,515 00			$14,515 00

Question 3.—What is the voting power of the several creditors of the estate at the meeting referred to, and how is this ascertained?

A.—The votes of creditors are calculated as follows:

For every claim of or over $100 00, and not exceeding $ 200 00, 1 vote
" " " " 200 00, " " 500 00, 2 votes
" " " " 500 00, " " 1,000 00, 3 "
" additional 1,000 00, or fraction thereof 1 vote

A creditor, however, whose vote is disputed, shall not be entitled to vote until he has filed with the Assignee an affidavit in proof of his claim, stating the amount and nature thereof, and proper vouchers.

The Secured Creditors would rank as regards voting on the value of their unsecured claim (if any); that is, on the difference between the admitted value (see section 20, clause 4 of the Act) of the security and the gross amount of the claim.

Applying these rules to the estate referred to, the Creditors would vote as follows:—

A. 7 votes.
B. 6 "
C. 6 "
D. 4 "
E. 3 "
F. 3 "
G. 2 "
H. 0 "
K. 2 " subject to his making a proper affidavit proving claim.

Question 4.—The Creditors decide to wind up the Estate. The Real Estate, Merchandise and Fixtures and Merchandise in Warehouse are to be sold by auction, and the Book Accounts collected. This having been done, they realize respectively $8,400, $4,800, $200, $560, and $1,900. The Bank realizes $1,250 from their securities. The expenses are : Assignee $200, Advertising $150, Auctioneer $270, Taking Stock $40, and Sundries $25. Prepare a Statement showing the Assignee's Account with the Estate, properly classified for the consideration of the Inspectors.

A.—STATEMENT BY ASSIGNEE, SHOWING RESULT OF REALIZATION OF ASSETS.

Nature of Property Sold.	Estimated Value.	Realized.		
		Secured to Creditors.	Unsecured.	Total.
Real Estate................	$10,000 00	$6,300 00	$2,100 00	$8,400 00
Merchandise................	8,000 00		4,800 00	4,800 00
Fixtures.....................	250 00		200 00	200 00
Merchandise (subject to hypothecation	1,000 00	300 00	260 00	560 00
Book Debts. ...	2,000 00		1,900 00	1,900 00
Bills Receivable (secured to bank)................	1,400 00	1,050 00	200 00	1,250 00
Cash on Hand..............	25 00		25 00	25 00
	$22,675 00	$7,650 00	$9,485 00	$17,135 00

Expenses:
Assignee.........$200 00				
Advertising...... 150 00				
Auctioneer 270 00				
Taking Stock.... 40 00				
Sundries 25 00				
$685 00	....	....	....	685 00
Available for Secured Creditors. $7,650 00			Balance..	$16,450 00

Unsecured Creditors.... ....$9,485 00
Less............... 685 00

$8,800 00

Question 5.—This Statement having been approved, prepare Statements showing the distribution among those entitled to the same.

Distribution of Cash Realized.

A.—Secured Creditors paid **in full**:

Mortgagee.	$6,300 00
Bank	1,050 00
Advance on Merchandise.....................	300 00
	$7,650 00

INSOLVENCY.

Unsecured Creditors paid as follows, receiving a Dividend of 60 cents on the dollar. Memo.—No further mention being made of the Unsecured Disputed Claim, K. $300, it has been assumed that it has been settled at $91 cash.

A., $4,700 00 receives	....	$2,820 00
B., 3,200 00	"	....	1,920 00
C., 3,050 00	"	....	1,830 00
D., 1,850 00	"	....	1,110 00
E., 800 00	"	....	480 00
F., 650 00	"	....	390 00
G., 225 00	"	....	135 00
H., 40 00	"	....	24 00
			$8,709 00

Question 6.—The Encumbered Assets of the Estate failing to realize the amount of such encumbrances respectively, what is the position of the parties and the Estate with respect to these several matters?

A.—In this Estate there are three Creditors, who are respectively secured as follows:

	Debt.	Value.
Mortgage, Real Estate	$6,420 00	$10,000 00
" Mdse.	300 00	1,000 00
Lien on Bills	1,050 00	1,400 00

In general practice, when there is a good margin of security as in this example, the Assignee, acting under the authority of the Creditors, would arrange with the Secured Creditors as to the disposal of it, and the Secured Creditors would be paid in full as a matter of course, or the Assignee could pay the debt and take the property. The Debtor can only assign the equity of redemption, and the Assignee might sell the property subject to the Mortgage.

In the question now being answered, we are asked to consider the position of these Creditors if their securities failed to realize the amount of their claim.

First, we will assume a fresh valuation of the securities, which will probably leave very little margin over the Debts, if any.

In cases where the Secured Creditor, anticipating that the security will not cover his Debt, puts in a claim for the Debt; he is required to value his security.

The Assignee may agree with this valuation and the Creditor would then rank as an Unsecured Creditor for the difference between his total debt and the amount of valuation, or the Assignee may require the Creditor to assign his security at an advance of ten per cent. upon the value so specified, to be paid out of the Estate as soon as such security is realized.

The Bank would also put in its claim in a similar way, but the security being based on negotiable instruments, the claim can be amended on the maturity of any of the bills.

Supposing Mortgagee valued his security at $5,000, and the debt was $6,420, if the Assignee agrees with this valuation the Mortgagee can rank as Unsecured Creditor for $1,420. Should the security realize at the sale referred to $5,500, this Creditor would receive all of it, and rank then as Unsecured for $920. Supposing, however, the Creditor valued the security at $4,500, the Assignee could act as before or make him assign the security to him (the Assignee) at $4,950 (valuation with advance of ten per cent.), he would then rank as Unsecured for $6,420—$4,950=$1,470; and would receive the $4,950 when security was realized, whatever it sold for.

Further, if the Creditor valued his security at say $6,000, the Assignee being satisfied that the valuation was a full one, could, under the authority of the Inspector or Creditors, let him retain the security and prove for the $420.

Question 7.—It is learned that the Insolvent is also a partner in another business. How would you exhibit this interest in the Statement prepared for the Creditors?

A.—The Act provides that on a motion passed by the Creditors at a regularly called meeting or on the request of the majority of the inspectors either in writing or by resolution, the Assignee can demand a proper Statement of the Debtor's affairs and his position in the partnership.

This would appear in the Statement either as an Asset or a Liability, probably the Insolvent would himself estimate the amount in the Statement and the Assignee's duty would be afterwards to confirm, as above, such valuation, etc.

Question 8.—The aforesaid Estate having been that of an incorporated Joint Stock Company, with Capital Stock subscribed $10,000, paid in $6,000 as follows:

L.	$2,000 00, paid in	$1,800 00
M	300 00, "	300 00
N	3,000 00, "	900 00
O	2,000 00, "	2,000 00
P	2,700 00, "	1,000 00

what alteration, if any, would be made in the form of statement prepared for the creditors?

A.—The form of Statement would be the same, with this addition, viz., that the Assets would be increased by an item of $4,000 (subject, of course, to realization). This Asset might be described as amount due by Contributories on their Stock.

The Asset would then be shown at $18,210.00 (see answer to Question 2).

Question 9.—What is the procedure in dealing with Shareholders in winding up a Joint Stock Company.

A.—The Liquidator settles the list of Contributories.

(a) Every Shareholder is liable to contribute the amount unpaid on his shares of the Capital.

(b) Where a Shareholder has transferred his shares under circumstances which do not by law free him from liability in respect thereof, or where he is by law liable to the Company or its Contributories or any of them, to an amount beyond the amount unpaid on his shares, he shall be deemed a member of the Company for the purposes of this Act, and shall be liable to contribute as aforesaid to the extent of his Liabilities to the Company or the Contributories independently of this Act, and the amount which he is so liable to contribute shall be deemed Assets and a Debt as aforesaid.

(c) The list of Contributories shall distinguish between persons who are Contributories as being representatives of or liable for others.

(d) It shall not be necessary where the personal representative of a deceased contributory is placed on the list to add the heirs or devisees of such contributory; nevertheless such heirs or devisees may be added at any time afterwards.

Any list so settled shall be prima facie evidence of the liability of the persons named therein to be Contributories.

The list may further be settled by the Court; see Revised Statutes of Ontario, cap. 222, section 15.

The Liquidators have the power at any time to call on all or any of the Contributories, as they may deem necessary. See same Act, section 17.

Question 10.—If, after realizing upon the Company's Assets there is sufficient to pay the Creditors, and $1,000 to spare, without making a further call upon the Shareholders, prepare a Statement exhibiting their interests respectively, also Statement showing final contribution.

A.—This $1,000 would be divisible amongst the Shareholders in proportion to their number of shares, if all were on an equal footing. To adjust the Accounts the $4,000 unpaid must be added to this amount, as if duly collected.

L...............	$2,000 00	receives	1-5th	=	$1,000 00
M...............	300 00	"	3-100ths	=	150 00
N...............	3,000 00	"	3-10ths	=	1,500 00
O...............	2,000 00	"	1-5th	=	1,000 00
P...............	2,700 00	"	27-100ths	=	1,350 00
	$10,000 00				$5,000 00

This division is, however, subject to the unpaid calls, which must be adjusted as per next Statement, to settle the Contributories' Accounts amongst themselves.

	Amount Subscribed.	Amount Unpaid on Shares.	Amount of Dividend.	BALANCES.	
				Net Balance Due.	Amount to credit of Shareholder.
L.	$2,000 00	$ 200 00	$1,000 00		$ 800 00
M.	300 00		150 00		150 00
N.	3,000 00	2,100 00	1,500 00	$600 00	
O.	2,000 00		1,000 00		1,000 00
P.	2,700 00	1,700 00	1,350 00	350 00	

FINAL BALANCE SHEET.

Liabilities.			Assets.		
L., due to him.	$ 800 00		Cash on hand		$1,000 00
M. " "	150 00		N. owes..	$600	
O. " "	1,000 00		P. " ..	350	950 00
		$1,950 00			$1,950 00

MEMO.—If N. or P. are unable to pay their Debts, the accounts of L., M., & O. would require further adjustment, as any further loss would have to be borne by them pro rata.

CHAPTER XVI.

INSOLVENCY.

Question 1.—What are the advantages, or otherwise, of a Federal Bankruptcy Act?

For answer to this question see page 198.

Question 2.—What are the duties and powers of Inspectors of an Insolvent Estate?

A.—Under the Assignments and Preferences Act, the Inspector's duties are not very distinctly defined. His duties consist in seeing that the Estate is disposed of in accordance with the directions of the Creditors, as given in General Meeting, and failing any instructions can remunerate the Assignee. He can require the Assignee to pay a dividend whenever he considers the funds available, and it can safely be paid, making allowances for disputed claims, etc.

He, or a majority of the Inspectors, can give the necessary authority to the Assignee to obtain from the Debtor any Books or Statements required to ascertain his affairs.

In short, his duties would be to advise the Assignee generally in dealing with the Assets, which, by the way, he cannot himself purchase.

Under the Winding-up Companies Act, R. S. O. 1897, cap. 222, his duties and powers are more clearly defined, if such an appointment is made.

His, or their duties are to superintend and direct the proceedings of the Liquidator in the Management and Winding up of the Estate; and all the powers of the Liquidator must be exercised subject to the advice and direction of the Inspectors, or Inspector, if only one is appointed.

His appointment is subject to revocation by the Members of the Company at any meeting subsequent to the one in which he was appointed.

The Inspector has power, in the absence of instructions being given by the Members of the Company, to instruct the Liquidator how to dispose of the property, real or personal, of the Company.

Question 3.—(a) What does a General Assignment under the Assignments and Preferences Act vest in the Assignee?

(b) Need a Deed of Assignment, to be operative under the Act, include the whole of a Debtor's effects except those exempt from seizure or sale under execution?

A.—(a) It vests in the Assignee all the real and personal estate, rights, property, credits and effects, whether vested or contingent, belonging at the time of the assignment to the Assignor, except such as are by law exempt from seizure, or sale under execution, subject however as regards lands, to the provisions of the registry law as to the registration of the Assignment.

(b) No, section 6 of the Act provides that such an assignment would hold and the effects so assigned would come under the provisions of said Act.

Question 4.—In case of an Assignment by two persons who were co-partners, and who had individual Assets and Liabilities as well as Partnership Assets and Liabilities, how would these be dealt with?

A.—The rule in this case is that the claims shall rank first upon the Estate by which the debts they represent were contracted, and shall only rank upon the other or others after all the Creditors of such other Estate or Estates have been paid in full.

Question 5.—What do you understand by a "fraudulent preference"? Give examples.

A.—When any person is unable to pay his debts as they become due, or knowing himself to be on the eve of insolvency, voluntarily or by collusion with a creditor or creditors, gives a confession of judgment, cognovit actionem or warrant of attorney to confess judgment with intent, in giving such confession, cognovit actionem, or warrant of attorney to confess judgment, to defeat or delay his creditors wholly or in part, or with intent thereby to give one or more of the creditors of any such person a preference over his other creditors, or over any one or more of such creditors, such preference is termed a fraudulent preference. Also any gifts, transfer, etc., of the debtor's property made with the intent to defraud or prejudice creditors, and any gift, transfer, etc., made to one creditor to give him an unjust preference over another creditor, are fraudulent preferences.

Examples.

A debtor giving a chattel mortgage when he is insolvent to a creditor knowing his position.

A debtor returning goods to the wholesale merchant from whom he bought after he knows himself to be insolvent, such return of goods being in the shape or in lieu of a payment.

Question 6.—What do you understand by the "double ranking" of Chartered Banks?

A.—In the event of the property and assets of the Bank being insufficient to pay its debts and liabilities, each Shareholder of the Bank shall be liable for the deficiency to an amount equal to the par value of the shares held by him, in addition to any amount not paid up on such shares.

This is double the liability of a Shareholder in an ordinary Joint Stock Company, hence the term, "double ranking."

Question 7.—What are the rights of the first execution creditor as to his costs, and how should he proceed to collect them?

A.—He has a lien for his costs on the property seized under the execution which he could retain until paid, or obtain the amount from the assignee or his guarantee or undertaking to pay the same.

Question 8.—(a) How are Rent and Wages preferred, and to what extent?

(b) Have preference creditors for Rent, Wages, etc., any vote at a meeting of creditors, their claims being only proven?

A.—(a) Rent is preferred for one year previous to the date of assignment and three months following, and as long as assignee shall occupy the premises.

Should, however, there be no distrainable effects on said premises the landlord would only rank as an ordinary creditor. Wages or salaries of all employees at date of assignment or within one month previous, not exceeding three month's Wages or Salary will rank as preferred claims. For any further balance owing they would rank as ordinary claims.

(b) Generally speaking, all creditors who have proved their claims by affidavit, and such vouchers as the nature of the case admits of, are entitled to vote in accordance with the regulations laid down in the Act, R. S. O. 1897, cap. 147, section 20.

It might perhaps here be noticed that in the case of a Joint Stock Company, the Directors are liable for one year's Wages due, subject to certain conditions for recovering the same.

See The Ontario Companies Act, section 85.

See The Ontario Companies Mining Companies Incorporation Act, section 8.

Under "The Companies Act" (Dom.), however, six months Wages due is the limit. See the Act, section 60.

Question 9.—The Assets of an Insolvent Estate realize $20,000. The total expenses to be deducted therefrom are $1,200. The liabilities to creditors are $35,000, and the bills of customers under discount with the Bank (endorsed by the Insolvent firm) amount to $10,000. How would you proceed to distribute the Assets available for dividend?

A.—The amount available for dividend to the creditors is $20,000 less $1,200, viz., $18,800.

The liabilities to creditors are $35,000 and the Bank has a claim to rank as a creditor for any loss on the bills discounted, which amount to $10,000.

Assuming that none of the bills will be paid, the amount due to creditors would be $45,000, which is the $35,000 mentioned and the $10,000 against Bills. It is taken for granted also that none of the Bank's claim has been included in the said $35,000.

The Bank in the case assumed would be entitled to 10-45 of the dividend, or say, $4,178; so by retaining this amount to pay the Bank, when its claim is fixed, an equal dividend with the other creditors, and making the largest provision therefor which could be required, the balance, $14,622 could be safely distributed amongst the creditors whose claims amount to $35,000.

When the value of the Bills is settled at their maturity, the Bank would be paid dividend at same rate as the creditors have received, on its unsecured claim, and the balance of cash on hand (probably a fair amount) would be equally divided amongst all the creditors (including the Bank).

Question 10.—What is meant by a discharge in Bankruptcy? How can an Insolvent Trader obtain a complete discharge?

A.—A discharge in Bankruptcy cannot at present date be obtained in Canada, as there is no Bankruptcy Act in force as regards Insolvent Traders. Such a discharge means that the Insolvent is released from any further liability as to the debts created prior to the date of his becoming bankrupt and surrendering his estate for the benefit of his creditors. Such a discharge would only be given on proof that such Bankruptcy was not fraudulent; and is usually refused (except perhaps at some future date) where a very small dividend is only payable to the creditors.

An Insolvent Trader in Ontario can obtain a complete discharge by all his creditors undertaking to release him, or accepting a composition of so many cents on the dollar in full discharge of his debts.

CHAPTER XVII.

INSOLVENCY.

Companies.

Question 1.—Describe the procedure necessary to place a Company in voluntary liquidation.

A.—A general meeting of the Shareholders for the special purpose must be called in accordance with the Act or by the By-laws of the Company, if mentioned therein.

If the period for which the Company was incorporated has expired, or where the event (if any) has occurred, the occurrence of which provided in the Charter that the Company is to be dissolved, and the Company in general meeting has passed a resolution requiring the Company to be wound up, then the Company can be wound up under the "Joint Stock Companies Winding-up Act," R. S. O. cap. 222, sec. 4, and may proceed to liquidate.

"Where the Company (though it may be solvent as respects creditors) has passed an extraordinary resolution to the effect that it has been proved to their satisfaction that the Company cannot by reason of its liabilities continue its business, and that it is advisable to wind up the same, it may also be wound up under said Act.

Where the Company has passed a "special resolution" requiring the Company to be wound up, it may be wound up under such Act.

"'Extraordinary resolution' shall mean a resolution passed by a majority of not less than three-fourths of such members of the Company, for the time being entitled to vote, as may be present in person, or by proxy (in cases where by the Act or Charter or instrument of incorporation or the regulations of the Company proxies are allowed), at any general meeting of which notice specifying the intention to propose such resolution has been duly given."

" Special resolution " shall mean a resolution passed in the manner necessary for an extraordinary resolution, where the resolution after having been so passed as aforesaid, has been confirmed by a majority of such members (entitled according to the Act, Charter or instrument of incorporation or the regulations of the Company to vote) as may be present, in person or by proxy, at a subsequent general meeting of which notice has been duly given, and held at an interval of not less than fourteen days, or more than one month from the date of meeting at which the resolution was first passed. R. S. O. 1897, cap. 222, sec. 3."

N.B.—The winding up or liquidation of the Company shall be deemed to commence at the time of the passing of the resolution authorizing the winding up.

Question 2.—(a) Having been appointed Liquidator of a Company provisionally, what is the extent of your authority for the purpose of dealing with the estate?

(b) What, if any, further powers are vested in you upon confirmation of your appointment?

A.—(a) **Subject to the superintendence and** direction of the Inspector, or **Inspectors,** if any are appointed, the Provisional Liquidator's powers would be:

To settle a list of contributories:

To bring or defend actions;

To carry on business as far as beneficial to the winding up;

To sell the property of the Company;

To sell the debts, due to the Company, " en bloc," if all efforts have been made to collect them severally;

To draw, accept, etc., Notes and Bills of Exchange on behalf of the Company;

To take out, if necessary, letters of administration to deceased contributories, and collect debt;

To execute deeds, receipts and other documents in name of Company;

To do everything that may be necessary for the winding up of the affairs of the Company, and the distribution of its Assets.

(b) No further powers are vested. The members of the Company have power to retain the liquidator, or dispense with his services, after remunerating him therefor.

Question 3.—What is the authority for staying liquidation proceedings when it is contemplated resuming operations under the Company's Charter?

A.—The Court, upon application by any Contributory, and upon proper proof to the satisfaction of the Court, may make an order staying all proceedings in relation to the winding up of the Company, subject, however, to such terms as the Court deems fit. R. S. O. 1897, cap. 222, sec. 33.

Question 4.—Prepare a statement of the affairs of a Joint Stock Company for a meeting of Shareholders, a winding-up order having been made. The following is substantially the Company's position :—

Sundry Creditors, unsecured	$10,000 00
Rent Payable	100 00
Capital subscribed, 65 % paid in	15,000 00
Provision for doubtful Book Accounts	800 00
Profit and Loss Account, Dr.	1,000 00
Merchandise	2,000 00
Book Accounts	4,000 00
Real Estate	3,500 00
Mortgaged for $1,500.	
Bills under Discount	1,850 00
Cash in Bank	50 00

Write out a short review (say 200 words) of the Company's position, you being Liquidator, and presumed to have gone critically into every feature.

A.— STATEMENT.

Liabilities.			Assets.		
SUNDRY CREDITORS, UNSECURED		$10,000 00	PROPERTY, Cash in Bank	$ 50 00	
SECURED CREDITORS.. Real Estate	$1,500 00 3,500 00		Merchandise on hand	2,000 00	$2,050 00
Carried to contra	2,000 00		BOOK ACCOUNTS Less provision	4,000 00 800 00	3,200 00
PREFERRED CREDITOR, Rent payable	100 00		CONTRIBUTORIES, 35 % on Capital subscribed		5,250 00
Carried to contra					
CONTINGENT LIABIL'TY Bills under discount	1,850 00		SURPLUS FROM REAL ESTATE, as per contra		2,000 00
CAPITAL SUBSCRIBED..	15,000 00				12,500 00
		15,000 00	LESS PREFERRED PAYMENTS, Distrainable Rent..		100 00
			Assets available for Dividend to Creditors....		12,400 00
			Balance at Dr., Profit and Loss	1,000 00	
			Deficiency, as per special report, showing causes therefor	11,000 00	12,600 00
		$25,000 00			$25,000 00

Liquidator's Review.

As shown by the statement which is appended hereto the Unsecured Liabilities amount to $10,000. The Secured Creditors are well covered at the valuations affixed, and the securities held by them seem thoroughly reliable. As regards the Bills under discount at the Bank, they may be regarded as safe, any other than A1 paper having been for some time refused by the Manager.

The Merchandise should realize about $1,200, as, unfortunately, owing to the glut in the market and fall in prices in this particular line, it is difficult to find purchasers.

The Books and Statements, and all Vouchers have been carefully examined into. The provision of $800 made for the Book Debts seems ample. There are a few outstanding liabilities, however, which, having only just been ascertained, could not be included in the statement which was printed for distribution in accordance with directions. They are as follows:

Wages, due and owing, as per Wages Book	$ 35 00
Salaries	48 00
Taxes	83 00
Interest owing on Mortgage and accrued	117 60
	$283 60

This amount will have to be deducted from the Assets available for dividend to the Unsecured Creditors. There appears good reason for hoping that the Creditors will receive a big dividend, as the Contributories are men of good average means. I have only touched on a few points, but have reported fully as to the causes of the deficiency in my special report on the Deficiency Account.

Question 5.—(a) What classes of persons may be Contributories in winding-up proceedings?

(b) What is the legal effect of the settlement of a person's name upon a list of Contributories?

A.—(a) Shareholders of the Company at time of winding-up.

Shareholders who have transferred their shares under circumstances which do not by law free them from liability in respect thereof.

Shareholders who are by law liable to the Company or its Contributories, or any of them, to an amount beyond the amount unpaid on their shares.

Contributories may be also divided into two classes, those who are Contributories as being representatives of or liable for others, and those who are Contributories as being liable in their own right.

(b) It is prima facie evidence of the liability of the person named therein to be a Contributory.

Question 6.—You are asked to advise whether an Insolvent Company can more effectively and equitably be wound up under the provisions of the Federal or the Provincial Acts in that behalf. State clearly the circumstances upon which your opinion would be based, and your conclusions therefrom.

A.—The answer to this question is one of fact as to which Act the Company must be wound up under, and not as to considering whether the Company can more effectively and equitably be wound up under the provisions of the Federal or the Provincial Acts in that behalf.

If the Creditors are going to wind up the Company they must apply under the Dominion Winding-up Act, cap. 129, as this Act is in the nature of an Insolvency Law, but if the Company is going to voluntarily wind up, or a Shareholder is petitioning therefor it must be wound up under the Provincial Act.

On a petition of certain Shareholders of a Company praying for a winding-up order under the Dominion Winding-up Act, cap. 129, it was held that that statute was intended to be put into operation at the instance of Creditors only.

If the Company had a choice it would certainly elect to be wound up under the Provincial Act, as therein it is provided that it conducts the winding-up, appoints inspectors, liquidators, etc. Under the Dominion Act, cap. 129, the winding-up may be briefly summarised as being conducted under the directions of the Court.

It has been assumed that "the Company" referred to was incorporated under the Provincial Companies Act. In the case of a Trading Company, incorporated under the Dominion Act, applying to be wound up either on its own petition or on the petition of a Shareholder, it would be wound up under the "Winding-up Amendment Act, 1889."

Traders.

Question 7.—How may claims be **legally** barred when Creditors decline to value their security within the specified time?

A.—" In case a person claiming to be entitled to rank on the estate assigned holds security **for his claim or any part** thereof, of such a nature that he is required by **the Act to value** the same, and he fails to value such security, the Judge of the County Court of the county wherein **the** debtor at the time of making the assignment **resided** or carried **on** business, may, upon summary application by the assignee or by any other person interested in the debtor's estate of which application three days' notice shall be given to such claimant, order that unless a specified value shall be placed on such security and notified in writing to the assignee within a time to be limited by the order, such claimant shall, in respect of the claim, or the part thereof for which the security is held, in case the security is held for part only of the claim, be wholly barred of any right to share in the proceeds of such estate; and if a specified value is not placed on such security, and notified in writing to the assignee according to the exigency of the said order, or within such further time as the said Judge may by subsequent order allow, the said claim, or the said part, as the case may be, shall be wholly barred as against such estate, but without prejudice to the liability of the debtor thereof." R. S. O. 1897, cap. 147, sec. 20.

Question 8.—What is the status, at a meeting of creditors, of a Creditor :—

(a) Whose claim has not been formally proven?

(b) Whose claim is disputed?

(c) Whose claim is for an account not yet matured?

A.—(a) He could vote if his claim is admitted, in accordance with the rules laid down in the Assignments and Preferences Act.

Memo.—Only creditors having proved claims can vote on a motion to change the assignee.

See section 8 of the Act.

(b) He cannot so vote until he has filed with the Assignee an affidavit, and in proof of his claim stating the amount and nature thereof.

(c) He is entitled to prove under the assignment and vote at meetings of Creditors, but in ascertaining the amount of any such claim a deduction for interest shall be made for the time which has to run until the claim becomes due.

Question 9.—State clearly the rights of an Assignee, with respect to Hypothecated Securities composing a portion of the estate?

A.—The Assignee has had assigned to him all the Debtor's property, and included therein the equity of redemption in all Hypothecated Securities. He has, then, the power, if authorized, to sell the securities subject to mortgages on them, to redeem the mortgages if they are payable on demand, or by their conditions, or to arrange with the mortgagee so that the properties can be sold to the best advantage, the mortgagee dealing with the Assignee as he would have done with the debtor before he assigned.

Further, the Assignee can require the Secured Creditor to put a specific value on his security, and (under the authority of the Creditors) he may either consent to the right of the Creditor to rank for the claim after deducting such valuation, or he may require from the Creditor an assignment of the security at an advance of ten per cent. upon such value, to be paid out of the estate as soon as the Assignee has realized such security.

If a Creditor holds a claim based upon negotiable instruments upon which the Debtor is only indirectly or secondarily liable, and which is not mature, such Creditor shall put a value on the liability of the party primarily liable therein; but after the maturity of such liability and its non-payment he shall be entitled to amend and revalue his claim; and the Creditors' rights will be the same as in the preceding paragraph.

Where the Creditor holding the security fails to value the same, the Assignee may make summary application to the Judge of the County Court of the county wherein the Debtor at the time of making the assignment resided or carried on business, three days notice of such application being given to such Creditor, and the Judge may order that unless a specified value be placed on such security and notified in writing to the Assignee within a term to be limited by the order, such Creditor shall, in respect of his claim, or the secured part thereof, in case part only is secured, be wholly barred of any right to share in the proceeds of such estate; and if a specified value is not placed on such security, and notified in writing to the Assignee, according to the exigency of the said order, or within such further time as the said Judge may by subsequent order allow, the said claim, or the said part, as the case may be, shall be wholly barred as against such estate, but without prejudice to the liability of the Debtor thereof.

Question 10.—If a Bankrupt refuses to execute an Assignment of his estate for the benefit of his Creditors, what course should be pursued in their interests generally?

A.—As a general practice each Creditor looks after his own interests, but in such a case as mentioned, where the Creditors appear to have met and the Debtor has refused to Assign his estate, one of them should obtain an execution against the Debtor's property and place it in the hands of the Sheriff for him to realize the amount thereof, and the rest of the Creditors should prove at once their claims against the Debtor in the manner prescribed by the Creditors' Relief Act (R. S. O. 1897, cap. 78), and the Sheriff would then divide the moneys realized under the execution among all the Creditors pro rata. If the debtor has other property not sold by the Sheriff under the execution, the Sheriff would make further sales of the Debtor's property to realize enough to pay the Creditor's claims.

In the question the term Bankrupt is used which seems to imply that the Debtor has committed an act of insolvency. Probably, then, writs have already been taken out. The remaining Creditors would then have to follow suit and do likewise or prove their claims as above mentioned to come under this Act. If it becomes necessary to follow up any property unlawfully transferred or disposed of, one Creditor can represent the other Creditors in a suit at law, and the benefits obtained, if any, will accrue to them all. Creditors for debts not due, and payable at some future date, have practically no remedy under the circumstances narrated.

CHAPTER XVIII.

INSOLVENCY.

Question 1.—Give your views as concisely as possible as to the benefit to be derived from Federal rather than Provincial Bankruptcy Laws.

A.—The question seems to imply that each Province could pass its own Bankruptcy Act, which is not the case, as by the provisions of the British North America Act this privilege is reserved to the Dominion Parliament.

If, however, each Province could do so, it is obvious that the disadvantages which would arise from the different laws thus enforced would be far counterbalanced by a uniform Federal Bankruptcy Act, especially considering how interwoven is the trade between the various provinces.

Foreign countries, too, would have far more confidence in trading with Canada as a whole, knowing that her merchants were subject to the provisions of a wise Dominion Bankruptcy Act.

Question 2.—(a) Under what circumstances is the giving of security under pressure to a Creditor, by a Debtor who knows he is on the eve of Insolvency, presumed to have been given with intent to give the Creditor an unjust preference?

(b) Would pressure by the Creditor validate such a transaction if it occurred more than sixty days before proceedings were taken to set it aside or an assignment made?

A.—(a) Every assignment or transfer of property, real or personal, made by a person at a time when he is in insolvent circumstances, or is unable to pay his debts in full, or knows that he is on the eve of Insolvency, to or for a Creditor with intent to give such Creditor an unjust preference over his other Creditors, or over any one or more of them, shall, as against the Creditor or Creditors injured or prejudiced, be utterly void.

If such transaction with or for a Creditor has the effect of giving that Creditor a preference over the other Creditors or over any one or more of them, it shall be presumed prima facie to have been made with the intent aforesaid, and to be an unjust preference within the meaning of the Act, whether the same be made voluntarily or under pressure, if the Debtor within sixty days after the transaction makes an assignment for the benefit of his Creditors, or if any action or proceeding is brought within sixty days after such transaction to impeach or set aside such transaction. R. S. O. 1897, cap. 147, sec. 2.

(b) Yes, pressure would validate such a transaction.

Question 3.—A Creditor obtains judgment and execution against his Debtor and places it in the Sheriff's hands. The Sheriff seizes the Debtor's goods and realizes the amount of the judgment. The Debtor assigns. Is the Creditor or Assignee entitled to the money in the Sheriff's hands, and why?

A.—The Assignee is entitled to the money in the Sheriff's hands, subject to the lien of the Execution Creditor for his costs, because an assignment for the benefit of Creditors takes precedence over an Execution Creditor. R. S. O. 1897, cap. 147, sec. 11.

Question 4.—(A) Are there any differences between a Sole Trader and a Limited Company as to a condition of Insolvency? If so, enumerate them.

A.—(A) The appended statement marked (1) will define a condition of Insolvency in a Sole Trader; the Winding-up Act states what constitutes a Company Insolvent. Statement (2) gives the various points as laid down in Act referred to.

Now, we are asked what differences there are between the Sole Trader and the Limited Company as to a "condition of Insolvency." Practically speaking there are not many, but there are one or two.

In the case of the Limited Company there is an Act provided, in the case of the Trader there is none (at present) in Canada. If he once gets into the condition of Insolvency he can, as a rule, remain there; true, he can assign his estate, but is not released from paying his Creditors in full.

The Act provides that a Company is deemed Insolvent under clause (h), see statement (2). This would not prove a Trader to be in a condition of Insolvency, though it might be evidence in that direction.

Further, a Company is deemed to be unable to pay its debts as they become due, and, therefore, insolvent, whenever a Creditor to whom the Company is indebted in a sum exceeding two hundred dollars then due, has served on the Company in the manner in which process may legally be served on it in the place where service is made, a demand in writing, requiring the Company to pay the sum so due, and the Company has, for ninety days, in the case of a Bank, and for sixty days in all other cases, next succeeding the service of the demand, neglected to pay such sum or to secure or compound for the same to the satisfaction of the Creditor.

A Sole Trader is subject to no such test as this, whereby he is rendered insolvent.

Statement 1.

A Sole Trader may be deemed in insolvent circumstances if he does not pay his way, and is unable to meet the current demands of Creditors, and if he has not the means of paying them in full out of his Assets realized upon a sale for cash or its equivalent.

Statement 2.

By the Dominion Winding-up Act, R. S. O. cap. 129, sec. 5, a Company is deemed insolvent,

(a) If it is unable to pay its debts as they become due;

(b) If it calls a meeting of its Creditors for the purpose of compounding with them;

(c) If it exhibits a statement showing its inability to meet its liabilities;

(d) If it has otherwise acknowledged its insolvency;

(e) If it assigns, removes or disposes of or attempts, or is about to assign, remove or dispose of, any of its property, with intent to defraud, defeat or delay its creditors, or any of them;

(f) If, with such intent, it has procured its money, goods, chattels, lands or property, to be seized, levied on or taken, under or by any process or execution.

(g) If it has made any general conveyance or assignment of its property for the benefit of its Creditors, or if, being unable to meet its liabilities in full, it makes any sale or conveyance of the whole or the main part of its stock in trade or assets, without the consent of its Creditors or without satisfying their claims.

(h) If it permits any execution issued against it, under which any of its goods, chattels, land or property are seized, levied upon or taken in execution, to remain unsatisfied till within four days of the time fixed by the Sheriff or proper officer for the sale thereof, or for fifteen days after such seizure.

(B) The Balance Sheet of a firm is summarized as under:—

Liabilities.		Assets.	
To Creditors	$16,500 00	Cash, Stock and Debts	$22,500 00
" Capital	12,500 00	Fixed Assets	5,000 00
	$29,000 00		$27,500 00

Would you consider this firm Insolvent? Give your reasons.

A.—(B) Presuming that all Liabilities and Assets are shown in this statement, there is a deficiency or impairment of Capital to the extent of $1,500. This would affect the Shareholders, certainly, as proprietors of the business, but as regards its Creditors the firm is absolutely solvent on the face of it, if the valuations of the Assets are correct, and even if not there is a large margin in reserve. The amount of Debts or Stock is not stated, and no Chartered Accountant would give an opinion as asked for without proper details and full information.

Under the "Winding-up Amendment Act, 1889," if this Company should be incorporated under the Dominion Act:

The Court may make a winding-up order—" inter alia ";

When the Capital Stock of the Company is impaired to the extent of twenty-five per cent. thereof, and when it is shown to the satisfaction of the Court that the lost Capital will not likely be restored within one year.

This does not apply to the Company in question, as taking the total Assets as correct, their capital is only impaired $1,500.

Question 5.—(a) Creditors may substitute one Assignee for another. What proportion in number or value of Creditors is required?

(b) Must such proportion be represented at the meeting at which the change of Assignee be made?

A.—(a) A majority in number and value of the Creditors who have proved claims to the amount of $100 and upwards.

(b) Yes, necessarily, either personally or by proxy.

Question 6.—(a) What claims upon an Insolvent Estate are "preferred," and to what extent?

(b) Would an Auditor's fee be a preferred claim in your opinion?

(c) John Brown is an agent on commission for Joyce & Co. The firm fails, owing Brown $500. How would you class his claim in the Statement of Affairs, and why?

A.—(a) *Rent*—The landlord is a Preferential Creditor as regards rent, provided there are distrainable effects, otherwise he ranks as a general Creditor only.

His claim is preferred as follows:

Arrears of rent due during the period of one year last previous to, and for three months following the execution of the assignment, and from thence so long as the Assignee shall retain possession of the premises leased.

Wages of all persons in the employment of the Debtor at the time of making the assignment, or within one month before the making thereof, are preferred as follows:

> Not exceeding three months wages or salary, and such persons to whom these wages are owing are entitled to rank as Ordinary and General Creditors for the residue, if any, of their claims.

Taxes cannot strictly be called "preferred claims," as the Assignee must pay such, the assignment not protecting him against this being duly collected, or charged against the property in question.

Such claims as Gas and Telephone are practically, though not by enactment preferred, as to save such services being discontinued the Assignee may have to pay what is owing.

(b) An Auditor's fee is not a preferred claim.

(c) He would rank as a General Creditor, because his claim for $500 could not, even if for commission, rank as preferred.

Question 7.—A Creditor proves a claim against an Estate for $8,000, and values his security at $2,000. The Assignee elects to take the security at $2,000 and the prescribed advance of 10%.

(a) When is the $2,000 and the 10% advance, or $200, to be paid to the Creditor?

(b) What is the Creditor's remedy in case of undue delay?

A.—(a) The $2,000 and the 10% advance is to be paid to the Creditor when the security is sold, which must be within a reasonable time.

(b) He can apply to the Court for an order demanding that the security be realized, or he could make an application to have the Assignee removed.

Question 8.—If an Assignee in carrying out a scheme of settlement of a Debtor's affairs, remains in charge of the business by keeping the Debtor on as Manager, and such person buys necessary goods on credit for the business, what is the legal position of the Assignee?

A.—The Assignee could, to enable the estate to be more profitably realized as a going concern, retain the Debtor on as Manager, as stated in the question. His position would entitle him to pay for such necessary goods, and also remunerate the Manager out of the funds of the Estate.

Memo.— If, however, the Assignee or Manager incurred more debts than the Estate could pay, the Assignee would be personally liable therefor.

Question 9.—If a Creditor of an Insolvent Trader wishes certain proceedings taken and the Assignee declines to take them, what remedy has the Creditor ? Wherein, if at all, is the right of the Creditor varied, if dealing with the Liquidator of a Joint Stock Company being wound up under R. S. O. cap. 222.

A.—Under the Ontario Assignment Act, if any Creditor desires to cause any proceedings to be taken which, in his opinion, would be for the benefit of the Estate, and the Assignee under the authority of the Creditors or Inspectors having refused to take such proceedings, the Creditor can obtain an order from the Judge authorizing him to take the proceedings in the name of the Assignee, at his own expense and risk, and upon such terms as to indemnity to the Assignee as the Judge may direct, and any benefit arising therefrom shall be for his own benefit to the extent of his claim and costs.

But if the Assignee expresses his willingness to the Judge to institute these proceedings before the order is granted, said order shall prescribe the time within which it shall be done; the benefits will then appertain to the Estate.

Under the Winding-up Act referred to, R. S. O. cap. 222, the Creditor would have no status as shown above, but he could appeal, no doubt, to the Court, which could issue the necessary instructions; but the Liquidator would carry out these instructions, not the Creditor, and presumably for the benefit of all concerned.

Question 10.—A claim is filed with an Assignee (of which he has no previous knowledge) after the Estate has been divided. What is the Assignee's liability to pay such Creditor the same rate of Dividend as was paid to the other Creditors?

A.—If the Assignee has carried out the proper regulations as to registration and published the proper notices, etc., in accordance with the Act, he would not personally be liable to pay such Creditor anything. It would appear, however that such Creditor has a right to compel the other Creditors to put him on an equal footing with then, and make them return sufficient for this purpose.

The Assignee should endeavour to ascertain all the Debts, whether they are proved or not.

CHAPTER XIX.

NEGOTIABLE INSTRUMENTS.

Question 1.—Define the difference between " Negotiable " Promissory Notes and " Not Negotiable " Promissory Notes. Illustrate by examples.

A.—" Negotiable " Promissory Notes are such as are transferable either by endorsement and delivery or by simple delivery. " Not Negotiable " Notes contain words prohibiting such a transfer or indicating an intention that they should not be transferable. When a Note is made payable either to a certain person, or to his order, it is negotiable by endorsement and delivery; when made payable to bearer, or to a certain person or bearer, it may then be negotiated by delivery without endorsement.

(NEGOTIABLE.)

$100.   Toronto, Nov. 1, 1898.

Three months after date, I promise to pay to the order of A. Brown, at the Bank of Commerce here, One Hundred Dollars, for value received.   John Smith.

The above Note is negotiable by endorsement and delivery, and would have exactly the same effect if, instead of " pay to the order of A. Brown," it read: " pay to A. Brown " or " pay to A. Brown or order." If it read " pay to A. Brown or bearer," it could then be negotiated by mere delivery without endorsement.

(NOT NEGOTIABLE.)

$100.   Toronto, Nov. 1, 1898.

Three months after date, I promise to pay to A. Brown only, at my office, 1 Brown Alley, the sum of One Hundred Dollars, for valued received.   John Smith.

This Note is not negotiable, as the word "only" is a clear indication of the intention of the maker to pay the sum promised to A. Brown and no one else; it can, however, be transferred by A. Brown to a third party, but it would carry with it any defects in title; for instance, if the maker were entitled to the benefits of any set off against A. Brown, the holder could only recover from him the amount actually owing. Whereas, with a negotiable note, the holder, for value, if a third party, could recover the face value of the note.

Question 2.—A Cheque is drawn on a Bank in favor of Cash or Order. Should the Bank pay this Cheque? Give your reasons.

A.—A Bank should certainly pay the Cheque as by the Bills of Exchange Act, 1890, the rule is laid down that "where the payee is a fictitious or non-existing person, the bill may be treated as payable to bearer." In this case, the Cheque being drawn in favor of Cash or Order, instead of to a person, is governed by the above clause and would be payable to the person presenting it, who, as a matter of practice, would generally be asked at the Bank to endorse it.

Question 3.—Give definition of the following:

    Cheque.
    Promissory Note.
    A Foreign Bill.
    Order.
    Bank Draft.
    Deposit Receipt.

A.—*A Cheque,*

Is a Bill of Exchange drawn on a Bank payable on demand.

A Promissory Note,

Is an unconditional promise in writing made by one person to another, signed by the maker, engaging to pay, on demand or at a fixed or determinable future time, a sum certain in money to or to the order of a specified person or bearer.

A Foreign Bill,

Any Bill which does not come under the following definition is a Foreign Bill. *Definition.*—An Inland Bill is a Bill which is, or on the face of it purports to be (a) both drawn and payable within Canada, or (b) drawn within Canada upon some person resident therein.

An Order,

Is a written request made by one person to another asking the latter to deliver to a third person certain goods or money and to charge the same to the Account of the person signing the Order.

A Bank Draft,

Is a Bill of Exchange drawn by one Bank upon another Bank or by one Branch on another Branch of same Bank, in which the latter is asked to pay a sum of money to a specified person and to charge the amount to the Account of the Bank issuing the Order.

A Deposit Receipt,

Is a form of acknowledgment given by a Bank to a Depositor for money deposited therein and is non-negotiable. They are also known as Certificates of Deposit, and usually bear interest at a specified rate stated therein.

Question 4.—What is the object or force of an endorsement on a Note or Bill of Exchange?

A.—The object or force of an endorsement on a Bill of Exchange or a Note by the holder thereof, is to transfer the property in it to some one else; it also has the effect of guaranteeing the subsequent holders against the default of the Acceptor or Maker, unless otherwise stated in the endorsement.

The object of an endorsement is also to render the document complete. A Cheque drawn to order, otherwise good, would not be payable by the Bank unless properly endorsed.

The endorser is precluded from denying to a holder in due course the genuineness and regularity in all respects of all signatures of previous parties to the Bill or Note, and also from denying to his immediate or a subsequent indorsee, that the Bill or Note was, at the time of his endorsement, a valid and subsisting Bill or Note, and that he had then a good title thereto.

Question 5.—Describe various ways of Endorsing Bills and give examples.

A.—

OPEN OR IN BLANK.	IN FULL OR SPECIAL.	RESTRICTIVE.	QUALIFIED.
C. R. McCullough	Pay D. Hoskins, or order, C. R. McCullough.	Pay D. Hoskins, only. C. R. McCullough.	Pay D. Hoskins, or order, without recourse to me. C. R. McCullough.

The principal kinds of Endorsements in use are shown in the above diagram. For the sake of clearness we will suppose the Note or Bill to have been made in favor of " C. R. McCullough or order." If McCullough Endorses it by simply writing his name across the back without indicating to whom he orders the Bill or Note to be paid (called " Endorsement in Blank," or " Open Endorsement "), it can afterwards be negotiated by mere delivery. If he indicates some person to whom the Bill or Note is to be paid, as " Pay D. Hoskins or order," or " Pay D. Hoskins " (called " Special Endorsement," or " Endorsement in Full "), then Hoskins must Endorse it in order to negotiate it further. Should McCullough, when Endorsing, add words prohibiting further negotiation or expressing that the Endorsement is merely an authority to deal with the Bill or Note as thereby directed, as " Pay D. Hoskins only," or " Pay D. Hoskins or order for collection " (called " Restrictive Endorsement "). The Endorsement gives Hoskins the right to receive payment of the Bill and to sue any party thereto that McCullough could have sued, but gives him no power to transfer his rights as Endorsee. Endorsing a Bill or Note in blank or specially, renders the Endorser liable on it to all subsequent parties to the Bill or Note unless words are added limiting the Endorser's liability (called

" Qualified Endorsement "), as " Pay D. Hoskins or order, without recourse to me, C. R. McCullough." When a Qualified Endorsement is used it operates to transfer the Bill, but does not render the Endorser liable in case the Bill or Note is not paid when due.

Question 6.—What do you mean by the holder of a Promissory Note? Does it affect his position or his rights, if he acquire it before or after its due date?

Supposing Brown gives Jones a Note and Smith is the Holder for value: What is Smith's position in above question?

A.—The Holder of a Promissory Note is the Payee or Endorsee who is in possession of it or the Bearer thereof. If he acquired it before maturity and in good faith and for value, and without notice of any defect in title, he is termed " a Holder in due course," and can enforce payment against all previous parties to the Bill. But if it has been acquired after maturity, he then holds it subject to any defects of title affecting it at or after its maturity, after which date he could neither acquire nor give a better title than that which the person had from whom he obtained the document.

If Brown gives Jones a Note and Smith is the Holder for value, Smith can enforce payment against either Brown or Jones for the full amount of the Note if he received it before maturity; but if he received it after maturity, he takes it subject to defects of title (if any).

Question 7.—What are Patent Right Bills? and how do they differ from an ordinary Bill?

A.—Patent Right Bills are Notes or Acceptances given in payment, or in partial payment, of a Patent Right or an interest in the same. The Bills of Exchange Act, 1890, enacts that any such Bills or Renewals thereof issued without the words " Given for a Patent Right " printed or written legibly and prominently across the face thereof shall be void, except in the hands of a Holder in due course, without notice of such consideration. Anyone knowingly issuing or transferring a Patent Right Bill, not having the above mentioned words thereon, is guilty of a misdemeanor, and liable to imprisonment or fine.

An important feature regarding Patent Right Bills is the fact that when negotiated they are subject to any defences or set-offs that may exist between the original parties, unless not marked "given for a Patent Right" as aforesaid.

Question 8.—How does the Statute of Limitations apply to—

(1) A Cheque;
(2) A Promissory Note;
(3) A Bank Note or Bank Bill?

A.—(1) An action may be commenced for the collection of a dishonored Check any time within six years from date of receiving same.

(2) An action to collect a dishonored Promissory Note may be commenced any time within six years from the date it is payable.

(3) The Statute of Limitations does not apply to Bank Notes or other evidences of Debt issued by Banks.

A subsequent written promise to pay, or partial payment on Account of either the dishonored Check or Note above mentioned, would suffice to extend the time for action for six years after the date of such promise, or partial payment. See page 224.

Question 9.—In the course of business you, "C.," have received a Note made by "A." in favor of "B." At maturity this Note is Dishonored. Show all the Journal entries you would make, and also describe the necessary steps to protect your interests.

A.—When the Note is Dishonored either of the following entries may be made in the Journal:—

(a) B. (the person from whom it is received) Dr.
        To Bills Receivable.
Stating particulars of the transaction.

(b) Overdue Bills Receivable, **Dr.**
          To Bills Receivable.
With full particulars of Bill, etc.

In either case, the Note should be no longer included among the current Bills Receivable.

To protect my interests it would be necessary to give B. notice of Dishonor either on the maturity date or the following business day, as by so doing I can hold him liable on his Endorsement for the amount of the Bill. Failure to do this would release B. from all liability and I would have to look to A. alone for payment.

Question 10.—Briefly describe some "Negotiable Instruments" not mentioned in this paper.

A.—In a Negotiable Instrument the person who is liable to pay it, must do so to the lawful Holder thereof, when payment is legally due.

Taking a Negotiable Instrument in this sense then it is difficult to name any not mentioned in this paper, with the exception of

Bank Notes and Dominion Notes,

Which are Negotiable Instruments, and may be termed "gilt edged" ones.

Some Debentures and Coupons are Payable to Bearer and Negotiable.

A recent case gives some light as to the negotiability of Debentures. The Owner lost a Debenture payable to Bearer—he stopped payment of it—meanwhile the Debenture matured. Some person had stolen the Debenture and sold it to an innocent purchaser for value. Said purchaser was refused payment and failed to recover same on appealing to the Courts. The original owner recovered his rights.

The following Extract from a paper read by Mr. W. R. Wilson, B.A., Barrister-at-Law, before the Chartered Accountants Student Society of London (Eng.), and published in "The Accountant" of 3rd December, 1898, will be of interest on the subject:—

When, however, we come to consider Debentures to Bearer, we approach another thorny question.

Now, the chief object in issuing a Debenture to Bearer is, as far as possible, to endow it with the characteristics of a Negotiable Instrument, and in particular,—

(a) To make it transferable free from equities as between the Company and the person to whom it is issued.

(b) To enable the Bearer to sue the Company in his own name.

(c) To ensure a good title to any person who acquires the Debentures bona fide for valuable consideration, notwithstanding any defect in the title of the person from whom he acquires it.

Now, can this be done? I think it is indisputable that it can to a certain extent. For, from a consideration of the following cases, viz., Re Agra & Masterman's Bank, 2 Ch. 397; Re Blakeley Ordnance Company, 3 Ch. 154; Re Natal Investment Company, 3 Ch. 361; Re Imperial Land Company, 11 Eq. 487; and Crouch v. Credit Foncier, L. R. 8 Q. B., 385, it seems clear that as against itself, by virtue of the doctrine of estoppel, a Company may issue Debentures to Bearer on which it will be liable and against which it cannot set up any equities existing between it and the original Debenture Holder; in other words, should the Company set up such a defence good as against the original contractee, and, therefore, generally good as against the Assignee also, it would be a good reply to say that the Company had, with a view to inducing persons to become Assignees of such Instruments, represented that there were no such equities.

Can, however, a Company go further than this and claim, by issuing Debentures to Bearer, not only the power to alter or abandon their own rights, but also to alter and abandon the rights of those who may become holders of the Debentures, and to declare that such persons shall, contrary to the general law, hold them on a precarious title liable to be divested thereof if a thief or finder can discover a bona fide purchaser of the Debenture; and further, can they give a right of action in his own name to any holder in due course? The question, which is involved in this wider one, viz., "Whether the class of English Negotiable Instruments, negotiable by virtue of the old lex mercatoria is capable of expansion or not," has given rise to much discussion, and to what may be called two schools of opinion. The one, which may be called the conservative school, adhering to the views expressed by Blackburn, J., in delivering the judgment of the Court in Crouch v. Credit Foncier, L. R., 8 Q. B. 374, wherein he says: "We have already intimated our opinion that it is beyond the competency of the parties to a contract by express words to confer on an Assignee of that contract a right to sue in his own name. And we also think it beyond the competency of the parties by express stipulation to deprive the Assignee of either the contract or the property represented by it; of his right to take back his property to anyone to whom a thief may have transferred it, even though the transferee took it bona fide and for value."

This view, I may say, has lately been upheld by Mr. Willis, Q.C., now His Honour Judge Willis, in his able lectures on Negotiable Instruments. The other, or progressive school, represents the opinions expressed by Cockburn, C.J., in the celebrated judgment delivered by him in the case of Goodwin v. Robarts, L.R. Ex. 337, in the course of which he says: "Having given the fullest consideration to this argument (i.e., that the list of English Negotiable Instruments is finally closed), we are of opinion that it cannot prevail. It is founded on the view that the law merchant is fixed and stereotyped and incapable of being expanded and enlarged so as to meet the wants and requirements of trade in the varying circumstances of commerce.

"It is true that the law merchant is sometimes spoken of as a fixed body of law forming part of the common law, and, as it were, co-eval with it; but, as a matter of legal history, this view is altogether incorrect. The law merchant thus spoken of with reference to Bills of Exchange and other Negotiable Securities, though forming part of the general body of the law merchant, is of comparatively recent origin. It is neither more nor less than the usage of merchants and traders in the different departments of trade, ratified by the decisions of Courts of law, which upon such usages being proved before them, have adopted them as settled law with a view to the interests of trade and the public convenience.

"By this process what before was usage only, unsanctioned by legal decision, has become engrafted upon or incorporated into the common law, and may thus be said to form a part of it.

"Usage adopted by the Courts having been thus the origin of the whole of the so-called Lex M. as to Negotiable Securities, what is there to prevent our acting on the principle acted on by our predecessors and followed in the precedents they have left us? Why is it to be said that a new usage which has sprung up under altered circumstances is to be less admissible than the usage of past times? Why is the door to be now shut to the admission and adoption of usage in a matter of altogether cognate character as though the law had been finally stereotyped and settled by some positive and peremptory enactment. I may just add in conclusion on this subject that Mr. Palmer, in his recent book on Companies, warmly champions the theory upheld in these last quoted cases—that the list of Negotiable Instruments, negotiable by virtue of the law merchant is not finally closed, and gives a list of important London banks and bankers who consider that Debentures to Bearer are negotiable by mercantile custom, and who act on that view in the ordinary course of business."

A Bill of Lading

Is supposed commonly to be "Negotiable"—but a transfer by endorsement carries with it all defects, and the holder would have to prove his title to the goods therein represented.

CHAPTER XX.

NEGOTIABLE INSTRUMENTS.

Question 1.—What do you understand by Negotiable Instruments? What are some of their advantages? Give examples.

A.—Such Instruments representing on their face a certain sum of money as give the holder thereof a good title and the right to recover the amounts therein mentioned to be paid by the persons liable, and may be transferred by endorsement and delivery, or by delivery alone.

The question may well ask for only some of their advantages. The enormous growth in business in late years may safely be credited to " Negotiable Instruments." A merchant by their use is entitled to practically use Capital to extend his business in much the same proportion as the wealth of a country may be compared to its available gold currency (where used).

The most frequent examples in common use are where a man sells his goods on credit, and can convert this Debt immediately into its present value in Cash by taking from the Purchaser his promise to pay at a fixed date (known as a Promissory Note) the amount of the Debt, possibly with interest added, and discounting same, provided that the credit of the parties thereto is good.

A Bank Note or Bill is a Negotiable Instrument of such a recognized value or quality that it passes as readily as a gold coin, nay even more so in ordinary times, where it represents a large amount, as it is so much more convenient in every respect than a bag of gold coins or gold dollars.

In business transactions between parties at a distance the Cheque or Bank Draft affords a good example of the advantages of negotiable paper in thus being able to remit in a letter the equivalent of Cash.

Question 2.—Can a Non-Negotiable Note be transferred to anyone? If so, how and what would be the effect of such transfer?

A.—A Non-Transferable Note or Cheque can be practically transferred to any one by an assignment or transfer, but the holder could not demand and enforce payment if the party liable could show that he did not owe the debt. In other words, the holder would hold it subject to all defects in title, etc.

Question 3.—What constitutes proper Presentation for Payment, of a Bill?

A.—Presenting it on its due date by the Holder, either personally or through an agent, at the place mentioned therein for payment, or where no place for payment is specified, on the Drawer or Maker himself, or at his place of residence, or last known place of residence.

If the Drawer or Maker could not be found after this reasonable search, Proper Presentment would have been duly made.

This question is answered fully on page 231.

Question 4.—Black and Brown are Trading Partners and owe Smith $1,000. Black gives Smith a Promissory Note for the amount at four months, and by mistake Brown gives him a second Note for the same amount. Each was signed " Black & Brown." Smith has these Notes discounted at his Bank and before the due date fails badly, leaving no Assets. What is the Bank's position?

A.—The Bank can evidently get nothing from Smith, but it can duly recover both Notes from Black and Brown. The Bank is a Holder in due course for value.

It might, perhaps, be noted that Smith however could only have recovered payment of one of the Notes, as he improperly obtained both, and could under the circumstances detailed be held liable for obtaining money presumably under false pretenses.

Question 5.—(a) **State** what is meant by Endorsement.

(b) **How does it affect the party** Endorsing?

(c) **In how many ways** may Endorsing be done?

A.—Endorsement is the **act of a person** writing **his** name on a Bill when it is payable to him or his order for the purpose of negotiating it.

(b) **It renders him liable for** the amount of the Bill to any future holders, unless when he Negotiates it he qualifies **his** Endorsement by such **words as** "Sans **Recours**," or "Without Recourse." He could further endorse it as shown in the answer to (c).

(c) For full **answer to** this, see page 209.

Question 6.—(a) What is meant by Protesting a Bill of Exchange?

(b) Who may Protest it?

(c) What are the essential features of a Protest?

A.—For full **answer to this question, see page** 225.

Question 7.—**Three months after** date I promise to pay John **Jones** One hundred dollars.   (sgd.)   W. Smith.

Is this **Note** valid? If not, **point out** wherein it is defective.

A.—The Note is valid, but **not complete.** It can however be legally rendered so **by John** Jones filling in the proper date, or of course Smith could **do so.**

Question 8.—Is Notice of Dishonor of a Bill or Note ever dispensed **with?** If so, when and **how?**

A.—Notice of Dishonor of a Bill is dispensed with when the Endorser waives Notice, that is, **undertakes to** be responsible whether **he** receives Notice of Dishonor **or** not.

Further, when the Maker has signed merely to accommodate the other party, he could still be entitled to be repaid, if a subsequent Holder had enforced payment from him (the Maker) and neglected to notify the party accommodated, viz., the first Endorser.

When, after the exercise of reasonable diligence, Notice as required by the Bills of Exchange Act, cannot be given to or does not reach the Drawer or Endorser sought to be charged.

As regards the *Drawer* in the following cases, namely, (1) Where the Drawer and Drawee are the same person; (2) Where the Drawee is a fictitious person, or a person not having capacity to contract; (3) Where the Drawer is the person to whom the Bill is presented for payment; (4) Where the Drawee or Acceptor is, as between himself and the Drawer, under no obligation to pay the Bill; (5) Where the Drawer has countermanded payment.

As regards the *Endorser*, in the following cases, namely (1) Where the Drawee is a fictitious person, or a person not having capacity to contract, and the Endorser was aware of the fact at the time he endorsed the Bill; (2) Where the endorser is the person to whom the Bill is presented for payment; (3) where the Bill was accepted or made for his accommodation.

Question 9.—" Three months after date I promise to pay A. " Brown, or order, One hundred dollars, with interest at 7 per cent. " per annum, value received. (sgd.) W. Bell."

Brown being unable to collect the Note sues Bell on 31st Dec., 1898, for the face of the Note and interest. State how you would compute the claim, and your reasons.

A.—This Note, like its valid predecessor in Question 7, is not dated, but presuming that it matured before the 31st December, the claim would be for the $100 and interest thereon computed from the date of Bill to 31st December at 7 per cent., though it is more than probable that Brown would only recover interest at the rate of 6 per cent. (rate regulated by the laws of particular country) from the due date of Bill to date of payment.

Question 10.—Explain what is meant by a Cheque being crossed "Generally" and crossed "Specially." What are the duties of Bankers as to Crossed Cheques?

A.—A Cheque being crossed Generally means that two parallel transverse lines are written across with the word "Bank," or without it, written between as follows:

meaning that instructions are thereby given to the paying Bank to only honor the Cheque when it is presented for payment through a Bank. It bars the Cheque being paid in Cash over the counter.

A Cheque crossed Specially has the name of the Bank written between the lines as above, thereby specifying the Bank through whose hands it must pass before being paid. In countries where Crossed Cheques are the rule and not the exception, as is not the case in Canada, these instructions in the latter case, though rigidly observed in the General Crossing, are more honored in the breach than the observance, that is, the Cheque is usually treated as Generally Crossed, unless drawn for a large amount.

CHAPTER XXI.

MERCANTILE LAW.

Question 1.—What is a Contract?

Give two examples of Contracts, which are " per se " void or illegal. State some kinds of Contracts which must be in writing.

A.—A Contract can be defined as an agreement between two or more persons, which is enforceable at law, such an agreement being a compact or undertaking between certain individuals to do or perform something or to render some benefit to the other party, direct or indirect, for a consideration. The consideration therefore being an essential part to render the agreement binding at law.

A Contract to perform an impossible undertaking would " per se " be void.

A Contract entered into to retail liquors without a proper license, or commit a robbery, would be illegal, and consequently void.

For the kinds of Contracts which must be in writing, see p. 222.

Question 2.—Define the term " Consideration," and explain the difference between Legal and Moral Consideration.

A.—" Consideration " is part of a Contract which is necessary to make it enforceable at law.

The exceptions to this are Contracts under Seal and Negotiable Instruments.

Consideration may be defined as the benefit to be derived, either directly or indirectly, by any party to the Contract who promises or undertakes to do or not to do something, such benefit being given or promised him by the other party.

A standard definition is as follows:

"Some right, interest, profit or benefit accruing to the one party or some forbearance, detriment, loss or responsibility given, suffered or undertaken by the other."

A Legal Consideration is, as the name implies, one that is not contrary to law.

A Moral Consideration is one which is binding by the standard of what is right and honorable, but which is on a point of law not a Legal Consideration. Many things are illegal and at the same time not necessarily criminal.

Question 3.—What is "The Statute of Frauds"? Answer briefly and state its most important bearings on Commercial Transactions.

A.—What is known as the Statute of Frauds is an Act passed in the 29th year of Charles II., which in its main provisions is still in force. It regulated what Contracts must be in writing to make them enforceable at law, enumerating the different classes; also making provision as to Verbal Contracts for sale of goods, and limiting the cash value of such to make them legal.

A Verbal Contract (coming under the proper class) is limited in England to £10, in Canada to $40., unless there is a partial payment made thereon or a partial delivery and acceptance of the goods.

The Statute of Frauds enacts that no action shall be brought on any of the Contracts specified in the fourth section of the Act, unless the agreement upon which such action shall be brought or some memorandum or other note thereof shall be in writing and signed by the party to be charged therewith or some other person thereto, by him lawfully authorized.

The Contracts comprised in the fourth section are:—

    1. Any special promise by an Executor or Administrator to answer damages out of his own Estate.

2. Any special promise to answer for the Debt, Default or Miscarriage of another person.

3. Any Agreement made upon Consideration of Marriage.

4. Any Contract or Sale of Lands, Tenements or Hereditaments, or any Interest in or concerning them.

5. Any Agreement that is not to be performed within the space of one year from the making thereof. The 17th section of the Statute of Frauds enacts that no Contract for the sale of any Goods, Wares and Merchandise for the price of $40 sterling or upwards shall be allowed to be good, except the Buyer shall accept part of the goods so sold, and actually receive them, or give something in earnest to bind the bargain or in part payment, or except some Note or Memorandum in writing of the bargain be made and signed by the parties to be charged by such Contract, or their Agents thereunto lawfully authorized. By Lord Tenterden's Act (9 Geo. IV. c. 14, s. 7), this 17th section of Statute of Frauds was extended to include all executory (i.e., future) sales of goods to the value of $40 and upwards, whether the goods be in existence or not at the time of the Contract.

Question 4.—Explain briefly the effect of the Statute of Limitations on Debts.

A.—The effect of the Statute of Limitations is to limit the time in which a Debt can be recoverable at law.

In ordinary Debts, whether for trade or otherwise, the time is limited to six years, and after that period the Debt is said to be barred by the Statute. The limit differs in certain cases as follows: (R. S. O. 1897, cap. 72, sec. 1):

" Actions for penalties, damages, or sums of money given to the party aggrieved, by any Statute, within two years after the cause of such actions arose."

"Actions upon any Covenant contained in any Indenture of Mortgage, made on or after the 1st day of July, 1894, within ten years after the cause of such actions arose."

Actions for Rent, upon an Indenture of Lease, and

Actions upon Bonds and other Contracts under Seal (except the aforementioned Covenant in a Mortgage) must be commenced within twenty years.

Actions on Accounts must be commenced within six years.

Actions on Promissory Notes and Bills of Exchange must be commenced within six years after they are payable.

The important exception to the rule is the case of Banks. No Debt due by a Bank is barred for

(1) Notes Issued by it.

(2) Its Customers' Deposits.

(3) Dividends due Shareholders.

The Statute does not remove the Debt, the moral obligation to pay it still remains, but it takes away the power of collecting it by any legal process. The Debtor, however, can remove the "bar," as shown in the answer to Question six.

Question 5.—If A. owes B. several Debts and makes him a Payment, what are their respective rights as to the appropriation of this Payment.

A.—A., when he makes the Payment, has the right to say to which Debt or Debts it shall be applied. If he does not exercise this right, B. can apply it to any one or more of the Debts he pleases.

If, however, A. owed B. two Debts, one for $18, and the other for $13.36, and sent him a Payment for $13.36, it should be appropriated to the latter Debt, as it was clearly so intended.

If A. sent the Payment, stating how he wished it appropriated, B. must so deal with it, or he should return it to A. stating his objections.

The intention of A. ought to be notified to B. at or before the time of Payment, but B. need not apply it to any particular Debt at the moment of Payment; he has the right to make the application at any subsequent period.

Question 6.—In the former question if one of the Debts is barred by the Statute of Limitations, would it affect B.'s powers? How could this Debt be legally revived?

A.—If the Debt really exists (though the right of action is barred), it would not affect B.'s power in appropriating the Payment on the Barred Debt, subject, of course, to A. giving no directions, or implying any.

The Debt could be legally revived by a written acknowledgment of it, or by a part Payment.

The written acknowledgment must be in unconditional terms and such that an intention to pay when asked may be inferred.

And if when a Part Payment is made the Debtor showed plainly to his Creditor that he intended to pay nothing more, it would not operate to remove the bar.

Question 7.—What do you mean by "Protesting a Bill of Exchange"? What is required to make a Protest legal? Is it absolutely essential that all Bills or Notes, not paid at maturity, should be protested? And why?

A.—Protesting a Bill of Exchange is the noting and protesting thereof and the sending a formal notice of its Dishonor by a notary public to the parties who are liable to pay the same.

This Protest, in the absence of a notary public, can be made by any justice of the peace, resident in the place where the Bill is payable.

To make the Protest legal it must contain a copy of the Bill or the Original Bill may be annexed thereto, and the Protest must be signed by the notary making it, and must specify:—

(a) The person at whose request the Bill is Protested;

(b) The place and date of Protest, and cause or reason for Protesting the Bill, the demand made, and the answer given, if any, or the fact that the Drawee or Acceptor could not be found.

When a Bill is Protested, the Protest must be made or noted on the day of its Dishonor. It must be protested at the place where it is Dishonored, or at some other place in Canada situate within five miles of the place of Presentment and Dishonor of such Bill.

Except in the Province of Quebec, it is not necessary that all Dishonored Bills or Notes should be Protested as, in the case of an Inland Bill, the holder of the Bill when it is Dishonored can hold his recourse against the Endorsers by a simple notice of the Dishonor sent without delay. The Maker cannot demand this notice, and in certain cases the Endorser may dispense also with the notice by waving his right thereto.

The notice may be given as soon as the Bill is Dishonored, and must be given not later than the next following judicial or business day.

Where a party to a Bill receives due notice of Dishonor, he has, after the receipt of such notice, the same period of time for giving notice to antecedent parties to the Bill, that the holder has after the Dishonor;

The advantage of the Protest is that if the holder has to sue for payment it gives ready proof of the Dishonor and the other acts of the notary. In the case of Foreign Bills, however, when Dishonored they must be Protested.

Question 8.—Under what circumstances may an Endorser to a Note be discharged of his liability?

A.—(1) By the Note or Bill being paid by the Maker or any person antecedent to the Endorser in question.

(2) By the holder of the Note giving an extension of time to the Maker to pay, without his (the Endorser's) consent.

(There is an exception to this if the Maker or Acceptor has signed the Bill merely as a matter of accommodation for the Drawer, when if the holder thereof allowed him (the Maker or Acceptor) time and then made him pay the Bill, he (the Maker or Acceptor) would not lose his remedy against the party he had thus accommodated.)

(3) If he has not had proper notice of Dishonor. The Endorsers should be notified of the Dishonor as detailed in the previous answer.

(4) If the Note has not been Protested, if it is a Foreign Bill. (In the Province of Quebec all Bills must be Protested.)

(5) Where the Note has been materially altered without his consent, but if the alteration is not apparent on its face and the Note in the hands of a holder in due course, such holder may avail himself of the Bill as if it had not been altered.

(6) By Non-presentment of the Note for Payment.

Question 9.—What is meant by Stoppage in Transitu, and under what circumstances can the Seller's rights be annulled?

A.—Stoppage in Transitu is the right of the Seller to stop the delivery of Goods sold on credit, and while in course of being delivered, and in the carrier's hands, if meanwhile he receives notice or obtains information that the Purchaser of such Goods is Insolvent. The Purchaser must not have obtained possession of the Goods either actually or constructively. The Seller can not only stop the delivery, but resumes possession of the Goods until he receives payment for them, though the sale is not actually rescinded. The Purchaser might after all be in a position to pay for the Goods, and if he could not get them maintain an action for damages. Such a point as this would be a matter for the Seller to obtain legal advice upon.

The Seller's rights can be annulled by the Purchaser proving to be solvent, and if the Goods had been wrongfully delayed the Seller might not only have to deliver the Goods, but pay the expenses incurred.

If the Purchaser has sold the goods in good faith " to arrive " it would annul the Seller's rights.

The Seller's rights could also be annulled by not notifying the carrier who had the possession of the goods, also as before stated, by the Purchaser obtaining " actual or constructive " possession, possession by his agent would suffice.

In answering a question like this, there are so many distinctions in law as to the meaning of " actual or constructive " possession by the Purchaser, whereby the Seller's rights might be annulled, that only the main principles can here be dealt with, and the student could with advantage refer to some standard work on Mercantile Law for fuller information.

Question 10.—In a dispute submitted to Arbitration point out briefly the essentials of a proper award.

A.—That it must be according to the terms of the submission, and must only refer to the question or questions submitted, and must dispose of them all.

That it only affects the parties to the dispute.

That it covers all the matters submitted for arbitration.

That it is clear and certain in its meaning.

That it can be carried out at the time the award is made, that it is possible.

That it is legal.

That it is a reasonable award, and it must be final and conclusive.

That it must be in writing.

CHAPTER XXII

MERCANTILE LAW.

Question 1.—Define a Guaranty. What is necessary to make a Guaranty enforceable in law?

A.—A Guaranty is a promise or undertaking made by one person with another to be liable or answerable for the debt, default or miscarriage of a third person.

To make it enforceable at law it must be in writing and signed by the party chargeable therewith, and there must be a consideration unless the document is under seal.

Question 2.—What is Fraud? Give the main provisions of the Statute of Frauds affecting Contracts.

What are a Debtor's Rights in case he has given a secret preference to induce a Creditor to join in a Deed of Composition: (a) Where he has given security; (b) Where he has paid money.

A.—Fraud may be defined as a false statement made with knowledge of its falsehood, and with the intention that it should be acted upon, whereby any advantage is illegally or improperly obtained, or attempted to be obtained, or on the other hand whereby the party deceived has been damaged. For the provisions of the Statute of Frauds affecting Contracts see page 222.

The second part of question can be briefly answered as follows:
(a) The Creditor could not recover on or make use of such security.

(b) The Debtor could make such Creditor refund the money.

Question 3.—What is the General Law as to the Validity of Contracts made by a Minor? Give explanations.

Can a Minor act as an Agent? Explain.

A.—The General Law is that Contracts made by Minors, except for necessaries, are voidable, that is, that they cannot be enforced by law, unless ratified in writing when the person becomes of age.

It is supposed that a Minor is not capable of entering into trading or business transactions owing to tender years and business inexperience, but if he (or she) obtains necessaries, such as board, food and clothing on credit, it would be recoverable. However, a promissory note signed for them by a Minor would not, as it would come under the heading of a commercial transaction; though the seller could recover the amount of the note unless it represented more than the value of the goods supplied.

A minor can act as an Agent for another. The principal, if he considers the Minor competent to act for him, accepts the responsibility for his actions, acting as such, as if he performed them himself.

" Qui facit per alium, facit per se."

Question 4.—" A." and " B." are in partnership; " A.'s " capital is $20,000, "B.'s" is $10,000. Under their partnership articles they are each equally entitled to the profits, and are each equally liable for all losses. They decide to go out of business, and after realizing on all their assets and using up all their capital they still owe to third parties $5,000. " A." pays the balance of the debts; what does " B." owe " A." ?

A.—The losses from the question amount to $35,000, of which each bears half.

A. put $20,000 into the business, so it owes him this amount less his share of the losses, $17,500, viz., $2,500 plus the $5,000 he paid the third parties.

Memo.—B. should have paid this $5,000.

B. put $10,000 into the business and his share of losses is $17,500, so he has to pay $7,500, or owes this amount to A.

Question 5.—Define the meaning of the Application or Appropriation of Payments, and what are the rights in respect thereof: (a) of the Debtor; (b) of the Creditor?

In case neither Debtor or Creditor exercises the right, how are Payments applied in law?

A.—The Application or Appropriation of Payments refers to the treatment of the Payment made and the manner in which it is used in reduction of the one or more of the debts owing.

If there is only one debt no "appropriation" is made, as the Payment simply goes in reduction or satisfaction, but where there are two or more debts, the Payment can be appropriated to either debt as the Debtor may elect, or failing any instructions from him, as the Creditor chooses.

This question is fully answered on page 224.

If neither Debtor or Creditor exercises the right, the Payments are, as a general rule, applied by the Courts when appealed to as follows:

Providing it is not barred, the oldest debt is first paid off, and then the next oldest, and so on, as far as the payments will suffice, or as the Court may think just.

Question 6.—What is necessary to be done at the maturity of a Bill of Exchange to hold the Drawer and Endorser liable?

A.—It must be presented at the place of payment, if specified in the Bill.

If no place of payment is specified, but the address of the drawee or Acceptor is given in the Bill, it may be presented at that address.

If no place of payment is specified and no address is given, the Bill must be presented at the Drawee's or Acceptor's place of business, if known and if not, at his ordinary residence, if known.

In any other case it may be presented to the Drawee or Acceptor wherever he can be found, or at his last known place of business or address.

If dishonored, the Drawer or Endorser must be properly notified at once of the dishonor. In the case of a Foreign Bill it must be protested, when the Notary Public would send the proper notice of dishonor.

In the Province of Quebec all dishonored Bills must be protested to hold the Drawer and Endorsers liable.

Question 7.—Define a Warehouse Receipt; a Bill of Exchange, a Bill of Lading; a Promissory Note and a Cheque; and distinguish between a Negotiable Security and a Security which passes only by Assignment?

A.—*Warehouse Receipt,* is a receipt given by the proprietor of a warehouse, store, etc., acknowledging that certain goods as specified therein are warehoused, stored, or kept in his possession for the persons thus storing their property in said warehouse, etc.

The ownership in these goods may be transferred, for the purposes of security say to a Bank, or if sold, by delivery of the Warehouse Receipt duly endorsed.

Bill of Exchange, is an unconditional order in writing, addressed by one person to another, signed by the person giving it, requiring the person to whom it is addressed to pay, on demand or at a fixed or determinable future time, a sum certain in money to or to the order of a specified person, or to bearer.

Bill of Lading, is a receipt or document, which acknowledges the receipt of the goods as shipped, or to be shipped, and also contains the terms and conditions, including an undertaking, under which they are to be conveyed to their destination.

Where the goods are to be delivered by sea the receipt should contain the names of the shippers, of the vessel, giving details, etc., describing the goods with their distinguishing marks, and should be signed by the Master of the vessel.

Other Bills of Lading are usually signed by the agent of the Carrier or Company carrying the goods.

Bills of Lading give a title to the goods being conveyed, in a similar way to Warehouse Receipts.

A Promissory Note, is an unconditional promise in writing made by one person to another, signed by the maker, engaging to pay, on demand or at a fixed or determinable future date, a sum certain in money, to, or to the order of, a specified person, or to bearer.

A Cheque, is a Bill of Exchange drawn on a Bank, payable on demand.

A Negotiable Security, is one representing on its face a certain sum of money where the complete title thereto is contained in itself and passes by endorsement and delivery, or merely delivery.

A Security which passes only by assignment, passes the title thereto subject to any defects or set-offs which may belong to it.

A Promissory Note payable to order and endorsed and delivered to a third party would give him a good title.

A Promissory Note payable to a certain person only and assigned to a third party, would only give him the same title as the first endorser had, which might be subject to a set-off, etc.

Question 8.—Distinguish between **Void and Voidable Contracts**, giving illustrations of each kind.

A.—A Void Contract is "per se" null and void, rendered so through some defect; as to make a valid Contract certain regulations have to be observed, in other words, the agreement therein contained must be enforceable at law.

A Void Contract is one that has from the beginning no legal effect at all.

A Voidable Contract is one which can be rendered void by one of the parties thereto, who also has the power to render it binding.

A Contract which, not being under seal, contained no mention of consideration, there not being any, would be void.

A Contract for trading purposes entered into where one party was a minor would be voidable, at the option of the Minor, though he could ratify same when he became of age.

Question 9.—What do you understand by a Submission to Arbitration?

A.—Where parties cannot agree in any transaction and arrange to have the points on which they disagree referred to some person to settle the differences for them, and they agree to abide by this decision, such an agreement is known as a Submission to Arbitration.

Question 10.—What should the conduct of an Arbitrator be from the time he has accepted his appointment until the Award is delivered, in relation to all matters affected by the submission; and point out the important matters necessary to a valid Award.

A.—It is somewhat difficult to say what the Examiner here means by the term "Conduct," so the question is answered from a double standpoint.

His conduct, then, should be one of strict impartiality, being only guided in giving his award on the facts or evidences by his honest conviction, and not allowing any personal consideration to influence him.

He directs all proceedings necessary to the conduct of the Arbitration.

His procedure in conducting the Arbitration would be to study the matters contained in the submission; to summon witnesses, where necessary, and obtain all the information and documents which would be required to enable him to thoroughly understand the case. He would get advice and help from experts if wanted. If the submission was not clear he should have it made so by getting each party thereto to give him his views in writing before entering on the Arbitration.

He will have to be careful that he thoroughly understands the law in the matter, as his award must be in conformity therewith.

When the parties to the Arbitration have completed the presentation of their case, the Arbitrator should declare the Arbitration closed, after which no more evidence can be received. He then proceeds to make his award.

The important matters necessary to a valid award will be found in an answer to another question on page 228.

CHAPTER XXIII.

MERCANTILE ARITHMETIC.

Question 1.—A Trustee purchased at par five Municipal Debentures as follows:—

        No. 1....1 year.   Int. 4 % payable annually.
            2....2 "
            3....3 "
            4....4 "
            5....5 "

The amount payable annually by the Municipality to retire one Bond and Coupons on all Bonds is $1,100.

Find amount of each Bond.

A.—
Operation.

        Bond No. 5 = $1,100 00 ÷ 1.04 = $1,057 69.
        "   4 =   1,057 69 ÷ 1.04 = 1,017 01.
        "   3 =   1,017 01 ÷ 1.04 =   977 89.
        "   2 =   977 89 ÷ 1.04 =   940 28.
        "   1 =   940 28 ÷ 1.04 =   901 12.

Explanation.

Each payment of **$1,100** is made up of the maturing Bond and the last 4% Coupon attached to it, together with one 4% Coupon from each of the unmatured Bonds. It is evident, then, that the fifth payment of $1,100 is made up of Bond No. 5 and one Coupon of 4% thereon: 104% Bond No. 5=$1,100, and Bond No. 5=$1,100÷1.04=$1,057.69.

The fourth payment of **$1,100 is made** up of Bond No. 4, one Coupon of 4% thereon and **one Coupon of** 4% on Bond No. 5. But 4% on Bond No. 5=4%on $1,057.69=42.31, which deducted from

$1,100 leaves $1,057.69 as the sum of Bond No. 4 and one Coupon of 4% thereon. It will be observed that this is also the amount of Bond No. 5, and in like manner it may be shown that each Bond is equal to the sum of the preceding Bond and one of its Coupons. Therefore, all such questions may be worked as follows:

Divide the annual payment by the amount of $1 invested for one year at the given rate, thus obtaining the face of the last maturing Bond. This Bond divided by the same divisor gives the face of the Bond immediately preceding it. Similarly the face of all the other Bonds may be found by dividing the face of the Bond maturing immediately after it by the amount of $1 invested for one year at the given rate.

Question 2.—A Merchant is Mortgagor on Mortgage of $5,000, principal due in 1902. He has provided for interest but intends to pay principal out of proceeds of four mortgages of $1,250 each he holds, which expire, one in 1898, 1899, 1900, 1901. He proposes to invest sufficient of the principal of these at compound interest, 4% half-yearly, to provide for the $5,000 he owes in 1902.

How much of each did he invest?

A.—
Operation.

Each $1 invested in 1901 will by 1902 be worth $1 \times 1.02^2 = \$1.0404$
"   1   "   1900   "   "   " $1 \times 1.02^4 = 1.08243$
"   1   "   1899   "   "   " $1 \times 1.02^6 = 1.12616$
"   1   "   1898   "   "   " $1 \times 1.02^8 = 1.17166$

So that $1 invested annually for 4 years will by 1902 be worth $\underline{\underline{\$4.42065}}$

$\$5,000 \div 4.42065 = \$1,131.06.—Ans.$

Explanation.

This is simply another way of asking what sum set apart annually for 4 successive years and bearing interest at 4% per annum, compounded half-yearly, would amount to $5,000 at the end of the 4th year, which may readily be determined as follows:

Find the value at the end of the given time of an annual deposit of $1 at the given rate. This divided into the required sum will give the necessary annual investment to yield the same.

Higher Powers of Numbers.—In connection with such questions as the above a few hints on the method of obtaining the higher powers of a number may prove useful. Let us suppose for the purpose of such a calculation that we need the compound amount of $1 for 16 years. This just means that we have to multiply sixteen 1.04's together, in other words, raise it to the 16th power. 1.04 multiplied by itself gives what is known as the second power of 1.04, generally expressed 1.04^2; this multiplied by itself gives 1.04^4; the latter number multiplied by itself gives 1.04^8, which means eight 1.04's multiplied together; 1.04^8 multiplied by itself gives 1.04^{16}, thus arriving at the result by four multiplications instead of fifteen.

$1.04 \times 1.04 = 1.0816$; $1.0816 \times 1.0816 = 1.169859$ to six places $= 1.04^4$. Multiply 1.169859 by itself, carrying the answer correct to five places $= 1.04^8 = 1.368569$. Now multiply the latter number by itself to the same number of places $= 1.872980 = 1.04^{16}$.

Question 3.—What amount in currency will purchase a Bill of Exchange on London for £100, the current rate being 10%?

A.—"The current rate being 10%," means that Exchange on London is 10% advance on the Old Par, which was £1=$4.44 4-9.

Old par value of £100 = $4.44\frac{4}{9} \times 100 = \$444.44\frac{4}{9}$
Add 10 % exchange, = $44.44\frac{4}{9}$
Cost of bill would be.................. $488.88\frac{8}{9}$ or $488.89—*Ans.*

Second Method—

$\frac{10}{9} \times \frac{100}{1} \times \frac{110}{100} = \frac{1100}{9} = \$488.89.$—*Ans.*

Question 4.—Which is the most profitable way to invest money?

(a) Deposit in Savings Bank. Interest $3\frac{1}{2}$% per annum compounded half-yearly.

(b) Buy Imperial Bank Stock at 194. Dividend being 4% half-yearly.

(c) Buy Bank of Montreal Stock at 241. Dividend half-yearly 5%.

A.—Let us compare the half-yearly returns from an investment of $100 each.

(a) By depositing we get 1¾ per cent. per half year on $100 = **$1.75**.

(b) An investment of $194 in Imperial Stock yields $4 per half year, therefore $100 in Imperial Stock would yield $4 ÷ 1.94 = **$2.062** half-yearly.

(c) An investment of $241 in Montreal Stock yields $5 half-yearly, an investment of $100 in Montreal Stock would yield $5 ÷ 2.41 = **$2.075** half-yearly.

It is clear, then, that it would be most profitable to invest in Bank of Montreal Stock.

Question 5.—In the following account what percentage of the Sales does each item of the Debit side represent?

Dr.   FLOUR TRADING ACCOUNT.   *Cr.*

Purchases	$140,340 00	Sales		$189,340 25
Salaries	3,400 00			
Freight	2,000 00			
Departmental Charges	500 00			
Gross Profit	43,100 25			
	$189,340 25			$189,340 25

Purchases,	=	$140,340 00 ÷	$189,340 25	= 74.12	%.
Salaries,	=	3,400 00 ÷	"	= 1.79	%.
Freight,	=	2,000 00 ÷	"	= 1.056	%.
Charges,	=	500 00 ÷	"	= .264	%.
Gross Profit	=	43,100 25 ÷	"	= 22.77	%.
		Total		100.000	%.

Question 6.—The proceeds of a note discounted for 90 days (without grace) at 5% amount to $2,469.25.

What is the face value of the note?

A.—The Discount on any Note for 1 year (365 days) at 5% is 1-20 of its face, and the discount for 90 days would therefore be 90-365 of 1-20 face, which is 9-730 face of the note. Deduct this discount from the full face and we have as proceeds 721-730 face of Note, which according to question is $2,469.25.

If $\frac{721}{730}$ face = 2,469.25.
$\frac{1}{730}$ " = $\frac{2469.25}{721}$
$\frac{730}{730}$ " = $\frac{2469.25}{721}$ × 730 = $2,500.07 face of note.—*Ans.*

Another method of working this sum is to find the proceeds of say $100 discounted for the 90 days, and the result is obtained by simple proportion.

Thus. Interest on 90 days
$$= \frac{100 \times 5 \times 90}{365 \times 100}$$
= 1.233
Proceeds = $100 — 1.233 = $98.767,
then as 98.767 : 2469.25 :: 100 : the face of the note, which gives $2,500.07.—*Ans.*

Question 7.—A Merchant gave his clerk an Invoice of Saws he had purchased. The Invoice included four lines of goods, the net amount paid being:

Line No. 1	....	$ 90 85
" 2	....	74 25
" 3	....	34 72
" 4	....	134 84
		$334 66

The Invoice did not show the Manufacturer's list price, and the Merchant desired to compare the list with another maker's. The Discounts on each line were as follows:

No. 1	15	10	5		
" 2	25	20	10		
" 3	30	20			
" 4	30	25	20	10	5

What was the list price of each line?

What would Invoice amount to at list price?

A.—Any of the following methods may be used in obtaining the list price when the net price and discounts are given.

Line No. 1.—Net price, $90.85. Discounts, 15 %, 10 %, 5 %.
$90.85 \times \frac{100}{85} \times \frac{100}{90} \times \frac{100}{95} = \$125$, price list.

Line No. 2.—Net price, $74.25. Discounts, 25 %, 20 %, 10 %.
100 — 25 = 75.   100 — 20 = 80.   100 — 10 = 90.
.75 × .80 × .90 = .54 of list price.
$74.25 ÷ .54 = $137.50, list price.

Line No. 3.—Net price, $34.72. Discounts, 30 %, 20 %.
                100 % list.
    Less   30 "
                ___
                70 "
    Less 20 %   14 "
                ___
    Net,   56 "
56 % list price = $34.72
100 %   "   = $\frac{34.72}{56} \times 100 = \$62.00$, list price.

Line No. 4.—Net price, $134.84, Discounts, 30 %, 25 %, 20 %, 10 %, 5 %.
$134.84 \times \frac{10}{7} \times \frac{4}{3} \times \frac{5}{4} \times \frac{10}{9} \times \frac{20}{19} = \$375.50$, list price.

Invoice at list price = $125 00
                        137 50
                         62 00
                        375 50
                        _____
                        $700 00—*Ans.*

Question 8.—Find the cubic contents of a Bin, 12 ft., 6 in., by 6 ft. 2 in., and 6 ft. in height.

How many net tons (2,000 lbs.) of Anthracite Coal will it contain, a cubic foot of Coal weighing 58.25 lbs.?

A.—Multiply the three dimensions together.

$12\frac{1}{2} \times 6\frac{1}{6} \times 6$ ft. = $462\frac{1}{2}$ cubic feet.

It will hold the following quantity of Coal:

$$\frac{462.5 \times 58.25}{2,000} = 13.4703 \text{ tons.}$$

Question 9.—Find the value of the following:

.87942 of £1 sterling.
.6492 of a ton, avoirdupois.
.8543 of a bushel, dry measure.

A.—

£ .87942
20
―――――
s. 17.58840
12
―――――
d. 7.06080   Practically 17s. 7d.

.6492 ton.
2000
―――――
lbs. 1298.4
16
―――――
oz.   6.4   1,298 lbs. 6⅜ oz.

.8543 bushel.
4
―――――
pks. 3.4172
8
―――――
qts. 3.3376
2
―――――
pts. 0.6752   3 pks. 3 qts. 0⅔ pts.

Question 10.—What amount of Coffee, at 60c., 40c., 25c., and 15c., must a Merchant add to 40 lbs. at 75c. to make a mixture to sell at 30 cents?

A.—In such questions as this the losses on grades **worth more** than the actual selling price must be equalized by gains on grades worth **less** than the actual selling price. **It is** evident that there is a loss on the Coffees **quoted** at 75c., 60c. and 40c.; these **losses** can only be made up by putting in a sufficient quantity **of** 25c. **and** 15c. Let us begin with **the** quantity given in the question namely, 40 lbs. at 75c.:

On   1 lb. of 75c. coffee **there is a loss of** 45c.
" 40   " 75c.   "   "   "   45 × 40 = 1800c.

We can make this up by using 25c. **or** 15c. or both; for convenience we will use 15c. Coffee, **on which** we have the greater gain.

We gain 15c. on 1 lb. of the 15c. coffee.
" 1800c. on $\frac{1800}{15}$ or 120 lbs. of the 15c. coffee.

so that if we had only these two grades to deal with, our mixture would be 40 lbs. of 75c. and 120 lbs. of 15c. Coffee.

In a similar manner we could put in any quantity we chose of the 60c. Coffee and equalize the loss thereon by putting in either 25c. or 15c. Coffee.

On 1 lb. of 60c. Coffee there is a loss of 30c, and, as on each pound of 25c. Coffee we gain 5c., we should require 6 lbs. of the latter to equalize each pound of the former.

Again, it is seen that on 1 lb. at 40c. we lose 10c., to make up which it would require 2 lb. of the 25c., on which we gain 5c. per lb. It is clear we could have an indefinite number of answers to this question, as no limit is placed upon the quantities to be used other than of the 75c. Coffee. The following summarizes the above explanation, and shows the gains and losses side by side:

Losses.	*Gains.*
40 lbs. @ 75c. — loss 45c. × 40c. = 1800c.	Equalized by 120 lbs. @ 15c. — gain 15c. × 120 = 1800.
1 lb. @ 60c. — loss 30c. × 1 = 30c.	" " 6 lbs. @ 25c. — gain 5c. × 6 = 30.

He could put as many pounds at 60c. as he chose, so long as he put in six times as many pounds at 25c. to equalize them.

1 lb. @ 40c. — loss 10c. × 1 = 10c., equalized by 2 lbs. @ 25c. — gain 5c. × 2 = 10c.

He could put in as many lbs. at 40c. as he chose so long as he put in twice as many lbs. at 25c. to equalize them.

Answer—
40 @ 75c.
1 " 60c.
1 " 40c.
8 " 25c.
120 " 15c.

There are several other methods of working these questions, but they are all based upon the same principle, namely, equalization of the losses on the high priced grades by putting in a sufficient quantity of the low grades to yield gains of the same amount.

CHAPTER XXIV.

MERCANTILE ARITHMETIC.

Question 1.—The Steam barge "Elk" agrees to tow the barge B. for three trips. The Captain signs the following agreement:

It is understood and agreed between the undersigned Captains of the barges "Elk" and B. that in settling Tow Bills in going through the Welland Canal, the Gross Freights shall be taken, from which shall be deducted Canal Tolls and Canal Towing. One-third of the balance shall be the amount due Steamer "Elk." From this amount the B. is to retain $15 allowance for Harbor Tow Bills.

Under the above agreement two trips were made, 1st Trip, Duluth to Kingston, Rate of Freight, $3\frac{1}{4}$c. per bush. Cargo, 40,000 bush. Wheat.

2nd Trip, Duluth to Kingston, Rate of Freight, $3\frac{3}{8}$c. per bush. Cargo, 39,000 bush. Wheat.

On first trip, the Captain of barge B. collected Freight and paid Canal Towing, $156.60. Canal Tolls, $120, were paid by Captain of "Elk." On second trip, Captain of B. paid Canal Towing, $152.60 and collected Freight; Captain of Steam-barge paid Canal Tolls, $117. Captain of barge B. then paid on the following figures, contending that he was settling according to the agreement:

Trip 1. 40,000 Bush. at 3¼c. is $1,300
   Steam barge Elk, *Cr.* ⅓ is $433 33
     Dr.
   To Canal Towing $156 60
    " Harbour Tow Bills...... 15 00
    " Cash to balance 261 73
             ——— $433 33

Trip 2. 39,000 Bush. at 3⅝c. is $1,413 75
   Steam barge Elk, *Cr.*, ⅓ is $471 25
     Dr.
   To Canal Towing $152 60
    " Harbour Tow Bill 15 00
    " Cash to balance 303 65
             ——— $471 25

The Captain of Steam-barge claimed this was not right, that he should receive more Cash. What amount was he paid short, or was the settlement according to the agreement?

A.—Adopting the Captain's form of Account as an alternative method, the question may be worked as follows:

  Freight on Trip 1 = 40,000 × 3¼ = $1,300 00
  Deduct per agreement—
    Canal Towing $156 60
     " Tolls........... 120 00
            ———— = 276 60
                ————
     Net Freight........ = 1,023 40
  Elk's ⅓   "   .... = 341 13

The amount due the "Elk" can be best understood by adopting the Form of Account given in question:

TRIP 1.

Steam Barge Elk, Cr.		
By ⅓ Net Freight	$341 13	
" Canal Toll paid	120 00	
	————	$461 13
Contra, Dr.		
To Harbour Tow Bills..........................	15 00	
" Cash per question	261 73	
		276 73
Balance still due on Trip 1		$184 40

Freight on Trip 2 = 39,000 × 3⅝c.   = $1,413 75
Deduct per agreement—
    Canal Towing $152 60
    "   Tolls........... 117 00
                                        = 269 60

      Net Freight........   = $1,144 15
Elk's ⅓   "   ....   =   381 38

TRIP 2.

Steam Barge Elk Cr.

By ⅓ Net Freight $381 38
" Canal Tolls 117 00
                                                                                                       $498 38

Contra, Dr.

To Harbour Tow Bills 15 00
" Cash per question 303 65
                                                                         318 65

    Balance still due on Trip 2......... $179 78

Total shortage = $184 40 + $179 73 = $364 13.—*Answer.*

Answering same question in a more concise manner:
1st Trip—
    Freight = 40,000 × 3¼c. .... = $1,300 00
    Deduct per agreement—
        Canal Towing $156 60
        " Tolls 120 00
                                               = 276 60
                                                  $1,023 40

    Amount due Elk is ⅓................. = 341 13
    Less allowance for Harbour Tow Bills ..   15 00
                                                    $326 13

2nd Trip—
    Freight = 39,000 × 3⅝c. .... = $1,413 75
    Deduct per agreement—
        Canal Towing $152 60
        " Tolls 117 00
                                                    269 60
                                                    $1,144 15

    Due Elk ⅓ .... = $381 38
    Less allowance 15 00
                                                    $366 38

The "Elk's" Account, then, stands as follows. Due to Captain :

Account 1st Trip......................	$326 13
Cash advanced for Canal Tolls	120 00
" " "	117 00
Account, 2nd Trip	366 38
	$929 51
Deduct Cash paid by Barge "B". $261 73	
" " " .. 303 65	
	565 38
Amount short paid..	$364 13

The settlement made was not according to agreement. The "Elk" was not entitled to be charged with Canal Towing, and was not entitled to $\frac{1}{3}$ gross freights, but $\frac{1}{3}$ less charges as shown above.

Question 2.—A Ship carrying 1,000 tons dead weight and with 40,000 cubic feet capacity in its hold is to be freighted with Ore (occupying 15 cubic feet per ton) at $2.50 per ton, and Fruit (occupying 75 cubic feet per ton) at $9.00 per ton weight. How many tons of Ore and Fruit respectively should she carry so as to utilize her maximum capacity and tonnage, and what when so loaded would be her gross earnings?

A.—

Operation.

If loaded to carry 1,000 tons and occupy 40,000 cubic feet of space, the average space per ton = $\frac{40,000}{1000}$ = 40 cubic feet.

We must now find what proportion freight occupying 15 and 75 cubic feet respectively per ton must be taken to average 40 cubic feet per ton.

Averge, 40 $\begin{cases} 40 - 15 = 25 \text{ shortage, take 35 tons of this.} \\ 75 - 40 = 35 \text{ excess, } \quad\text{"}\quad 25 \quad\text{"} \\ \qquad\qquad\text{Total.......... 60 tons.} \end{cases}$

So that in each 60 tons 35 would be of the lighter material and 25 of the heavier. The amount required of each would just be—

$\frac{35}{60}$ of 1,000 = 583$\frac{1}{3}$ tons of the 15 feet freight.
$\frac{25}{60}$ of 1,000 = 416$\frac{2}{3}$ "   "   75   "   —*Ans.*

Gross Earnings

$583\frac{1}{3} \times 2.50 = \$1,458\ 33$
$416\frac{2}{3} \times 9.00 = 3,750\ 00$

$\$5,208\ 33.\text{—}Ans.$

Proof.

$583\frac{1}{3} \times$ **15 cubic feet** $= 8,750$ cubic feet.
$416\frac{2}{3} \times 75$ " $= 31,250$ "

$40,000$

Explanation.

Each ton which occupies 15 feet of space requires 25 feet less than average; a ton that occupies 75 feet requires 35 feet more than average. We must use just such a number of tons of each that the total quantity less than the average will be counterbalanced by the total quantity over the average. The easiest method of getting at this when there are only two quantities is what is commonly known as the Alligation Method, in which the shortage in the first would be multiplied by the number representing the excess in the second, and vice versa. If we reverse these numbers and multiply, we see that the total shortage exactly counterbalances the total excess, which proves that the right proportion has been found. It is then a simple matter to determine the quantity of each.

Question 3.—What amount of interest is due on the following Ledger balances? Interest allowed at 4% on Daily Balances.

1897.			Dr.	Cr.		Balance.
Jany.	1............	Bal.		$4,000 00	Cr.	$4,000 00
	8............	Cheque.	$ 500 00		"	3,500 00
	14...........	Dep..		100 00	"	3,600 00
	31...........	Cheque.	100 00		"	3,500 00
Feb.	6............	Dep.		325 00	"	3,825 00
	20...........	Cheque.	335 00		"	3,490 00
	24...........	"	80 00		"	3,410 00
Mch.	7............	"	133 80		"	3,276 20
	13...........	Dep.		224 12	"	3,500 32
	29...........	Cheque	125 00		"	3,375 32
	29...........	Balance	3,375 32			
			$4,649 12	$4,649 12		

N.B.—Answer must show clearly method of working calculation.

MERCANTILE ARITHMETIC.   249

A.—Reduce the various Balances to the equivalent number of Dollars, which, earning interest for one day, would yield same amount as the said Balances for the times given:

```
Jany.  1. . . . . . . . . . .  4,000   ×  7 = 28,000
       8. . . . . . . . . . .  3,500   ×  6 = 21,000
      14. . . . . . . . . . .  3,600   × 17 = 61,200
      31. . . . . . . . . . .  3,500   ×  6 = 21,000
Feb.   6. . . . . . . . . . .  3,825   × 14 = 53,550
      20. . . . . . . . . . .  3,490   ×  4 = 13,960
      24. . . . . . . . . . .  3,410   × 11 = 37,510
Mch.   7. . . . . . . . . . .  3,276.20 ×  6 = 19,657.20
      13. . . . . . . . . . .  3,500.32 × 16 = 56,005.12
      29. . . . . . . . . . .  3,575.32
                                        ──    ─────────
                                        87    311,882.32
```

$$\frac{311,882.32 \times 4}{365 \times 100} = \$34.18 \text{ —Answer.}$$

Question 4.—John Smith is Purchasing Agent in London, England, for two Canadian houses.

For A. he buys in Paris, France, goods amounting to Francs, 1168.11; for B. he buys in Hamburg, Germany, goods amounting to Marks, 76.50; his commission is 5% for buying.

What is the amount of the sterling Drafts A. and B. must remit and what is the amount of the Cheque they must pay the Bank issuing the Draft, Sterling Exchange selling at 10%, 21 Marks equal to £1, and 25 Francs equal to £1.

"Sterling Exchange selling at 10%" means at 10% advance on the old par of exchange which was £1 = $\$\frac{40}{9}$, so that in this case £1 cost $\$\frac{40}{9} \times \frac{110}{100} = \$\frac{44}{9}$.

A.'s invoice was 1168.11 francs, which reduced to sterling money on the basis of 25 francs = £1, gives $\frac{1168.11}{25}$ = £46.7244. 5% commission on this amount = £2.3362.

A.'s draft to Smith amounts to £46.7244 + £2.3362 = £49.0606 = £49 1s. 2½d.

A.'s £1 costs $\$\frac{44}{9}$, A. must give the Bank a cheque for £49.0606 × $\$\frac{44}{9}$ = $239.85.

B.'s invoice was 76.50 marks, **which must be reduced to sterling money on the basis of 21 marks = £1**, or including the 5% commission, on the basis of 21 **marks** = £1.05, which gives $\frac{76.50}{21}$ × £1.05 = £3.825 = £3 16s. 6d., the amount of B.'s **draft**.

B. must give the Bank a cheque for £3.825 × $4.88 = $18.70.

$$\left.\begin{array}{rl} \text{A.'s draft} = & \text{£49 1s. } 2\tfrac{1}{4}d. \\ \text{B.'s } = & 3\text{ 16}s.\text{ 6 }d. \\ \text{A.'s cheque} = & \$239\text{ 85} \\ \text{B.'s } = & 18\text{ 70} \end{array}\right\}-Answer.$$

Note.
The par value of £1 = $4.86¾.
" " 1 franc = .193.
" " 1 mark = .238.

Question 5.—Multiply by contracted method and give the answer to three places of decimals.

$$64.4235 \times 318.4851.$$

Operation.

```
         318.48510
            532446
         ---------
         19,109.1060
          1,273.9404
            127.3940
              6.3696
               .9552
               .1590
         ---------
         20,517.9242—Ans. 20,517.924.
```

Explanation.

The question calls **for three places of** decimals, **but to get the correct answer to three places it is better by the contracted method to** multiply **to** four places **on account of the "carrying figures." This is done** by reversing the multiplier and placing it under the multiplicand with the units figure under the **fourth** decimal place; **each of** the other figures then falls naturally into its proper position. Multiplying by the 6 tens gives us four decimal places in our product. Next multiply by **the** four units, commencing at the figure directly above it, which being a decimal of the fourth place gives a product of four decimal places; this product must be arranged under the previous one beginning at the extreme right. Now we multiply by 4, commencing at the 5 directly above it; this is really multiplying a decimal of 3 places by a decimal of 1 place, and gives, therefore, a decimal of four places for result, which is arranged as before at the extreme right. It will be noticed that all the results are in four decimal places, and when added give us an answer in four decimal places. The figures to the right of the one directly above that we are multiplying by are totally disregarded in the working.

Rule—*Reverse the multiplier, placing the unit figure thereof directly under the decimal to which it is intended to extend the work* (which should be one place further than an accurate answer is required to). Multiply as in ordinary multiplication, ignoring all figures in the multiplicand to the right of the figure we are multiplying by. Arrange the several products so that the figures on the extreme right are directly under each other. Add and point off the number of decimals to which work has been extended.

Question 6.—A Merchant holds a Mortgage of $6,250, Principal payable in four equal annual instalments of $1,562.50, Interest 5% payable annually. Being in need of money he offers to sell it to B. at a price that will give B. 8% on his investment. What amount did B. pay?

A.—The annual Payment on Principal being $1,562.50, the Payment of interest for the several years is as follows:

1st year, 5 % on $6,250 = $312 50. Total payment = $1,562.50 + $312 50 = $1,875.00.

2nd year, 5 % on $4,687 50.= $234 38. Total payment = $1,562 50 + $234 38 = $1,796.88.

3rd year, 5 % on $3,125.00 = 156 25. Total payment = $1,562 50 + $156 25 = $1,718 75.

4th year, 5 % on $1,562 50 = $78 12. Total payment = $1,562 50 + $78 12 = $1,640 62.

B. buys this mortgage at a price that will pay him 8% per annum on his money for the time it is invested. We must therefore find the present value of each of the above instalments.

Each $1 paid by B. for 1st instalment is worth $1.08 when 1st instalment is due: value of instalment No. 1 = $\frac{\$1875}{1.08}$ = $1736.11.

Each $1 paid for 2nd instalment is worth $1.08 × $1.08 = $1.1664 when 2nd instalment is due: value of instalment No. 2 = $\frac{\$1796.88}{1.1664}$ = $1540.53.

Each $1 paid for 3rd instalment is worth $1.08 × 1.08 × 1.08 = $1.2597 when 3rd instalment is due: value of instalment No. 3 = $\frac{\$1718.75}{1.2597}$ = $1364.40.

Each $1 paid for 4th instalment is worth $1.08 × 1.08 × 1.08 × 1.08 = $1.36049 when 4th instalment is due: value of instalment No. 4 = $\frac{\$1640.62}{1.36049}$ = $1205.90.

B. should pay for the mortgage $1736.11 + $1540.53 + $1364.40 + $1205.90 = $5846.94. Answer.

Question 7.—A Jeweller has 5 oz. Gold, 16 Carats fine, and melts it with 10 oz. Gold, 12 Carats fine. How much pure Gold must he add to his mixture to make it 20 Carats fine?

Operation.

Pure gold = 24 carats.
Standard required = 20 carats.
20 — 16 = 4 carats shortage on each oz. of 16 carat gold.
20 — 12 = 8   "   "   "   "   12   "
24 — 20 = 4   "   surplus   "   24   "
4 carats × 5 = 20 carats shortage on 16 carat gold.
8   "   × 10 = 80   "   "   "   12   "
————
100   "   = total shortage.
100 carats shortage ÷ 4 carats surplus = 25 oz.

Pure gold needed to raise the mixture to required standard 25 oz.—*Ans.*

Proof.

Oz.		Carats.		Carats.
25	×	24	=	600
5	×	16	=	80
10	×	12	=	120
40		)		800(20 carats.
				800

The fineness of Pure Gold is fixed at 24 Carats. Gold which is 20 Carats fine has only 20 parts out of 24 Gold, the rest of it is some other metal. In working this question each ounce is supposed to be divided into 24 parts. Each ounce of 16 Carat Gold contains only 16 parts Gold, which is 4 parts below the standard called for in the mixture. The shortage of Gold in 5 ounces would therefore be 4 parts × 5 = 20 parts. Similarly the shortage in each ounce of 12 Carat Gold is 8 parts, and in 10 ounces it would be 8 parts × 10 = 80 parts. Both together show a total shortage of 20 + 80 = 100 parts. This is to be made up by putting in Pure Gold, each ounce of which gives us a surplus of 4 parts as the average required is only 20 and Pure Gold is 24. The question thus becomes a very simple one, viz.: "How many ounces, each showing an excess of 4 parts Gold, will be needed to make up a shortage of 100 parts?" Just 100 divided by 4, or 25 ounces.

Question 8.—A Farmer has a Mortgage on his Farm of $5,340, Principal payable in five years from 1st January, 1898. Interest payable half-yearly, 5%. He desires to deposit in a Savings Bank an annual deposit which compounded at 4% every six months will give him enough to pay off the Mortgage at the end of five years.

1st. What amount of Interest does he pay on the Mortgage every six months?

2nd. How much must he deposit on the 1st of January, 1898, and four following years, to have $5,340 at the end of five years.

A.—1. His half-yearly Interest on Mortgage is just $2\frac{1}{2}\%$ on $5,340 = $133.50.

2. Each dollar deposited January 1, 1898, bears compound Interest at 2% half year for 10 half-years. Similarly each dollar deposited **January 1, 1899**, bears compound Interest at 2% per half-year for **8** half-years, etc.

$1 deposited Jan. 1/98 would at the end of the time be worth 1.02^{10} = 1.21899
1   "   Jan. 1/99   "   "   " 1.02^8 = 1.17166
1   "   Jan. 1/1900   "   "   " 1.02^6 = 1.12616
1   "   Jan. 1/1901   "   "   " 1.02^4 = 1.08243
1   "   Jan. 1/1902   "   "   " 1.02^2 = 1.0404

1   "   annually for five years "   " $5.63964

as often as $5.63964 is contained in $5340 there must be $1 in the annual deposit.

$$\$5{,}340 \div \$5.63964 = \$946.87. — Answer.$$

Second Method.

2% compounded half-yearly = 4.04% per annum.
1.0404^5 (or 1.02^{10}) = $1.2189944.
Compound interest on $1 for said time = .2189944.
.2189944 ÷ .0404 = $5.42065, final value of $1 annuity for 5 years paid at end of each year.
Add compound interest on $1 for time = .21899 + $5.63964 = final value of $1, invested annually for 5 years, at the beginning of each year.
$5340 ÷ $5.63964 = $946.87.—*Answer.*

Annuities and Sinking Funds.

Before calculations in **Annuities**, Sinking Funds, Debentures, etc., can be understood, it is first necessary to have a thorough grasp of the principles underlying Compound Interest. For instance, what causes an investment of $1 to amount to $1.36857 if out at Compound Interest for 8 years? Simply an annuity of 4 cents added to it, which in its turn gathers interest at the same rate. If, instead of leaving the first year's Interest in the same Bank as the $1, we withdrew the 4 cents and deposited it at the same rate in another Bank, and do likewise with each successive year's 4 cents as it becomes due, we shall then have at the end of eight years just $1 in the first Bank and $.36857 in the second Bank. The amount in the second Bank is simply an annual deposit of 4 cents at the **end of each year** for eight successive years, with the Interest on these deposits at **4%** compound added thereto.

MERCANTILE ARITHMETIC.   255

Now, an equal sum set apart annually for a number of years is an *Annuity*, therefore, the above .36857 is the Final Value or value at maturity of an Annuity of 4 cents for 8 years at 4%. Knowing the final value of an Annuity of 4 cents, it is, then, a simple matter to find the value of an annuity of 100 cents or $1.00 ; it is .36857×100÷4 divided by .04=$9.2142. From this we deduce the following useful rule:

To find the Value at Maturity of an Annuity of $1 for any given time at any given rate:

Calculate the Compound Interest of $1 for the given time at the given rate and divide it by the given rate expressed decimally.

Question 9.—A Merchant buys 1,000 yards of cloth from a Manufacturer, made up as follows:

>200 yards at 60 cents.
>300 yards at 50 cents.
>100 yards at 80 cents.
>125 yards at $1.00.
>100 yards at 90 cents.
>175 yards at 75 cents.

He retails it at an average price of 85 cents per yard.

What percentage of each sale was profit? How much did he make on the 1,000 yards? What percentage did he make or lose on each lot ?

A.—

200 yds. cost 60c., sold at 85c., gain =25c. = $\frac{25}{85}$ sale = $29\frac{7}{17}$% sale,
or gain = $\frac{25}{60}$ cost = $41\frac{2}{3}$% profit.
300 yds. cost 50c., sold at 85c., gain = 35c. = $\frac{35}{85}$ sale = $41\frac{7}{17}$% sale,
or gain = $\frac{35}{50}$ cost = 70% profit.
100 yds. cost 80c., sold at 85c., gain = 5c., = $\frac{5}{85}$ sale = $5\frac{5}{17}$% sale,
or gain = $\frac{5}{80}$ cost = $6\frac{1}{4}$% profit.
125 yds. cost $1.00, sold at 85c., loss = 15c. = $\frac{15}{85}$ sale = $15\frac{15}{17}$% sale *loss*,
or loss = $\frac{15}{100}$ cost = 15% loss.
100 yds. cost 90c., sold at 85c., loss = 5c, = $\frac{5}{85}$ sale = $5\frac{5}{17}$% sale *loss*,
or loss = $\frac{5}{90}$ cost = $5\frac{5}{9}$% loss.
175 yds. cost 75c., sold at 85c., gain = 10c. = $\frac{10}{85}$ sale = $10\frac{10}{17}$% sale.
or gain = $\frac{10}{75}$ cost = $13\frac{1}{3}$% gain.

Total cost = $120 + $150 + $80 + $125 + $90 + $131.25 = $696.25.
Total selling price = $1000 × 85c. = $850.00.

Total profit = $850 − 696.25 = $153.75.   *Answer.*

Question 10.—A Trustee has $10,000 to invest. He deposits $3,462 in Savings Bank at 3½% compounded half-yearly. With $3,500 he buys Dominion Bank Stock at $250 per $100 share, and receives Dividends of 3½% quarterly. With $3,038 he buys Bank of Nova Scotia Stock at $217 per $100 share, and receives Dividends of 4% half-yearly. At the end of the year, how much interest will he have received, and what rate does each investment pay?

Savings Bank :

$3,462 × (1.01¾)² = $3,584.23. Deduct $3,462 from this amount, which leaves as interest $122.23.

$$122.23 \div 3,462 = 3.53 \% \text{ per annum.}$$

Dominion Bank Stock :

$3,500 ÷ $250 = 14 shares. Each share pays $3.50 per quarter, or $14 per year. 14 × $14 = $196 income.

$$\$196 \div 3,500 = 5.60 \% \text{ per annum.}$$

Bank of Nova Scotia Stock :

$3,038 ÷ 217 = 14 shares. Each share pays $4 per half year, or $8 per year. 14 × $8 = $112 income.

$$\$112 \div \$3,038 = 3.69 \% \text{ per annum.}$$

Total income = $122 23
196 00
112 00
─────
$430 23

Total investment = $10,000.
Average rate of income = 430.23 ÷ 10,000 = 4.30 %.

www.ingramcontent.com/pod-product-compliance
Lightning Source LLC
Chambersburg PA
CBHW032104230426
43672CB00009B/1629